World War II in the Pacific

World War II
in the
Pacific

(second edition of *Never Look Back*)

MARK D. ROEHRS AND WILLIAM A. RENZI

M.E.Sharpe
Armonk, New York
London, England

Library of Congress Cataloging-in-Publication Data

Roehrs, Mark D., 1965–
   World War II in the Pacific / Mark D. Roehrs, William A. Renzi.
     p. cm.
   Includes bibliographical references and index.
   ISBN 0-7656-0835-9 (cloth: alk. paper) — ISBN 0-7656-0836-7 (pbk. : alk. paper)
    1. World War, 1939–1945—Campaigns—Pacific Area. 2. World War,
   1939–1945—United States. 3. World War, 1939–1945—Japan. 4. Pacific Area—
   History. I. Title: World War Two in the Pacific. II. Title: World War 2 in the Pacific.
   III. Renzi, William A., 1941– IV. Title.

   D767 .R64 2003
   940.54'26—dc21   2002036576

Contents

Preface to the
Second Edition

This second edition is offered both as an improvement upon the first and in response to the impressive volume of manuscripts added to the historiography of the Pacific War during the last decade. While few startling new revelations have been offered, much of the work is extremely thoughtful and has served to both broaden and deepen our understanding of the characters and events of that conflict. This is especially true regarding areas once overlooked or treated only peripherally by the standard texts, including the role of the comfort women, internment of American citizens of Japanese ancestry, the conduct and effects of the American firebombing campaign, eyewitness narratives, and the American approach to war termination without the atomic bomb. Certain biographies and memoir collections have also proven useful in shedding new light on key individuals in the struggle. Possibly the most interesting development of the past decade, however, has been the debate over the American use of the atomic bombs and their place in the public memory. These new studies have helped better explain a crucial period in history and, while not displacing the classic texts, have contributed significantly to the richness and fullness of our understanding.

More significantly, the addition of two new chapters dealing with the road to war and the war's conclusion greatly strengthens the narrative of this second edition. The opening chapter incorporates much of the rich new scholarship on Japan's development between the Meiji Restoration and the outbreak of World War I. Japan's ambitions and motives in the war are made clearer by greater study of the course of Japanese modernization. The chapter entitled "Allied Endgame" describes the Allied and American plans for war termination conceived of prior to the development of the atomic bomb, as well as the means for obtaining Japan's capitulation short of deployment of that weapon. It also reflects one of the most dynamic current trends of research on the Pacific War.

Preface to the First Edition

This book exists for several reasons. First, the authors have devoted years to the study of World War II, one having had his interest in the topic begun by the late Gordon W. Prange, for whom he was graduate assistant for five years. In the last decade, moreover, a spate of fresh primary and secondary source materials has become available. As our bibliography attests, we have made liberal use of these riches, together with, of course, the best of the old, or standard, works on the topic that are likely to remain classics.

We have concentrated on the Japanese-American episodes of the conflict in "The Great Pacific War" (which is what the war is called in Japan) for the simple reason that they were decisive. British participation, as well as Australian and New Zealander efforts in the struggle and the China–Burma–India theater, are all dealt with, but not to the same degree. We do not mean to negate or disparage the action in these other theaters, but since the conflict was primarily a Japanese-American one, this central perspective is maintained in order to retain a balanced narrative.

The reader will remember, of course, that Japan lies across the International Date Line. Like almost all other authors, we have retained zone times (also known as "local," "real," or "actual" times) in the narrative. Thus, December 7, 1941, was December 8 in Japan, and Pearl Harbor Day, a national holiday by imperial proclamation, was celebrated on December 8 in Japan during the war years. We have not used a standard system of transliteration for "oriental" names, for the simple reason that many of the actors are already well known and being doctrinaire in the matter might well be confusing; in most instances, we have employed the usual or most common transliteration for the family names involved.

We have tried to give both the Japanese and American points of view toward the conflict, in both its origins and actual conduct. The American side is relatively well known to many English-language readers; the Japanese side, perhaps less so. We have tried to keep a relatively even balance, but if we tend occasionally to explain Japanese motives and values a bit more than American ones, it is in the simple belief that they will be of greater interest to the reader.

Acknowledgments

I am greatly indebted to many people for their assistance in making this manuscript possible. I would like especially to thank my friends and colleagues Doctors Jim Lorrence and Chris McDonald for reading drafts of the text and offering valuable insights and suggestions. I am grateful to my editor, Andrew Gyory, for his patience, and for giving me the chance to accomplish this work. I am greatly in debt to my wife, Laurie, and daughter, Elizabeth, for allowing me the opportunity and inspiring the motivation to complete this task. Finally, I owe an unrepayable debt to the late Dr. William A. Renzi for encouraging me to pursue my love of history. He passed away when the first edition was released, and his absence in preparing this second edition has been sorely felt. Naturally, though many have contributed to the making of this text, any errors contained in it are my own.

Introduction

The Pacific War has provided subject matter for numerous textbooks, battle studies, personal memoirs, unit histories, and biographies. Collectively these works constitute a rich and enormous, if not exhaustive, reference resource base. And though they are very valuable within the field, the following weaknesses have tended to limit their usefulness within the typical classroom. These books, while well researched and often painstakingly documented, are often too detailed or specific for the general user, and often fail to deliver a broad context for the material they contain. A further significant drawback to many of these volumes is that they focus primarily, if not exclusively, on the Allied, or more often, American, experience of the war. Similarly, many of these books concentrate on specific aspects of the war, such as battles, weapon systems, individuals or groups, or political figures. Consequently, few of these works attempt to place the struggle in any form of historical or global context. The purpose of this text is to synthesize and present the vital elements of the history of the Pacific War in a format specifically suited to the novice historian, and, when appropriate, to suggest directions for further investigation.

This volume concisely bridges the gaps left by the other literature of the war and delivers a rational, systematic, and thorough survey of the entire scope of the Pacific War. Beginning with the background and situations that led up to the war, and proceeding through the course of the fighting, this survey gives special attention to the significant personalities and events affecting all parties involved in the conflict as well as the military, political, economic, and social developments during the war. It is the author's intention that this brief history of the Pacific War will serve to introduce readers to the various broad themes of the conflict and provide an evenhanded overview of the war's most significant features. To that end, the narrative begins over half a century before the attack on Pearl Harbor, or even the Japanese seizure of Manchuria.

Chapter 1 begins in mid-nineteenth-century Japan with the so-called "Meiji Restoration," which ousted the decrepit Tokugawa shogunate and brought a new, constitutional government to power under the nominal leadership of the boy emperor. This new leadership launched Japan into a period of unprecedented growth, and extended Japanese interests into China and the Northern and Central Pacific, where they encountered an expanding United States, also feeling the flush of expansionistic energy and the desire to exploit the resources of the vast Pacific basin. This contact resulted in mixed feelings on the parts of both nations as racism and ultra-nationalism fueled the natural rivalry between them. The chapter ends with Japan and the United States playing a limited military role in the primarily European conflict of 1914–19, though both countries profited from their participation in the war.

Chapter 2 begins with the victorious Allies establishing military limitations in 1921 in hopes of preventing a repeat of the events that had led to war in the previous decade. The U.S. and Japanese navies that confronted each other in the Pacific during the 1940s were very much a creation of these treaty stipulations. Close examination of the political situation in Japan during the 1920s reveals a growing militarism in political circles and increasing influence on the part of the active duty officers who held the posts of minister of the army and minister of the navy in the prime minister's cabinet. The Japanese were anxious to exploit the trade and territorial expansion that had accompanied the reduction of European influence in the Pacific during World War I. The Americans likewise hoped to increase their presence in the markets of Asia, and viewed the Japanese as both competitors and potential enemies, as is clear in American "Orange" plans for hostilities. The chapter ends with the Americans and Japanese viewing each other with barely concealed hostility as Japan sinks deeper into the China quagmire with little hope for an easy or immediate extrication.

Chapter 3 details the Japanese planning and execution of one of the most daring and successful military actions of all time, the attack on the U.S. naval forces stationed at Pearl Harbor. From the selection of Adm. Yamamoto Isoroku, through the extensive planning and preparation, to the nearly completely successful execution of the plan, the author draws from the landmark works of Gordon Prange to give insight into how the attack was accomplished, why it caught the Americans so thoroughly by surprise, and how it fulfilled the reasonably limited hopes of its author and designer, while at the same time leaving Japan susceptible to the rapid and devastating retaliation of the United States.

Chapter 4 is a litany of Allied defeats and Japanese successes. As Yamamoto had promised, his forces "ran wild" for the first six months after Pearl Harbor and captured an empire for Japan that reached from the Indian Ocean to the islands of the Central Pacific, and from the westernmost Aleutian Islands to the jungles of New Guinea. The forces of Great Britain, France, Holland, Australia, and the United States were nearly powerless in the face of the rapid Japanese onslaught, though some of the emperor's gains were dearly bought. The Japanese war machine surpassed all of its timetables and achieved a victory so vast that it left the citizens of the empire suffering from what some historians have termed "victory disease," or the feeling that defeat was impossible. Perhaps the Japanese fortunes in their subsequent campaigns were symptoms of this affliction.

The Japanese were not nearly as meticulous in the planning, nor as successful in the execution, of their next operations. Chapter 5 details the Allied successes in the Doolittle Raid, the Battle of the Coral Sea, and the turning point Battle of Midway. A combination of bravado, technology, and luck was responsible for turning the tide of the Pacific War during 1942. Col. James Doolittle's daring daytime raid of Tokyo in April 1942, employing long-range bombers flown from aircraft carriers, shook the Japanese high command's sense of invulnerability and negated a promise they had made to the citizenry of the empire that the war would never be brought to the homeland. The fighting in the Coral Sea witnessed the first battle in history in which the primary contestants never visually contacted one another. Carrier-based fighter and bomber forces struck at their foes over vast expanses of ocean with both sides managing to sink one of the other's precious aircraft carriers. The battle saved the Allied base at Port Moresby, but more importantly, it changed the face of naval warfare forever. Yamamoto's knockout blow, conceived to destroy U.S. naval strength in the Pacific at the tiny Central Pacific atoll called Midway, indeed achieved a devastating result, though not the one its designer had intended. American code-breakers learned of the Japanese plan and laid a trap for the massive Imperial force. The resulting struggle cost Japan four of its best aircraft carriers and, more importantly, the initiative for the remainder of the war. After Midway, the Allies would determine where and when the next fight would take place.

While Midway had disabled the Japanese navy, its land forces were still very much intact. Chapter 6 discusses the first significant Allied effort to wrest territories from the Japanese that they had conquered during their earlier advance through the Pacific. The remote and heretofore virtually unknown island of Guadalcanal became the site of some of the fiercest and most protracted land fighting of the Pacific War. Little quarter was asked or given in the brutal, often fanatical, fighting. Both the Allies and the Japanese committed their strength and determination to securing the island. Between August 1942 and February 1943, tens of thousands of American and Japanese soldiers fought and died in the malarial jungles of this tiny island in the South Pacific. After

Guadalcanal, the process of isolating or "hopping" islands became the standard technique of the advancing Allied forces, often stranding thousands of Japanese soldiers on island garrisons where they could not be resupplied or play any significant role in the remainder of the conflict. This process worked splendidly in the Solomon Island chain along the coast of New Guinea, and into the Marshall and Caroline Islands of the Central Pacific.

The campaigns of 1944 found the two prongs of the Allied advance approaching the Central Pacific's Mariana Island chain as well as the Philippines. Chapter 7 describes the desperate battles waged by the Japanese defenders of the regions they now considered the outer boundaries of the home islands. The Japanese had initiated a substantial colonization effort on Saipan in the Marianas, and had launched the largest surface action since Midway to try and safeguard it. The ensuing battle, known as the "Marianas Turkey Shoot" was a disaster for the Japanese, as were the suicidal defenses of the island's garrisons. The Allied threat to the Philippines and, by extension, Japan's lifeline to its southern resources region brought forth the largest naval battle of all time. The Battle of Leyte Gulf included the participation of hundreds of ships and thousands of aircraft, as well an amphibious landing. The struggle for the Philippines also produced the Japanese ultimate solution to the Allies' naval and air superiority, the kamikaze. Suicide pilots launched themselves and their crafts into the ships of the Allies in a vainglorious attempt to reverse the tide of the war. While certainly one of the most terrible weapons of the war, the kamikaze proved to be too little and too late to save the collapsing Japanese empire.

Chapter 8 breaks from following the course of battles and campaigns to examine the seemingly disparate topics of submarine warfare, life in Japan, and the empire during the war, as well as the condition of Japanese Americans in the United States. Submarines, while not the most romantic weapons of the Pacific War, proved to be the most effective. America's submarine effort denied Japan access to the vital resource wealth of its conquests. Once the problems resulting from faulty ordnance were worked out, American submarines took a devastating toll on Japanese merchant shipping, as well as gaining several notable victories against combat vessels. Due to wartime restrictions and the success of the submarine campaign, the average Japanese citizen enjoyed few of the benefits of mastery of a vast empire, and indeed suffered substantially from reduced food and fuel supplies by war's end. These deprivations did not, however, dampen the resolve of the emperor's subjects to sacrifice everything necessary to obtain victory, and in fact millions were enlisted in a national guard in preparation for the inevitable Allied invasion. But Japanese in the home islands were not the only ones subjected to brutal restrictions. Americans of Japanese ancestry were also victims of the war, as forced relocation and denial of fundamental rights was the U.S. government's response to a racist and paranoid West Coast. Tens of thousands of Japanese Americans were forced to abandon their homes and property and relocate to government camps with very little warning and no compensation. This wartime relocation program remains one of the most infamous actions of World War II.

Chapter 9 examines one of the most overlooked theaters of the war. The campaigns in China, Burma, and India provide several of the most colorful characters of the war and some of the most enduring images, but as a military theater the region almost certainly takes a secondary position to the naval warfare of the Central Pacific. The legacy of anti-European imperialism that continued after the war and led to the eventual withdrawal of all colonial governments in the following decades is certainly a significant, if not wholly intended, outcome of this campaign.

Chapter 10 concludes the land battle of the Pacific War. The bloody and dramatic conquests of Iwo Jima and Okinawa left the Allies at the very doorstep of the Japanese home islands, and placed the cities of Japan well within range of the new long-range bombers. The Imperial Navy made one last futile sortie, sacrificing its only remaining super-battleship to the desperate and doomed cause. Meanwhile, Allied bombers began to rain devastation upon the Japanese from the skies. The devastation wrought upon Japanese cities by the B-29 firebombing campaign from March through August 1945 is one of the most terrible examples of massive military and civilian destruction in the annals of war. Within the context of the bombing campaign, already highly successful in terms of sheer destruction, the atomic bombs provided emphatic punctuation to a line of devastation that had largely already been written. Ironically, neither bomber nor bombed appreciated all of the atomic devices' terrible destructive power, and therefore its real horror, radiation, was not an element of coercion forcing the Japanese decision to surrender.

Chapter 11 discusses the diplomatic and military planning efforts that proceeded simultaneously in the Allied capitals as the war reached its conclusion. Plans for a massive invasion of Kyushu were well advanced by late 1945, and troops were already being shifted from Europe to participate in the expected landings. The Soviet entry into the war was but another phase of the intended invasion, though it had a greater impact than even the Allied planners had anticipated.

Chapter 12 details the process through which surrender was accomplished and the collapse of the Japanese empire assured. In the face of determined resistance on the part of some military factions in the government, a coalition of civilian and military leaders brought about a surrender decision and used the emperor himself to make the decision known to the Japanese people.

The attempts by members of the cabinet and individuals in the army to stop the process, even up to the final hour before official surrender, are a testament to the tenacity with which the Japanese military clung to its hopes for a negotiated peace. Citizens' responses to the emperor's words also demonstrate that Japan, while physically devastated, was not yet broken and could have resisted even still, had the emperor called for such a sacrifice. The book concludes with the words of the emperor exhorting his people to look beyond the bitterness of the present and find a way to keep pace with the future.

Unfortunately this volume has had to omit, or only slightly cover, numerous fascinating details of the war. This was necessary to maintain the flow of the history and to stay within reasonable bounds for the typical survey course format. The author encourages readers to consult outside sources on specific aspects of the war, and, to this end, has included a list and brief description of the best, as well as the most up-to-date, appropriate secondary works at the end of each chapter.

World War II in the Pacific

1

Rising Sun

Japan Comes of Age

The year 1868 was as dramatic and important in Japanese history as the year 1941. For that year the boy emperor, Meiji, guided by a small group of warlord-noblemen, or *genro*, established the Japanese capital in Tokyo and began modernization of Japan. The motives that impelled the Japanese to begin industrialization were diverse. The traditional explanation on the American side of the Pacific has been that U.S. commodore Matthew Perry's arrival in 1853 had significant influence on Japan's decision to terminate its isolation. However, the internal factors that motivated the Japanese to abandon their traditional isolationism were more numerous and complex. Along with the arrival of the Americans were more pressing threats to the old order, including longstanding rivalries between various *daimyos* within the Tokugawa shogunate, as well as the regional ambitions of European powers, most dramatically demonstrated by the devastating British victory over China in the opium wars and the arrival of the Russian empire on Japan's Pacific seaboard. Russia's subsequent founding of the port of Vladivostok—its name may be literally translated as "rule over the East"—on the Sea of Japan, which had heretofore been a virtual Japanese lake, gave credence to Japanese fears of European intentions in Asia. Further, any influence the United States might have had was doubtless terminated by the U.S. Civil War, which seemed to Japan to demonstrate American weakness and incompetence.

The shogunate government, or *bakufu*, decision to sign a trade treaty with the Americans in 1858 may have provided the final impetus for its enemies' decision to revolt. Led by samurai of the Choshu and Satsuma *daimyos*, anti-*bakufu* forces denounced accommodation with the Westerners and called for reverence to the emperor and expulsion of the barbarians. In an ironic twist, the Tokugawa leadership, which had been the leading advocate of traditionalism and Confucian values, became associated with modernism and pro-Western sympathy. Attacks in 1864 on British and American shipping by forces from the Choshu faction resulted in reprisals and bombardment of coastal defenses, but not wholesale invasion and war, as had happened in China. Anti-Western demonstrations and the assassination of several prominent Westerners as well as members of the *bakufu* followed, but also failed to remove the "barbarian influences" from Japan.

Powerful samurai from numerous *daimyo* realized the futility of continued resistance to the Americans and Europeans and instead embraced the military and economic technology of the West as a means of self-strengthening. Cries of "rich country, strong army" replaced the calls for expulsion of the barbarians. Support for the *bakufu* was nearly nonexistent by the time samurai from Choshu and Satsuma called for the shogun's surrender of political leadership. The actual transfer of power from the *bakufu* to the rebels; then, was relatively bloodless. Consent of the young Meiji emperor justified the change and also ensured that rebel samurai would carry out the functions of government in his name.

The Meiji Restoration

The Meiji Restoration, as it came to be called, was a combination of traditional and modern elements. While adopting the technology and economics of the West, Meiji leaders were careful to preserve many of the values and traditions of Japan's heritage. A significant portion of the Japanese population found the changes wrought over the course of the next twenty-five years to be painful. In the end, no group was more affected than the very samurai who had begun the modernization. The samurai, Japan's traditional warrior class, had begun the process of transformation from standing military oligarchy to bureaucratic functionaries during Tokugawa's reign. Years of peace had already served to change many of the samurai into administrators and civil servants of the local *daimyo*. The restoration accelerated the completion of this process. One of the first orders of business of the new government was to break up the old *daimyos*, destroy the domain castles, and create a new provincial political order with centrally appointed governors. Thus, the emperor, not the local samurai, now became the focus of popular loyalty. Many of the petty samurai—those without extensive landholdings or political influence—were pensioned off and sent into unofficial retirement. These former samurai had the benefit of education and many opted to become teachers, artists, or bureaucratic officials. All of these were considered honorable professions, but they lacked the prestige associated with the samurais' former warrior status. The retirement system was suspended in 1876 when, in order to reduce government expenses, lifetime pensions were replaced by a one-time lump-sum payoff.

While the samurai class may have disappeared during the Meiji period, the spirit of the warrior caste did not. In fact, the leading political officials continued to be drawn from the samurai class and strove to prop up the faltering system on several occasions. It was, however, the adoption of conscript armies, more than any other element, that threatened to reduce the status of the samurai and was most hotly debated by the original restoration conspirators.

In 1873, debate coalesced around the question of Japan's relations with its nearest neighbor, Korea. Samurai from the Choshu and Satusuma regions, many of whom had initially been instigators of the restoration, called for a military campaign on the peninsula to open economic opportunities for Japan and to restore the position and respect of the samurai class. The government refused to endorse the venture, and in 1877 opposition samurai led by Saigo Takamori launched a desperate and ultimately futile revolt against the bureaucracy they had been instrumental in creating. The uprising ended with the siege of Kumamoto Castle and the victory of recently recruited conscript soldiers over the highly skilled but outnumbered samurai professionals. This marked the effective end of the samurai as a class, but the samurai spirit and warrior code (*bushido*) were adopted by future armies of Japan and remained a point of great national pride and reverence for future generations.

Another significant characteristic of the Japanese path to modernization included the leaders' refusal to become financially indebted to Western nations, though they were not adverse to borrowing heavily from Western technology. The Japanese had collected and studied Western science books throughout the seventeenth and eighteenth centuries, using their semi-annual contact with Dutch traders at the port of Nagasaki. After the "opening" of Japan to foreign commerce in the years following Perry's visit, Japan imported numerous Western experts and translated volumes of European texts. Japan imported technology and technicians from the West and sent its own students to Western universities to learn modern science and engineering. When the Japanese students returned, or Japanese technicians had been sufficiently trained by Western instructors, the Westerners were politely dismissed and technological progress continued independently. As a result, Japan experienced a remarkable lack of "brain drain" from these overseas ventures. Most Japanese students were anxious to return home to develop their skills, often forgoing more lucrative opportunities in the countries of their education.

As well as studying Western technology, Japanese leaders adopted the rhetoric of the Western enlightenment. Japanese city dwellers also began to mimic the tastes and fashions of European culture, often disparaging their country cousins as uncultured yokels. At the same time, however, the Japanese leaders reminded the people of the innate superiority and morality of traditional Japanese values and culture. One of the primary elements of enlightenment and nationalist thought adopted by the Japanese was the emphasis on education. While domestic institutions of higher education obviously served the needs of the growing industrial technological sector and staffed the increasing numbers of bureaucratic positions, the government also emphasized compulsory elementary education. The Imperial Rescript on Education issued in 1890 stressed learning directed at becoming a proper citizen and a proper Japanese, paying special attention to the uniqueness of Japanese culture and the Japanese people. Surprisingly, it even advocated the need for gender equity in education, though this was not observed before the mid-twentieth century. According to government leaders of the day, Japan had much to learn from the West technologically, but little morally.

Japan also borrowed heavily from Western models in its development of a new political structure. Peasant uprisings and political discontent led to calls for a constitution, which the leaders duly provided. Ito Hirobumi, the primary author of the Japanese constitution, borrowed heavily from the Bismarckian German model, which vested primary governing powers in the cabinet while also allowing for the creation of a representative body. The constitution was not a contract between the government and the governed, but rather a gift from the emperor to his subjects. As such, it contained clauses calling for a popularly elected parliament along with the directive that the decisions of that body would be subject to the will of the cabinet. The cabinet consisted of advisers to the emperor on both civilian and military issues as well as foreign affairs. Members were selected most often, not surprisingly, from the ranks of the former samurai leaders of the restoration, collectively known as the *genro*. The prime minister, again generally a member of the *genro*, was selected by the emperor and instructed to form a cabinet to carry out the imperial will. If the government failed to perform its assigned task, a new one was formed. The result of this situation saw the same individuals returned repeatedly to a variety of posts within the cabinet system. The generation of leaders who initiated the Meiji Restoration were relatively young at its inception and survived to oversee the first four decades of the transition. Despite frequent reshuffling, few new members and fewer new ideas were introduced before the opening of the twentieth century.

The growth and development of Japan's modern industrial base, like that of most industrialized nations, was accomplished on the backs of the peasantry. Unlike the case of industrialization in the Western world, however, the Japanese central government brought modern technology to a population that had just been liberated from several centuries of unbridled military despotism. The need for speed and efficiency in Japan's modernization dictated that industry would have to be supported and even directed by the central government to ensure the greatest productivity and discourage overlapping efforts. Japanese industry did not grow up in a laissez-faire or free trade environment, but rather was guided and stimulated by direct contact with the Meiji leaders and government. This support was enabled by a rather heavy tax burden imposed on Japan's traditional economic base, the farming peasantry. Japan's peasants were generally freeholders and the tax burden imposed in the 1870s and after—required in currency rather than rice, as had been the traditional norm—drove many peasants to poverty and often resulted in violent anti-government uprisings. Contact with the West, however, created greater demand and increased prices for such agricultural goods as silk, silkworms, and tea, and benefited certain sections of the peasantry, so that unrest was rarely widespread or unified.

The development of heavy industry followed the British model and eventually expanded from small shops of thirty employees or fewer to large factories with hundreds of workers. Early industries included textiles, mines, and railroads. The government took a special interest in the growth of the steel industry and supported expansion and standardization of the nation's railroad network. Government subsidies and guaranteed contracts, trading inexpensive production of military equipment for rights to all technological innovations, ensured that preferred companies grew with almost no internal or external competition. As the collaboration between select industries and the government grew, leaders of those industries branched into other areas—most often investment banking—and took advantage of the Meiji government's reluctance to purchase loans from foreign agencies to extend credits to the government themselves. These interconnected industries that depended on government support and in turn provided financial backing to the government were known as *zaibatsu*. The *zaibatsu* were (and remain, post–1945) targets of numerous foreign complaints about unfair trade practices, but they helped Japan achieve an economic miracle, accomplishing a total modernization of the industrial base in less than half a century. By the last decade of the nineteenth century, Japan had emerged as a rival to the Western powers for an economic stake in China and throughout Asia.

In less than fifty years Meiji's *genro* and their followers had industrialized the country. They had also copied the best of each European nation's contribution to modern society. The Japanese navy was built on the British model; the army was modeled on that of imperial Germany. From the United States very little was copied, for the simple reason that the recent Civil War made it seem unwise to do so. Meiji demolished isolation and brought the Japanese into the twentieth century. But the Japan that the *genro* modernized had been a feudal military dictatorship, and significant echoes of this remained.

The First Sino–Japanese War

Japan terminated its isolation and entered the world arena in the late nineteenth century. This period was the heyday of Western imperialism, when all of the great powers were engaged in conquering Africa and Asia. The Japanese adopted an imperialist agenda, but they did so rather late in the game. In a certain sense, it might be argued that World War II in the Pacific was, at least in the first instance, nothing more than the logical extension of nineteenth-century imperialism, albeit long after the rest of the world had begun to abandon imperialism as being overly aggressive, immoral, and, more importantly, unprofitable.

Japan's most important early colony was Korea. The Japanese engaged the Chinese in a rivalry for control of that strategic peninsula. Chinese military leader Yuan Shikai hoped to reduce Korea to a dependent state of the Manchu government and helped sponsor anti-Japanese revolts in Korean cities. The Japanese considered an independent or Japanese-controlled Korea imperative to their national security, often referring to the peninsula as "a dagger pointed at the heart of Japan." When the Japanese demanded that China put a stop to these uprisings the Chinese refused to yield. Japan used the revolts as a pretext to invade and attacked Chinese forces in Korea in July 1894, declaring war four days later. Most outside observers felt that China would easily hand the upstart Japanese a well-deserved bloodying, but the poorly trained and undisciplined Chinese armies retreated. Early defeat threatened to become a total rout when the capture of Beijing and collapse of the Chinese government were threatened by the end of the year. China's government indicated a willingness to negotiate and the Japanese accepted, fearing that a total dissolution of China would encourage a Western scramble to divide up the spoils. The ensuing negotiations produced the Treaty of Shimoneseki of March 1895. China gave Japan the right to exploit Korea as well as ceding outright several other territories, including Formosa.

Many Westerners, including the United States, viewed the Japanese victory as a positive development and hoped that the Japanese could impose some order on the chaos developing in East Asia. However, three European powers—France, Germany, and especially Russia—were determined to exploit or at least preserve the Korean peninsula for themselves. In 1895 these three powers informed the Japanese that Korea could not become a literal Japanese conquest. The "Triple Intervention," as the Japanese named it, constituted a body blow to Japanese prestige. Here for the first time was undeniable proof that the other great powers would not acknowledge Japan as an equal, at least not in the realm of colonial ambitions. The resultant shock was great in Japan and only encouraged further Japanese conquests.

Japan's inability to confront the coalition of European powers involved in the "Intervention," and the subsequent belief that Japan's modernization would not readily be acknowledged, caused political leaders to adopt a cooperative strategy for dealing with the West. When unrest in China culminated in the Boxer Rebellion in 1900, some 22,000 Japanese troops joined with American and European forces in protecting foreign legations in China and putting down the uprising. The Japanese troops received universal acclaim for their discipline and efficiency during the affair. The Japanese joined with the United States in hoping to restrict Russian influence in China, and not only participated in the suppression of the Boxers but further pleased the Americans by supporting the Open Door notes of 1899 and 1900. Relatively late entry into the race for China's markets and resources left both the Americans and the Japanese on the outside, looking in at the European imperialists who had already laid claim to much of China's coastal wealth. The Open Door plan promised access to those regions without the necessity of displacing the previous tenants, a situation that promised to benefit both new Pacific powers richly. Although, unlike the Americans, while the Japanese preferred to attempt peaceful means first, they were prepared to open the mainland markets by force if it proved necessary.

The "Open Door" was especially attractive to the industrially rich but resource poor Japanese. Japan consists of four home islands roughly the size of the state of Idaho. The islands have absolutely no natural resources, except for meager coal deposits and some "white coal," or hydroelectric power. From the Japanese standpoint in 1900, therefore, interest in the resources of continental Asia represented a version of what Americans termed Manifest Destiny. The regions surrounding Japan contained the iron ore, rice, rubber, tin, coal, oil, and other resources needed by Japanese industry in order to thrive. The governments of those areas, China included, were weak and poorly organized so that the Japanese could not enter into reliable trade arrangements with them to secure these goods. Nor were the native inhabitants putting those resources to good use. From the Japanese point of view it only made sense for an efficient, well-managed Asian power to exploit the bounty rather than allow the Europeans to take it for themselves. The Japanese even pictured themselves as working with the local inhabitants to produce a better situation for both countries, as opposed to the rapacious European imperialists who returned nothing to their colonies. But the Japanese (not totally unlike the Americans) approached exploitation of the mainland's resources without regard for the cultural integrity of the indigenous peoples they would have to conquer. Like the Europeans who had arrived centuries before, the Japanese paid lip service to respecting and preserving local customs and language, but such behavior remained no-tional. The Asian mainland—particularly Korea and Manchuria—beckoned as an area rich in resources. Japan's attention focused first on Korea, where Russia became its chief rival for domination of that timber-rich country.

The Russo–Japanese War

The Japanese were prepared to fight the Russians if necessary, especially after 1902, when a Japanese–British naval alliance was signed that would have benefited the Japanese had Russia acquired even one ally in the forthcoming war. The British were also pleased with this arrangement as the greatest threat to their Pacific holdings was thought to be from a potential coalition and not a single opponent. The treaty allowed the British to maintain a modest fleet in Asian waters and still remain secure. From the Japanese perspective, the treaty accomplished several valuable goals. In particular, the treaty specifically precluded French interference in any Russo–Japanese conflict. Prior to the treaty, the French alliance with Russia and its control of Indochina had meant that the Japanese would have been facing both northern and southern threats during any confrontation with St. Petersburg. The naval alliance also enhanced Japanese prestige and provided much desired international recognition to Japanese military strength.

Russia's participation in the "Triple Intervention" of 1895 set the stage for the conflict in 1904. The Japanese resented Russian arrogance and were further incensed when the Russians pressed the Chinese government for a ninety-nine-year lease of the strategic Liaotung peninsula and its strategic naval facilities at Port Arthur. The Russians had further threatened Japanese security by gaining the right to station troops in Manchuria. The significance of these insults was magnified in the eyes of a new generation of political leadership in Japan, more self-confident and aggressive than the aging *genro*. Violent encounters precipitated by the Russians against Japanese forces in Korea increased during 1903, leading military representatives to call for full-scale war. Japanese leaders attempted to negotiate with the Russians but eventually surrendered to growing internal pressure for more direct action. They refused to accept Russian intransigence in Korea and used the perceived threat to Japanese security as a pretext for a surprise attack at the heart of Russian military strength in the Pacific.

By January 1904 the Japanese had decided on war. On February 9, the Japanese fleet, under Adm. Togo Heihachiro, attacked the Russian Far Eastern Fleet while it was anchored at Port Arthur on the Yellow Sea. After using torpedo boats and land-based artillery to cripple the fleet, Japan declared war a day later. With the Russian navy no longer a threat, troops poured across Korea and entered Manchuria, China's industrial heart, on May 1.

Port Arthur was also besieged and eventually fell to the Japanese, but not before Japan suffered some 56,000 casualties. The Russians hastened to field an army in Siberia, 6,000 miles away from European Russia. The czar's forces were subsequently defeated in three major engagements, the largest of which took place at Mukden, Manchuria, in March of 1905, but retreated with their armies intact. The most celebrated battle of the war, however, was yet to come and would take place not in Manchuria or Siberia but at sea.

In the meantime, the war was producing various international reactions. The czarist government's hope that a successful campaign against Japan would deflect domestic criticism of economic and social policies turned into a disastrous military debacle that expanded disapproval and disillusionment with the entire regime. In Tokyo, though, the war was an unmitigated success. Patriotism and nationalistic expectations soared as news of the series of victories filled the headlines. Within the government, however, the situation appeared somewhat darker. While Japan was winning most of the military engagements, it could not afford to continue such costly victories against a strengthening foe, nor could it hope to force a general Russian surrender before Japan was bankrupt. Japan had committed nearly its entire army, and in a dramatic reversal of earlier fiscal policies was desperately seeking foreign loans to shore up an overheated wartime economy. Though this news was not shared with the general public, in early 1905 the government approached American bankers to secure a series of loans, and asked the American president, Theodore Roosevelt, to act as arbiter for a negotiated peace. Both the bankers and the president proved accommodating to Japanese wishes. Indeed, both the Americans and the British had favored the modern, industrious Japanese over the moribund, decadent Russian empire from the start. For his part, Roosevelt hoped Japanese victory in Korea and Manchuria would open China to greater trade access and encourage Japanese political interest and military activity in continental expansion, thereby removing the primary threat to American interests in the Pacific islands.

For their part, the Russians were unwilling to accept arbitration of the dispute until the power of a second Russian fleet was added to the military equation. Czar Nicholas II ordered the Russian Baltic Sea Fleet to the Pacific, an 18,000-mile voyage. The Russians, evidently unsure of victory, equipped each warship with a Japanese flag to hoist in the event of defeat. (Perhaps the Russians were not sure the Japanese would appreciate a white flag, even if it were hoisted as a token of surrender.) After a brutal world cruise, which included circumnavigating Africa because the British refused to allow them to use the Suez Canal, the Baltic fleet arrived in Japanese waters. The ensuing battle of Tsushima, on May 27, 1905, ended in a resounding Japanese victory. The Russians accepted Theodore Roosevelt's offer to act as mediator and the war ended in September 1905 with the signing of the Treaty of Portsmouth (New Hampshire). As a result of the settlement, Japan gained recognition of its right to incorporate Korea into its empire, a lease on the Liaotung peninsula, and possession of the southern half of Sakhalin Island.

Victory over a European foe was a tremendous accomplishment for the Japanese, who less than half a century before had been locked in a feudal government and society. As a result of miscommunication between the Japanese government and its people, however, the victory seemed less important than it should have. The Japanese public was led to believe that the government would secure both land and indemnification from the Russians, as they had from China in 1895. The treaty settlement provided less territory and none of the money the people had been led to expect. It thus caused an immediate public outcry. Mobs rioted in Tokyo accusing Foreign Minister Komura Jutaro, one of the younger generation of political leaders, and Roosevelt of having robbed Japan of its victory and selling out the country. Roosevelt dispatched Secretary of War William Howard Taft to Japan later in 1905 to soothe anti-American sentiments. Though Taft was able to help avert a crisis, the reaction violently demonstrated the tenuousness of good feelings toward the United States in Japan. The treaty had riveted Japanese attention on the United States, as well it might have. While Japan and the United States had interacted with one another on numerous occasions, and had generally favorable perceptions of each other, clearly neither country had a truly accurate understanding of the other. The Portsmouth Treaty was a hallmark event in the developing relationship between the countries, which was characterized by both competition and mutual interest.

America's Growing Pacific Empire

During the decades after the Civil War, American interest in the Pacific had been limited to a small but significant China trade and whaling. Aside from Secretary of State William Seward's near mania to acquire Alaska from the Russians in the 1860s, America had expended little energy acquiring possessions beyond its continental borders. However, in 1885, Cdr. Alfred T. Mahan's seminal *Influence of Sea Power on History* intruded on American complacency regarding the security and future direction of foreign economic expansion. Arguing that modern nations required naval strength to ensure access to vital foreign resources and markets during wartime, Mahan's work launched a global naval building race that included the United States. During the later 1880s and the 1890s, Americans had joined with the European empires in laying claim to every rock and atoll in the Pacific for use as coaling stations and naval facilities for their burgeoning fleets. At the same time, American interest in the strategically located Hawaiian Islands grew beyond just pineapples and sugar cane. The natural harbor at the mouth of the Pearl River and the deep-water anchorage at Lahaina were very attractive potential facilities for a Western outpost in the Pacific. In Hawaii as in other affairs, Japanese and U.S. interests were growing apace. America's anticipated annexation of Hawaii in the early 1890s brought criticism from the Japanese government, which worried about the civil rights of the nearly 25,000 Japanese citizens residing on the islands. This was on top of the sentiments of some Japanese nationalists who felt that Hawaii would make just as satisfactory an eastern outpost of the Japanese empire as it would a Western one for the United States.

Though the Japanese government eventually acquiesced to American annexation of the islands in 1898, after assurances of equal treatment for Japanese nationals, there was no denying that Japan and the United States were now competitors in the Pacific arena. Similarly, though the Japanese preferred U.S. domination of the Philippines, a prize of the 1898 Spanish–American War, to that of a more aggressive European power, they were loathe to see the decrepit Spanish replaced by the dynamic Americans in a territory that lay along the path of one potential avenue of Japanese expansion. Since the 1880s, in fact, Japanese newspapers had spoken of Japan's "frontier" in the Hawaiian Islands. Even the U.S. "Open Door" proclamations of 1899–1900 had been made in part to discourage Japan from further aggression against a China toward which the United States had shown a measure of good will for several decades. The U.S. acquisitions made America a Pacific power in every sense of the word. Americans realized that they faced potentially stiff economic and territorial competition from a modernized and industrialized Japanese nation. This new competition blended with traditional racial biases to produce one of the first real crises in Japanese–American relations.

In the first decade of the century, the state of California, urged on by native jingoists including the Oakland-born novelist Jack London, all but declared war on Japan. Anti-Japanese sentiment existed on the West Coast and even in Hawaii, the most tolerant of American possessions, to such an extent that on America's western seaboard Japanese were forbidden to buy or lease land in some neighborhoods, and in more than a few they were not welcomed even as visitors. In part, the jingoists focused on the "yellow peril," which the Japanese were sometimes made to exemplify particularly (perhaps because Japanese immigrants were a bit wealthier than the Chinese and sometimes purchased farmland). The first "yellow peril" discussions in the United States had been bruited about during the Sino–Japanese War, when images of a massive Chinese population industrialized and militarized under Japanese leadership caused some Americans to fear for the security of America's West Coast. The "yellow peril" had again been raised during the Russo–Japanese War as Americans were appalled at stories of Japanese military barbarity during the conflict. The upshot of such talk was the call, especially from western state representatives, for limitation or even total stoppage of Asian immigration to the United States. Sometimes these racial attitudes and fears took the form of discrimination and reprisals on the domestic Asian population.

Somehow blaming them for the earthquake in 1906, San Francisco residents nearly banished the city's Japanese to Los Angeles. This occurred in spite of the fact that the Japanese Red Cross raised over $250,000 in emergency relief that was forwarded to the devastated city. The most distressing episode occurred later in that same year when President Roosevelt was compelled to intervene to persuade the San Francisco school board not to force Japanese schoolchildren to attend a specifically segregated school with their Chinese classmates, even though the number of Japanese schoolchildren affected was small. Extremists on both sides of the Pacific called for war to preserve their rights and dignity. This talk did not carry much weight in official military circles, but to calm public outcry Roosevelt had the State Department work out a voluntary solution to the problem of increasing numbers of Japanese along the U.S. West Coast with the Japanese government. The so-called Gentleman's Agreement of 1908 restricted Japanese blue-collar immigration to the United States, and this mollified some of the more ardent anti-Japanese forces in this country, who evidently believed that a "racial mongrelization" would eventually occur as a result of intermarriages between Japanese and Americans, unions then prohibited by law. During his last year in office, Roosevelt became so concerned over anti-Japanese sentiment, particularly on the West Coast, that he sent an American battleship fleet on a world cruise with a stop in Tokyo included to "show the flag" and calm nationalist bluster. The Tokyo reception was stage-managed beautifully, including Japanese schoolchildren waving small American flags and singing the U.S. national anthem. And while the cruise did little to relieve Japanese–American tensions, it did provide some valuable lessons to the United States Navy.

"We were near war with Japan in 1913," wrote Secretary of the Navy Josephus Daniels with pardonable exaggeration. But if war had come in 1913, the Americans would not have been completely unprepared. While Roosevelt tended to downplay the worst of the racist rhetoric and worked diligently to reduce tensions between the Pacific powers, he was not blind to the potential threat of American–Japanese hostilities. After the graphic demonstration of the destructive capabilities of the Japanese Navy at Port Arthur and the Tsushima Straits, in 1906 Roosevelt called upon the United States Navy's general staff to prepare war plans anticipating Japan as the principal enemy. This was the first time that specific orders were given naming Japan as a potential and likely foe. The resulting scenario was designated the Orange Plan and largely anticipated the scope and course of the 1941–45 Pacific War. From the beginning, naval planners envisioned a three-phase conflict in which, during the first phase, Japan conquered or controlled most of the western Pacific. After about six months phase two would begin in which the Americans would begin a step-by-step reconquest of the central Pacific that would last two to three years. The final phase would include a blockade and air bombardment of the home islands that could last as long as five years. Though the original plan anticipated only a U.S.–Japanese struggle, and the details of the plan were modified to accommodate improved weapons and technology, the basic plan remained intact from its inception until 1945.

Orange plans were only a minor element of American political thinking toward Asia in the 1910s and 1920s. The new administration of President William Howard Taft was the first of several to adopt a blatantly pro-Chinese outlook. Taft's primary foreign policymakers considered China a better potential investment opportunity for American businessmen and they impressed this notion on the president. Taft led the call for the creation of a consortium to take advantage of China's financial and territorial development. This was specifically intended to secure American and European interests in China, while discounting Japanese claims to a "special relationship" to its large continental neighbor. Woodrow Wilson continued the pro-China policies, but for other reasons. Wilson saw China under the ascendancy of Sun Yat-sen, a Christian convert, as more righteous than Japan. Wilson even withdrew American participation in the China consortium, preferring to operate on a moral rather than financial basis. Wilson's defeat in 1920 returned the Republicans to power and Americans to the China consortium. The Republican administrations of the 1920s supported a pro-China policy for the same reasons Taft had started down that path before 1910. Also, the Chinese seemed more benign and a less threatening rival to American interests than the rapidly expanding Japanese, who had acquired Korea in 1910, and made a bid for more Chinese territory in 1915. Many Americans felt the Japanese were pursuing a dangerously aggressive foreign policy and could not be trusted.

The Japanese contended that since the United States had acquired a Pacific empire by annexing Hawaii and conquering the Philippines, Japan had a perfect right to pursue similar ambitions. A few American jingoists actually called for war, being particularly concerned to protect the great powers' freedom of trade in China. A conflict might have erupted in the second decade of the century, especially after 1912 when the emperor Meiji died and was succeeded by his son Taisho, who was mentally defective and possibly also an alcoholic. Taisho was less effective in counseling restraint on Japanese nationalists. The period from the ascendancy of Taisho in 1913 to his son Hirohito's regency, begun in 1922, witnessed the steady growth of the power and influence of political parties in Japanese politics. The final passing of the *genro* also caused a leadership vacuum that was eventually filled by members of the military. But the outbreak of World War I in August 1914 gave the Japanese other priorities.

World War I

Japanese diplomats have always enjoyed an international reputation for objective factual reporting. This era was not an exception. The Japanese cabinet met several times that August and, based partially on information available from their European embassies, determined that the Allies would win the war after a conflict that would last approximately three years. They were determined to take advantage of the European war to achieve further gains in Asia and settle some old scores, reasoning that the great powers would now be preoccupied. Hence, they delivered an ultimatum to Germany and entered the war against it on August 23, 1914. This was especially satisfying, as it represented vindication against a second of the Triple Interventionists.

The Japanese had no intention of actively participating in the European theater of the conflict. Their purpose was to take advantage of the colonial power's preoccupation with the crisis in Europe. Their plan was threefold, beginning with besieging Tsingtao, the only German naval base in China, which fell on November 7, 1914. They then gained their first experience of amphibious operations by seizing German colonies north of the equator, including the Marshall, Mariana, Palau, and Caroline islands. The Japanese also moved into the economic markets abandoned by the Europeans, both friend and foe. They found ready consumers of Japanese made goods and enjoyed an expanding and profitable relationship with many of their Asian neighbors. Finally, the Japanese moved diplomatically against neutral China. Their interest in China was natural because of its size, the fact that the Chinese revolution of 1911 had left China politically fragmented and unstable, and because recent Japanese immigration into northern China had placed nearly 140,000 Japanese in the area. And the Japanese had designs on Manchuria's western neighbor, Mongolia, which was huge and underpopulated by Japanese standards.

In January 1915 the Japanese ambassador in Peking, taking advantage of "the chance of 1,000 years," delivered an ultimatum to the Chinese government, subsequently known as the Twenty-one Demands. The ultimatum was typed on paper literally watermarked with armaments. The demands were separated into five sections. The first dictated transfer of the German concessions in Tsingtas to Japan. The second required further concessions in Southern Manchuria and Inner Mongolia. The third part called for a ninety-nine–year lease on the Southern Manchurian Railroad for Japan, and access to iron and coal deposits in central China. The fourth part demanded concession of Fukien Province to the Japanese. The fifth and final part demanded that the Chinese employ Japanese political, military, and financial experts in their national government. It also called for Japan to receive privileges to build temples, schools, and three additional railways in China.

These demands were neither new nor totally unexpected, as various nations had made similar requests over the past century. However in this case China could not fall back on its traditional technique of blocking the aggressors by playing off one great power against another to maintain its sovereignty. Both the British and Americans denounced the demands and called upon Japan to wait for final settlement of the European crisis before attempting any transfers of territory or sovereignty in China. Ironically, both Britain and the United States felt that parts one through four were probably reasonable and even potentially stabilizing and profitable for all nations interested in the China trade. It was the fifth part, that constituted a virtual surrender of Chinese sovereignty to the Japanese, that proved most offensive and led to the denunciation.

Though the Japanese retreated from their position on the demands, after the armistice of 1918 ended World War I they were determined that the forthcoming peace treaty should ratify their possession of the former German colonies. Prince Saionji Kimmochi attended the Versailles Conference in 1919 as Japan's representative and a member of the "big five" powers. The Japanese easily obtained the German islands north of the equator, but they were unable to obtain a coveted racial equality clause specifically requested by Emperor Taisho. The Japanese hoped to obtain international recognition and great power status through international law. But even without the equality clause, Japanese diplomats managed to secure recognition of Japan's "special relationship" with Manchuria through secret deals with the Allied nations during 1916. Similarly, the Lansing–Ishii agreements of 1917 secured American recognition of Japan's role in Manchuria in return for a Japanese reaffirmation of the "Open Door" in China.

President Wilson fueled the growing animosity by accepting common descriptions of Japan as the "Germany" of Asia. Wilson's personal religious bigotry led him to view Japan as an obstacle to peace and to accept the notion of inevitable conflict between the two countries. Even Wilson's advisers differed over how to handle the Japanese. Presidential adviser Edward M. House recommended working with the Japanese and integrating them into a common front for stability, while Secretary of State Robert Lansing encouraged the president's view that China should be America's primary friend in Asia. In the end, Wilson himself denied Japanese calls for the racial equality clause, believing that the American Senate would never accept a treaty based on such a principle. Indeed, the Senate did not accept the Versailles Treaty, but it was not a racial equality clause that they found so offensive. Failure of the racial equality clause was painful to many Japanese unfamiliar with the other secret deals, however, and blaming this largely on President Woodrow Wilson, they engaged in a spate of jingoism, evidently encouraged by the government.

American distrust of Japanese motives was exacerbated by the Siberian intervention of 1918 and after. Japan joined with the other allies in invading and occupying portions of Russia after the Bolshevik Revolution. Eventually some 70,000–80,000 Japanese troops were stationed in Siberia, ostensibly to protect Japanese nationals and possessions, and to assist in the escape of the Czechoslovakian battalion. The size and behavior of the Japanese force angered Americans, even though the Japanese had refrained from intervening until after receiving U.S. encouragement. Further complicating the situation was the fact that the Japanese chose to remain in Siberia until 1922, some two years after the substantially smaller American force had departed.

The outcome of deteriorating U.S.–Japanese relations during the 1910s was a refocusing of defensive perceptions by both nations. Although the United States had begun to perceive Japan as a serious military threat as early as 1907, little had come of this outside of initial Orange plans. The naval building program of 1916 can be seen as the first real policy aimed at U.S. preparations to meet a threat in the Pacific, as most of the fleet to be built was intended for the Pacific. In fact, after the war in Europe ended, Wilson transferred the bulk of the American fleet to the Pacific, where it remained until 1941. Even if naval planners always accepted that the western Pacific would be outside of America's reasonable defensive perimeter, after 1919 they had every intention of making the eastern Pacific an unquestioned U.S. preserve.

Similarly, the Japanese military establishment reconsidered its perception of Russia as Japan's primary foe after World War I. While the army continued to prepare for a continental war against traditional foes like China and Russia, the navy won new support for its own building program, pointing to the United States as a potential rival for the resources of the central and western Pacific. After 1919, Japan entered into a naval arms-building race with the United States and Britain to secure its future as a maritime power in Asia. Once again, Japan opted to confront Western aggression with its own tools, and undertook a program of self-strengthening in preparation for what it felt was an inevitable confrontation.

These rivalries underlay the conflict in Asia and the Pacific for the next two and a half decades. American and Japanese interests clashed frequently as Japan attempted to implement its own "manifest destiny," a destiny that required the territory and workforce of continental Asia and the resources of the southern Pacific islands. At the same time, the United States attempted to retain rights of free trade and open access to the lucrative markets of China and the Pacific Rim.

Suggestions for Further Reading

Edwin Reischauer, former U.S. ambassador to Japan, provides a useful introduction to Japanese culture and folkways in *The Japanese* (Cambridge, MA: Harvard University Press, 1981). Some very good general studies of Japanese development after the Meiji Restoration have been added recently as well including Marius Jensen, *The Making of Modern Japan* (Cambridge, MA: Belknap Press, 2000); and Masayo Duus, *Modern Japan* (New York: Houghton Mifflin, 1998). The standard work on the place of the military in Japanese society remains Ruth Benedict, *The Chrysanthemum and the Sword* (Boston: Little, Brown, 1946). Joining Charles E. Neu, *The Troubled Encounter: The United States and Japan* (Malibar, FL: Kreiger, 1981), as one of the best surveys of Japanese–American relations prior to the conflict is Walter LaFeber's *The Clash: U.S.–Japanese Relations Throughout History* (New York: W.W. Norton, 1997). For the Japanese theory and way of war, Tsunetomo Yamamoto's *Hagakure: The Book of the Samurai* (New York: Kodansha, no date) is invaluable, but see also S.R. Turnbull, *The Samurai: A Military History* (New York: Macmillan, 1977).

2

The Road to Pearl Harbor

War between Japan and the United States was neither inevitable nor unavoidable. Consequently, the progress of international relations that culminated in the surprise attack on the American fleet at Pearl Harbor on the morning of December 7, 1941, was not such that a single turning point or crucial incident marked the start of irreconcilable differences. In fact, the very opposite seems to be true. There were numerous instances of real cooperation and opportunities to forestall hostilities in the two decades between the conclusion of World War I and the opening volley of the Pacific War. As a result, the history of this period is better seen as one of gradual shifts of attitude and incremental movement toward confrontation. Most ironically, on the very eve of the war between the two great Pacific powers, influential factions in both countries were aware of the potential for conflict and were working diligently to prevent it.

One area of misunderstanding and conflict that plagued U.S.–Japanese relations throughout the interwar period was Japan's expanded role in Asia after 1920. Japanese economic and military interests in Korea and southern Manchuria were already well established by the end of World War I, but acquisition of the German mandated territories in the central and southern Pacific, as well as the leasehold on the Shantung peninsula, expanded Tokyo's imperial vision. The new territories promised to relieve some of the pressure of Japan's expanding population and industrial growth. In return, the Asian mainland could provide both much-needed raw materials and outposts for expanded military and economic ventures. To Americans, these new Japanese ambitions represented a potential threat not only to the United States, but also to European empires and resources in the Pacific. Because of this perceived predatory expansionism, some American authors even began to refer to Japan as the "Germany of the Pacific." Other Americans saw the twenty-one demands of 1915 coupled with Japan's new acquisitions as part of a unified effort to dominate all of Asia and its precious trade markets and natural resources. Though many of these American voices were still on the fringe, their dire predictions of future conflict between the United States and Japan represented a powerful anti-Japanese sentiment in the American public that was to surface from time to time between 1921 and 1941.

What appeared to some in the United States as Japan's "unified" effort to dominate all of Asia was, for Japan, far from well organized. Japan entered the postwar period in a state of relative political drift for numerous reasons. By 1920, most of the *genro* responsible for leading Japan through the Meiji Restoration and the subsequent modernization of Japan's industrial, economic, and political structure, were dead. Functionaries of the nascent political parties and members of the military officer corps increasingly filled their positions in the government. New political parties of the left appeared, while the collapse of the postwar economic boom in 1921 began a decade-long inflationary period as competition for the markets surrendered by the Europeans after 1914 once again became fierce. Though Japan had unquestionably positioned itself as one the great powers, it was suffering from a lack of leadership to guide it in this new international situation. Or perhaps it would be more correct to say that Japan suffered from too many leaders, as politicians, military commanders, and economic leaders of the powerful *zaibatsu* increasingly became powers unto themselves in the following decades. These different agencies used a variety of means to appeal to public sentiment, though none more successfully than the military.

This crisis of leadership was complicated by the deteriorating health of the emperor. After a severe stroke in 1919, Taisho became increasingly unstable, his condition worsened by his heavy drinking. Subsequent less debilitating strokes in 1919 and 1921 impaired Taisho's memory as well as his ability to speak and walk, and on several occasions may have even caused him to fall from his horse. In 1921, after, among other oddities, the emperor rolled up a scroll and peeked through it at members of the Diet, his son, Hirohito, assumed power as regent. While Hirohito was quite healthy and quite sane, he had lived a sheltered life and was largely unacquainted with political affairs. Though personally inclined to pacifism, Hirohito was often unwilling to intervene in the daily business of government. Indeed, constant intervention was not the role envisioned for the emperor under the Japanese constitution, but it may have been better had the emperor assumed more direct leadership in the events that followed.

The Washington Treaty System

In 1917, the United States announced a naval building program that would create an American navy "second to none." After the crisis of war passed, however, the fiscally conservative Republican Congress, led by Senator William H. Borah, evidenced no desire to pay the construction and maintenance costs entailed in such a program, to say nothing of facing the international ill-will engendered by the policy. Instead, Congress hoped to stave off the burdensome expense and the arms race such a program had already begun through international cooperation. In November 1921, the United States invited representatives from Great Britain and Japan to discuss naval arms limitations in Washington. The invitation was received warmly in London and Tokyo for different reasons. Like the Americans, the British were anxious to cut defense spending and wanted to avoid a disastrous naval arms race with the United States. Britain was even willing to trade the beneficial Anglo-Japanese Naval Treaty, which it knew the Americans disliked, if it meant an end to the new arms race. At the same time, postwar inflation in Japan made a series of U.S.-sponsored loans by the Morgan Bank attractive enough to lure the Japanese to the bargaining table. The primary accomplishment of the conference was agreement on a 10 : 10 : 6 ratio for capital ships (excluding aircraft carriers, which were covered by a different ratio), meaning that if each power built to treaty strength the Japanese navy would be three-fifths the size of the American and British navies. In addition, a ten-year moratorium was placed on all new capital ship construction. Erection of new fortifications in the Pacific was also forbidden, with exceptions made for the U.S. base of Pearl Harbor on Oahu, Hawaii, the British fortress at Singapore, and several Japanese possessions.

More significantly for the Americans, the Washington conference accomplished other substantial goals of U.S. foreign policy including ending the Anglo–Japanese Alliance, which members of the U.S. State Department had targeted for destruction because of its implied threat against American interests in the Pacific. Also, the Five and Nine Power Treaties, signed by the three primary participants along with other nations with Pacific interests, reestablished the principle of the "Open Door " while avoiding discussion of Japan's role in Korea and Manchuria. The United States also received permission to build a communications outpost on the island of Yap. Finally, in a gesture both satisfying to American jingoes and financially and militarily economical for Japan, Tokyo unilaterally surrendered its concession on Shantung and announced the end of its Siberian occupation during the conference.

Though Japan's navy had hoped for a 10 : 10 : 7 ratio, if not absolute parity, and was disappointed with the limitations placed upon it, the Japanese government was generally satisfied with the system. From the Japanese navy's standpoint, however, insult was added to injury when a few years later they discovered that the American delegation had learned via cryptography that Japanese representatives had been instructed to accept 10 : 10 : 6 as a last resort. The one glaring failure of the Washington system was its inability to deal with more than just capital ship ratios. For various reasons, the moratorium on capital ships failed to include cruisers, and those became the focus of naval building during the 1920s until the London Conference of 1930 placed a similar 10 : 10 : 6 cap on them. So while the race to build battleships and aircraft carriers was suspended, by the end of the 1920s all of the signatory powers were engaged in significant cruiser construction efforts.

Internationally, the results of the Washington conference were greeted with praise and high hopes. It initiated a decade of peace and generally good relations among the signatories, often in spite of political ineptitude. For instance, the conference had scarcely concluded when the United States enacted the Immigration Act of 1924, which forbade further Japanese immigration. Had the Americans chosen to submit Japanese immigrants to the same quotas placed on Europeans—a fate Japan would have submitted to with little cause for animosity—the number would have been less than 200 per year. However, exclusion of "orientals" was the order of the day, and representatives from the West Coast were adamant. While the exclusion act gave ultra nationalists in both countries plenty of fuel for war talk, it did little to change thinking in military circles. The United States Navy had perceived Japan as its most likely enemy since the 1910s and, similarly, the Japanese placed the United States at the top of its list of potential foes. Neither, however, saw this particular legislative crisis as a potential *causus belli*; consequently, neither raised its own preparedness significantly.

Victory of the Japanese Militarists

With the demise of Taisho, who had lived in seclusion since 1921, on Christmas Day 1926, Emperor Hirohito's reign officially began. From the outset the new emperor, who had chosen the motto *Showa*—enlightened peace—as his posthumous "throne name," disliked the plans his military was obviously hatching.

As a cure-all for Japan's problems, a Japanese "expedition" to occupy and "bring order" to Chinese Manchuria, which was admittedly in disarray, was openly bruited about Tokyo in the late 1920s. There is no doubt that barbarism and banditry were the order of the day in Manchuria. Civil war tore China throughout the 1920s and 1930s as warlords vied with nationalists and communists for control of the remnants of the deceased Qing empire. Many Westerners viewed Japanese control of Manchuria as a potentially stabilizing force and were receptive to any program that promised to bring order to the Asian mainland. But in actual fact the Japanese coveted Manchuria

23

for its extensive iron ore, coal, and oil resources. Such resources would free Japan from its dependence on foreign nations (particularly the United States) for raw materials, and would ensure its status as a great power.

During the 1920s, Japanese policymakers developed a foreign policy that envisioned creating an Asian empire for Japan similar to those held by Western powers. Japan even spoke of this empire in terms not dissimilar to America's idea of Manifest Destiny. Japan's egocentrism led Japanese to believe that they were the most advanced Asian race and that therefore it was both their right and their obligation to dominate and lead the other Asian nations. In the 1920s, that vision focused primarily on the conquest of the Asian mainland, a notion that American presidents as early as Theodore Roosevelt had actually endorsed and encouraged. Prime Minister Tanaka Giichi became the spokesman for this vision and advocated a harsh line against both Chinese corruption and instability, and Asian communism. Most Japanese political and military leaders came to accept as axiomatic that expansionist foreign policy was their nation's only hope of survival.

This assumption became an absolute necessity after the collapse of the Japanese economy following 1929. Farmers and peasants, who had only been on the margins of the economic boom of the 1920s, were overwhelmed by the economic disaster of the Great Depression. Most Japanese raised silkworms as a secondary income source, and the greatest consumer of Japanese silk was the United States. The onset of the Great Depression destroyed the silk market in the United States and meant the loss of an income for many Japanese that represented the difference between survival and starvation. The economic crisis revealed the depth of Japanese dependence on foreign markets and resources and led many to believe that expansion and conquest were not a military luxury but rather an economic necessity. The Japanese began operating on these beliefs, however, without ever fully reconciling them with the economic and security considerations of the other great powers with significant previously existing interests in the Pacific. This fundamental incompatibility would eventually lead to conflict. Initially though, most Japanese saw their involvement in Manchuria as a logical extension of their natural interests.

Some Japanese, admittedly a minority, viewed bringing order to China's northern provinces as a duty, since the government in Peking obviously could not do so. Emperor Hirohito reigned, but he did not rule and hence had no voice in the actual formulation of policy; he could only watch the drift toward conquest and war, as helpless as any civilian. If the emperor objected to any particular military stratagem, the army, via the time-honored doctrine of *gekokujo*, could simply declare that the emperor was being ill-advised and that true obedience dictated the course the military had chosen. And some Japanese viewed the emperor's position as so lofty that they considered mundane affairs of state to be beneath him. In any event, it would be easy to fabricate an excuse for military action in Manchuria, since Japanese troops had occupied Korea and exercised the right to guard Manchuria's rail lines since 1905. The prolonged existence of this occupation force, the Kwantung army, had given it a life and personality of its own. Populated mostly with the sons of peasants and farmers, the ranks of the Kwantung officer corps and soldiery were more than willing to manufacture the means to alleviate the suffering of their families and friends back home, even if it meant risking war.

On the night of September 18, 1931, the plot against Manchuria began to unfold. An explosive charge was planted under a rail line near Mukden; it duly exploded, although it merely scattered some of the roadbed's ballast. Nonetheless, that same evening the Japanese army occupied Mukden and seized the Chinese arsenal in that city. A subsequent investigation of the incident by the League of Nations disclosed that a train had passed safely over the line only twenty minutes after the explosion and revealed the fabricated nature of the entire episode. Japan withdrew from the League, however, when the findings were made public.

The Japanese government's policy during the 1920s had been one of cooperation with the Peking government, with all attempts at economic development carried out through appropriate agencies. They reversed this policy in the early 1930s, however, and began supporting individual Chinese warlords and encouraging the individual efforts of powerful Koumintang generals. Kwantung leaders took this policy so far, that when warlord general Chang Tso-lin refused to cooperate and turned on the Koumintang, they had him assassinated. Like the Mukden Incident, this act of rogue policymaking was excused by the general public and went virtually unpunished, making the cabinet and even the throne guilty after the fact of complicity with the radical militarists. Japan's leaders were not alone in dismissing the actions of the Kwantung army. The international community did nothing to castigate the Japanese for their actions either. In fact, America's Stimson Doctrine, a policy of nonrecognition of territorial gains acquired by force, was the harshest of the international responses.

The Mukden Incident marked the ascendancy of the Japanese military in national politics and in the cabinet itself. When coupled with several army-inspired assassinations of political figures opposed to war, it brought about the end of the power of the political parties and began the domination of the government by the military. Both the army and the navy could bring down any cabinet by ordering their own service ministers (Ministry of War and Navy) to resign. This right, inherent in the Japanese governmental structure by common accord, was henceforward greatly abused. The extent of the military's power over the course of Japanese policy may be inferred from the fact that it could enjoy the luxury of internecine warfare among its own factions after 1931.

Though Japan had conquered Manchuria, it did not end all of the region's difficulties, for bandits still plundered the countryside by night. Also, Manchuria did not prove the boon to the Japanese economy that had been anticipated, as Japan's rule cost its economy as much in iron and oil as it obtained from Manchuria. Indeed, Manchuria, or Manchuko as the Japanese renamed it, was virtually self-sufficient. The expected windfall of natural resources and wealth was never forthcoming. However, by dominating the resources and manufacturing of the region, the Kwantung army and Nissan, the *zaibatsu* organization created to govern Manchuko's economy, became virtually independent both economically and politically. Neither the army nor the throne made any strong moves to counter this development either. The Manchurian Incident was a great popular success in Japan, and denunciation or disciplining of its leaders would have met with sharp disapproval among the Japanese masses. In fact, Japanese control of China's northern provinces did begin to alleviate one concern of the expansionists: The opportunities for Japanese citizens to find lucrative jobs in the expanding bureaucracy of empire led to mass emigration from the home islands that would continue throughout 1945 into all of Japan's acquired territories. This talent drain proved to be both a blessing and a curse, as the relief to Japan's burgeoning population came at the cost of the loss of some of its most able citizens.

Given the mixed success of the Manchurian Incident it is a small wonder that two factions emerged among the staff officers in Tokyo, both calling for further expansion to find Japan a suitable area for exploitation and possible colonization. A large majority of the adherents of both groups were majors and colonels, although it was generals who determined membership and ideology. The *Kodo,* or Imperial Way, faction held that the Soviet Union was Japan's primary enemy, and that after Manchuria had been pacified, Japanese expansion should take place at the expense of the USSR. The opposing *Tosei,* Control, group also desired that gains in Manchuria be consolidated, but believed that Japan's destiny lay to the south. Specifically, the *Tosei* believed that the Philippines, Hong Kong, the Malay peninsula, Thailand, Burma, and particularly the Dutch East Indies constituted Japan's version of Manifest Destiny. In the early 1930s officers of both schools first used the term "El Dorado of the South" to describe the latter areas. Some officers actually subscribed to both schools of thought, and debate between them at first seemed routine. By early 1936, however, the *Kodo* felt they had lost ground. They saw an opportunity to strengthen their position when a group of young officers launched an insurrection in the heart of Tokyo. The young officers hoped to force the government to cease cutting the military budget and adopt an expansionist foreign policy. Though the *Kodo* generals had nothing to do with the initiation of the uprising, they did attempt to coopt the movement once it had begun. In the early morning hours of February 26, 1936, just after a severe snowstorm had blanketed the city, troops commanded by *Kodo* officers seized control of a portion of the capital adjacent to several of the foreign embassies. They hoisted helium-filled balloons with streamers proclaiming the virtues of their cause and assassinated some high-level officials, including several of cabinet rank who had been publicly opposed to their imperial vision.

Hirohito determined that he would not remain a spectator. He demanded the insurrectionists' surrender and reportedly ordered his own palace guard units to mobilize fully. The siege dissolved as ordinary soldiers, who had not been informed of the intent of their officers, returned to their barracks upon promises of full amnesty. The young officers petitioned the emperor to allow them to commit ritual suicide rather than surrender, but were refused and opted to have their day in court and make their cases fully known there. Order was restored late in the evening of February 29, and the emperor ordered harsh treatment, including the institution of court martials, for the officers involved. Yet the army, however divided, closed ranks and looked after its own. It circumvented the emperor's orders without his knowledge, and the young officers were portrayed as pure-spirited, self-sacrificing patriots working only for the well-being of the empire. But the back of the *Kodo* had been forever broken. As many of the foreign ambassadors in Tokyo reported, future Japanese overseas expansion was now more likely to be southward.

The year 1936 also witnessed Japan's official withdrawal from terms of the Washington and London naval treaties. The emerging naval arms race in alternative classes of weapons as well as worsening relations with Western powers, including U.S. commitment to a major new building program, led Tokyo to discard the pretense of the limitations agreements. In reality, Japan had ignored much of the treaty from the very start. However, the British and the Americans had never bothered to check on reports of those violations. Japan had placed numerous island fortifications on restricted territories and stretched the limits for naval tonnage on numerous classes of vessels.

Early in 1937 Hirohito resolved to stem further military adventures. He returned to tradition by appointing a nobleman, Prince Konoe Fumimaro, as premier. Konoe was in every way an unusual choice. One of the emperor's few personal friends, he was a reputed socialist and virtually a professional pacifist. A youthful bout with tuberculosis had left him with a streak of laziness and indifference that was to prove frustrating. Konoe accepted much of the expansionist vision of the military, but was also sincerely dedicated to

27

avoiding conflict with the Western powers, a contradiction he never successfully reconciled. Konoe took office with the intention of making the military
his servant. When he could not realize this ambition, he lapsed into indifference without giving up the seals of office. The greatest irony of his several
premierships would be his approval of Operation Hawaii, the surprise attack
of December 7, 1941.

Konoe had scarcely taken office when a crisis erupted in China, sparked
by the Marco Polo Bridge Incident. Continued incremental incursions into
northern China had brought Japanese troops south of the Great Wall and to
the very gates of Peking. On July 7, 1937, in a demilitarized zone near Peking, a Japanese soldier disappeared during night maneuvers in the treaty
port of Tientsin. The Japanese demanded Chinese help in finding the missing
soldier, implying that he had been kidnapped. Local fighting between Chinese and Japanese ensued, and each side believed itself the aggrieved party.
(The soldier reportedly turned up several hours later.) After a series of high-
level conferences in Tokyo, the Japanese military responded to this incident
with force. The military assured the government that the conquest of additional Chinese provinces would take no more than six weeks. Believing that
Japanese national pride was involved, Konoe adopted a very hard-line attitude toward China, evidenced in his subsequent dealings with Chiang Kai-
shek and his response to U.S. overtures to end the hostilities on the continent.

Sino–Japanese hostilities also began in the southern provinces as Chiang
attempted to expel Japanese military and civilian personnel from Shanghai.
Shanghai was an important economic and symbolic center of nationalist
power, and Chiang felt compelled to commit the bulk of his best troops to
expelling the Japanese from this vital center. The Shanghai campaign expanded rapidly and disastrously for the Chinese. While the defense of Shanghai demonstrated impressive Chinese resolve and exacted considerable
casualties on the Japanese, its final outcome was a crucial loss for Chiang
and ultimately led to the taking of his capital at Nanking. Shanghai also
demonstrated a pattern that would be repeated throughout the Japanese campaign in China. Japanese forces were extremely successful while operating
in urban areas along China's extensive coastline, but once the line of battle
moved inland, beyond easily maintained supply lines and out of the range of
the navy's guns, progress slowed and pacification of the countryside became
very difficult.

Tokyo was pleased with the impressive gains that were quickly achieved,
and the emperor ultimately forgave Konoe, but not his military. In consequence he refused to declare war against China, hoping that the Western
world would perceive that he had not desired a major conflict. His signals
were misread. World opinion presumed that the lacking declaration of hos-

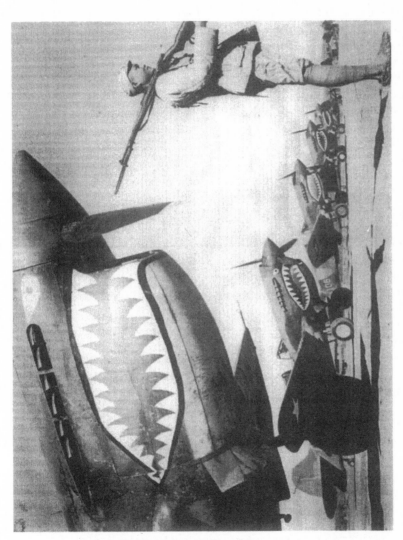

A Chinese sentry stands over a squadron of P-40 fighter planes ornamented with the distinctive "Flying Tiger" nose art. (*National Archives*)

tilities was a manifestation of Japanese duplicity, and embarrassed Japanese diplomats were forced to refer to hostilities in China as the "China Incident," as if using a singular noun would somehow terminate the conflict. American opinion was particularly aroused. Again Japan seemed to be following the fascist pattern of Mussolini in Abyssinia against an equally helpless China. Sentiment on the U.S. West Coast was particularly strong, and more than one Sunday school class contributed funds to help the Chinese government.

Konoe further obliged the military in November 1937 by issuing the Greater East Asia Co-Prosperity Sphere proclamation, more commonly known in Japan as *Dai Nippon*, meaning literally (and much more simply) "Greater Japan." As originally worded and conceived by Konoe, this document proclaimed Asia for the Asians and an end to white colonialism. But the common Japanese expression *Dai Nippon* conveyed the military's (if not Konoe's) true intent. The Chinese government responded by ordering a full military mobilization, and a full-scale war in China began. For the Japanese the war in the Pacific began in 1937, reputedly as a result of Chinese aggression.

In Japan many household commodities and foodstuffs became scarce as the war weakened the economy. Ironically, the expansion initially launched to help relieve Japan's crippling lack of raw materials caused even greater demands to be made on the resources and population of the home islands. By 1938, Japan's growing military commitments had produced a classic trap for the Tokyo government. The territorial gains that had promised to alleviate shortfalls of resources crucial to Japan's industry and economy, were actually costing more to obtain that they were providing. At the same time, Japan could not afford to disengage itself from these military obligations for those same economic reasons, as well as those of national honor. After having successfully recovered from the worst of the depression by 1936, Japan was once again accumulating an enormous debt as a result of its increasing military operations.

The China Incident

Japanese behavior in China became atrocious. Chinese soldiers attempting to surrender were frequently executed on sight. Civilians were openly massacred, the slaughter following the fall of Nanking in December 1937 being only the most notorious example. There, approximately 250,000 civilians and POWs were raped and slaughtered in a fortnight's murderous debauch. Konoe attempted to halt the conflict through diplomatic initiatives, but his efforts failed. Worse, in early December 1937, Japanese planes flying from an aircraft carrier deliberately attacked Britain's HMS *Ladybird*, killing one sailor, and sank the American gunboat *Panay* in the Yangtze River. President

Franklin D. Roosevelt was outraged. He gave a speech calling on America's friends to "quarantine aggression," the reference in part being to Japanese involvement in China.

Roosevelt's secondary response was to write to American industrialists and request that they begin curtailing trade with the Japanese. This he could plausibly do because American manufacturers knew they could easily market the same materials to customers in Europe. American companies, including Standard Oil, complied with Roosevelt's request, although at first the Japanese did not know of his role in the matter. When Roosevelt's role was appreciated, the Japanese grew fearful lest a complete trade embargo leave them stranded in their home islands with no raw materials.

In consequence, Konoe submitted his resignation to the emperor in January 1939. At the emperor's personal request, Konoe returned to the government as prime minister and formed a new government specifically intended to resolve the war in China while at the same time advocating further enlargement of the military. Worse, Konoe's choice for foreign minister, Matsuoka Yosuke, was a strident militarist and advocate of regional power blocs. Matsuoka envisioned a Pacific power bloc under Japanese control as a natural addition to U.S., German, and Russian power blocs in other parts of the world. Although apparently desirous of peace with all nations, Matsuoka was greatly impressed by Nazi Germany and became a firm advocate of a direct military alliance between Japan and Germany. This alliance, he hoped, would neutralize the United States while Japan acquired its Pacific empire. He found allies among many army staff officers in Tokyo who deluged Konoe with letters and phone calls advocating such an alignment. When Konoe objected that such an alliance would be resented in the United States and would brand Japan as a fascist aggressor, Matsuoka, who had been educated in Oregon, replied that he knew American public opinion better than anyone else in the cabinet and that the United States would not be alienated. The foreign minister voiced this opinion so vehemently and with such unction that his cabinet colleagues began to doubt his mental stability. On one occasion, a close friend asked Konoe if Matsuoka were insane; Konoe replied that this was unfortunately not the case, as insanity would at least furnish precedent for removing him from office. (When Matsuoka died in 1946, he was clearly psychotic.) But Konoe could not remove him, for Matsuoka had many army allies in Tokyo.

In the end Matsuoka had his way. Since the cancellation of the Anglo–Japanese Alliance in 1922, Japan had felt itself a nation without friends. Germany was not a perfect solution. In fact, in many ways, Germany was exactly wrong for that role, but its growing strength made it a formidable force to be associated with. A military alliance with Germany, and Italy as well, was signed in Berlin in September 1940. Of ten years' duration, the Tripartite Agreement pledged the signatories to aid one another if attacked by a power not yet involved in warfare in the Orient or Europe. Years later, in reviewing prewar events, Hirohito specified the signature of the alliance as the most important cause of war with the United States. He may have been wrong, but from this point forward the American press openly viewed Japan as a fascist state. On more than one occasion it even assumed that Hitler was dictating Japanese policy! No assumption could have been more mistaken, but the idea was not implausible.

The U.S. response to the alliance was simple but dramatic. Having already abrogated America's trade treaty with Japan, Roosevelt instructed the State Department to begin specifically (and rather stiffly) limiting the licensing of those firms that would be allowed to trade with the Japanese. In effect, the Roosevelt administration began undisguised, direct control of the materials being shipped to Japan from the United States. Matsuoka's frantic explanations to the Japanese cabinet did nothing to alleviate the situation. Sensing the nearness of war, Matsuoka traveled in March of 1941 to Berlin and Moscow. With Hitler's consent, he negotiated a neutrality pact with Soviet leader Josef Stalin. (The Nazi attack on the Soviet Union in June came as a complete surprise to the Japanese and a personal humiliation for Matsuoka.) Signed on April 13, 1941, the pact was a pledge of mutual neutrality in which the Soviet Union recognized Japan's conquest of Manchuria in return for a Japanese promise to respect Soviet sovereignty over Mongolia. The agreement was valid for five years. When Matsuoka entrained in Moscow for Vladivostok, Stalin made a surprise appearance on the platform and openly proclaimed: "Japan can now expand southward."

In a last attempt to preserve peace, the emperor ordered that the Japanese embassy in Washington ask the U.S. State Department under what conditions normal trade could be restored. The task was almost hopeless. Roosevelt had committed his prestige to opposing further Japanese expansion. And Cordell Hull, his secretary of state, was notoriously anti-Japanese. Ambassador Nomura Kichisaburo nonetheless complied, opening trade negotiations in Washington in early March 1941. The talks proceeded slowly. Hull bluntly told the cabinet that he did not believe the Japanese were sincere and that he thought they were negotiating merely to gain time. Nomura dutifully did as Tokyo ordered, even though Hull's racial views might have proved offensive to him. He lived in the same building as Hull, the Wardman Park Hotel, and they frequently met on Sundays in the informal surroundings of Hull's quarters. The results of these talks were often disappointing for both parties. Hull believed in the efficacy of teaching proper behavior to intransigent foreign governments by preaching his personal opinions to them. This approach generally yielded few or no practical results. On the other hand, Nomura had the unprofessional tendency to misrepresent his conversations with Hull when reporting to his superiors. He tended to err on the side of presenting a far more conciliatory American attitude than actually existed, leading to a false sense of optimism in the foreign office in Tokyo.

In entering into trade talks with the Japanese, the United States enjoyed one advantage unknown to the Tokyo government: In September 1940 American cryptographers had penetrated Japan's most complex diplomatic cipher system, named simply the "purple" cipher by the American cryptographic team. Operation Magic, as the American decrypting effort was entitled, was the most secret matter in Washington at the time. Worked jointly by the United States Army and Navy, the fruits of Magic yielded to American leadership every telegram exchanged between the foreign ministry in Tokyo and all Japanese embassies abroad. Only twelve American leaders were cleared to read the resultant intercepted traffic. These included President Roosevelt, Secretary of State Hull, and several military leaders, none of whom held overseas commands. But Magic could not give specific warnings of the Pearl Harbor attack for two reasons: the Japanese diplomats in Washington were not told of the operation because, first, they had no need to know, and second, had they been told, they might inadvertently have revealed the plan to the Americans.

In this instance, information actually served to lessen American preparedness. The flow of decrypted traffic gave the American leadership a false sense of security. Reading the other fellow's mail is a time-honored intelligence technique, but the Americans were new at the game. Very careful scrutiny, analysis, and experience are necessary. Various messages beyond the routine were intercepted. But as will be seen, no warning specific enough was detected to warrant transmitting it verbatim to the commanders at Pearl *at the time.*

In July 1940 the Japanese had occupied the northern portion of French Indochina (Vietnam), an area technically under the control of the collaborationist French Vichy government. Washington was not pleased, but the Japanese could argue that they needed the area as a strategic base for directing further hostilities in China. In July 1941 the Japanese decided on further action, but this time the United States reacted sharply. First, Konoe resigned and then reconstructed his government in a single day, dropping the troublesome Matsuoka as foreign minister and replacing him with the relatively easy-going Adm. Toyoda Teijiro. Virtually the first act of the new government was to order the occupation of the southern half of Indochina, making it perfectly clear that Japan intended to use the former French colony as a springboard for further conquest in Southeast Asia.

President Roosevelt reacted immediately. He began implementing a series of executive decisions that resulted in the suspension of all trade with Japan. All Japanese assets in the United States were frozen on July 26, 1941. Britain and the Netherlands followed suit, thereby depriving the Japanese of any other major trading partners. This move created both panic and confusion in Tokyo. The Japanese government held that its actions were legal under the existing precepts of international law—which, perhaps, they were. But the Japanese navy had carefully calculated that it had only a two-year supply of diesel fuel accumulated, and this was by peacetime consumption standards. No one knew how much fuel might be burned in wartime operations.

The American blow was a stunning one, and the Japanese press universally echoed one theme: the American eagle had bared its claws and shown its aggressive intent toward the Japanese people. The Japanese maintained that they were merely fulfilling their vision of Manifest Destiny, as the Americans had done a century before. The U.S. government thought otherwise. It may well be that the United States failed to appreciate fully the seriousness of Japan's economic situation. The United States, after all, could afford to be relatively complacent about its own natural resources: it was nearly self-sufficient, and the 120 million Americans enjoyed a gross national product five times that of Japan proper.

Washington had issued several war alerts to its various Pacific commands before freezing Japan's assets. Thus, the commanders at Pearl Harbor would later state that the situation seemed more tense in July than at the beginning of December, and perhaps superficially it was. Even then, however, most military observers assumed that the Japanese first strike would be against either British or Dutch possessions in the South Pacific and not against American bases. Consequently, representatives of the Dutch and British governments began making overtures to Roosevelt inquiring whether a Japanese strike against their Pacific possessions would be sufficient to secure a military response from the United States. Roosevelt refused to give definite guarantees of a U.S. response in the event of an attack on European colonial possessions, but clearly understood the threat to American security implicit in Japanese southward expansion. The Japanese were aware of these talks and began consideration of southern initiatives as well. While there was no one point in time at which a majority of the Japanese cabinet agreed that war was inevitable, July marked a turning point in their collective thought patterns. War with America was now viewed as much more likely, the only question being: if it could not be avoided, at what date should hostilities commence?

Secretary of State Hull informed the U.S. military that the Japanese were continuing trade negotiations only to gain time and that he would like to wash his hands of the entire affair. Everyone in Washington cleared to receive Magic knew that war was almost a certainty. Obviously, it would come at the convenience of the Japanese. The most important question remaining for the Americans was: Would the Japanese leave their flank open if they moved to conquer the El Dorado of the South by leaving the Philippines untouched, or would the Japanese seize those islands as well, bringing instant war with America? No one in Washington knew the answer, but they did know that the Japanese had never left their flank open at the beginning of a conflict in the past.

By early September 1941, the emperor determined that a decision for war or peace must be made soon. He was prompted by nothing more complex than the calendar. Since high summer was approaching south of the equator it was the ideal time for conquest of the Dutch East Indies. Furthermore, north of the equator, particularly in Burma, an invasion in mid-winter would pose no real obstacles and would avoid the monsoon rains that dominate the summer months there. The Japanese navy added that if war must occur, the sooner it came the better, since the navy was running on reserve fuel supplies obtained before the trade embargo.

Premier Konoe grew frantic. He reiterated a longstanding proposal for a summit meeting with President Roosevelt, possibly in Alaska. Initially Roosevelt was receptive to the idea and spoke in terms of summit diplomacy. Hull rejected the possibility, though, and convinced the president that the gulf between the Japanese and American bargaining positions was still such that a meeting of national leaders could accomplish little. Additionally, while Roosevelt and Hull did not doubt that Konoe himself sincerely desired to avoid conflict, they feared that any promises Konoe made would be repudiated by the Japanese military as soon as Konoe returned to Tokyo. Ambassador Joseph Grew, America's representative in Tokyo, argued otherwise, pleading the case for Konoe's credibility with the Japanese military, but Roosevelt remained unconvinced. Grew repeatedly referred to the moderate element of the Japanese government, which he hoped would prevail against the militarists at some future date. This, however, was wishful thinking on his part, and had little basis in reality. Such thinking was encouraged by the fact that Grew tended to patronize those members of Japanese society who supported his sentiments. In Japan in 1940, even the moderates supported an expansionistic outlook though not necessarily by military means.

Hoping to save Japan from the wholesale destruction of total war, the emperor was moved to action. Earlier he had called for a series of special Liaison Conferences to include the more important cabinet members as well as the chiefs of staff of the Japanese army and navy. The emperor preferred the format of the Liaison Conferences, because there was little protocol for them and the participants would more readily voice their individual opinions. One such conference met on September 3, 1941. The emperor remained silent and listened as his service chiefs outlined the need for war. Another conference was held on September 6, and the emperor had the meeting prefaced with a statement to the effect that there was too much emphasis on armed conflict rather than on diplomacy as a means for settling grievances. Unknown to the conferees, Hirohito had brought with him the emperor Meiji's famous poem:

> If all men are brothers,
> Why are the winds and waves of the world so troubled,
> Why cannot all men live in peace?

The emperor broke tradition and read the poem to the assembled military personnel, some of whom had never before heard his voice. At the end of the conference, nonetheless, all present agreed that war was inevitable if there was no "reasonable hope" that the United States would restore trade with Japan.

Since the Japanese were unwilling even to consider withdrawing from China or Indochina, which was bound to be America's minimum price for the restoration of trade, the situation remained deadlocked. Further conquest suggested itself as the only plausible alternative to economic stagnation. Neither the Americans nor the Japanese ever fully appreciated the differences in their basic positions on the situation in the Pacific. Japan pursued a policy originally formulated after the first Sino–Japanese War in 1895 seeking recognition of Japan's special place on the Asian mainland. The American position was based on the only slightly younger "Open Door" policy as formulated in 1900. The disagreement was essentially an economic question, but had come to include a great deal more, including national prestige, human rights, and international policy.

Konoe's next move was to summon Ambassador Grew for a confidential off-the-record meeting whose only other participant was, evidently, Konoe's mistress. The Japanese premier reiterated his desire for a summit meeting with Roosevelt, insisting he would bring enough military leaders with him to ensure that any decisions rendered would not be rescinded upon his return to Tokyo. It was evidently after this meeting in which Konoe determined that a summit meeting was ruled out that he decided to submit his resignation to the throne. On October 16 Konoe returned the seals of office to the emperor, pleading that far from terminating the China Incident he had brought Japan to the verge of war and could not control the military leaders. In the course of a twenty-minute conversation with the monarch, Konoe, amid other suggestions, recommended Minister of the Army Tojo Hideki as his successor, on the grounds that Tojo was a respected army leader who was relatively moderate and not automatically in favor of war.

When others subsequently suggested Tojo as well, the emperor made him premier. The American press headlined that the military had taken over the government. In actual fact, Tojo, for all of his fire-eating bluster, was a moderate compared to many other ranking army officers. And Tojo's selection of Togo Shigenori as foreign minister was also a hopeful sign in that Togo was genuinely committed to further negotiation with the United States and got along well with Ambassador Grew. Through his private secretary, Kido Koichi, the emperor communicated his only command to the new cabinet: "Go back to blank paper." In effect, Hirohito had rescinded the decisions of the imperial Liaison Conferences and had instructed his ministers to restart negotiations with the United States, beginning at square one.

From Washington's standpoint, however, Tojo's first really significant act concerned embassy personnel in the American capital. Ambassador Nomura, like all educated Japanese, read English with dispatch and had a fair oral grasp of the language as well. However, Hull's particular Tennessee accent was often incomprehensible to the ambassador and was reportedly worsened by ill-fitting dentures. Only on the rarest occasions were translators employed. Further, Nomura deeply regretted the lack of progress in negotiations and had several times unsuccessfully offered his resignation. When Togo learned that Nomura's physician believed him to be nearing a mental and physical breakdown, a second envoy was dispatched.

Kurusu Saburo was a career diplomat who had served as ambassador to Germany and had signed the Tripartite Alliance with Germany and Italy in 1940, though he was opposed to the pact. Thereafter, Kurusu repaired to Japan and lived in seclusion with his American wife. Since English was his household language, Foreign Minister Togo sent him to the United States in early October. Via a Pan Am clipper from Hong Kong, Hawaii, and San Francisco, he eventually reached Washington. Hull regarded his coming with distaste. Kurusu may have known idiomatic English, but Hull viewed his marriage to a white woman with disdain. The secretary of state was also offended by the fact that Kurusu had signed the Tripartite Pact.

Hull was also ignorant of another crucial fact. The translators who worked Operation Magic labored at a very difficult task. Diplomatic Japanese is susceptible to numerous translations, and precise shades of meaning were sometimes lost on the Magic personnel. Whenever they were faced with two or more possible translations for any particular sentence, for their own professional protection they inevitably chose the more belligerent version, evidently assuming that the cryptographers in the Japanese embassy less than a mile away on Massachusetts Avenue would do the same. They were often wrong. When Hull noted that Nomura and Kurusu often seemed to voice less belligerent language than their instructions apparently ordered, he assumed that they were following a policy of deliberate duplicity. Thus, Hull fell victim to inaccurate translations that historians and researchers noted only in the late 1960s.

Basically, Hull, like Roosevelt, was wedded to a policy of deterrence, hoping that maintaining the U.S. Pacific Fleet at Pearl Harbor and enlarging the Army Air Corps in the Philippines would suffice to deter Japanese aggression. But as a result of U-boat activity, the United States was fighting an undeclared naval war with Nazi Germany in the Atlantic, and the Pacific Fleet had been weakened. Roosevelt's assertive policy failed. But even stationing every major American warship in Pearl Harbor, assuming that the United States possessed the tankers to refuel them during subsequent operations, would be unlikely to have any substantial impact. Adm. Yamamoto Isoroko, author of the Pearl Harbor attack plan, was a gambler by nature and instinct. The strike at Pearl would have occurred regardless of the size of the force stationed there. Conversely, moving the entire fleet back to San Diego would have prevented a surprise attack against it that fateful Sunday morning, but it ran contrary to the policy of deterrence, and would have dismayed America's possessions and Allies in the Pacific, from Hawaii to Guam to Australia and New Zealand.

The Magic personnel were electrified on November 22 when they intercepted a message to the ambassadors in Washington from Tokyo indicating that the situation had so deteriorated that the deadline for any further negotiations would be November 29. (Tokyo had several times set deadlines, then revised them.) The telegram concluded, "It is absolutely certain that this deadline cannot be changed, *because after November 29 things are automatically going to happen*" (emphasis added). Here was as clear an indication as would ever be had that a war plan was afoot and, by inference, that, as was the Japanese tradition, hostilities would not be proceeded by a declaration of war. Col. Rufus Bratton of the U.S. Army Signal Corps read the intercept in his office and was instantly alarmed. When this information was added to the details of Japanese naval troop movements shared with the United States by British intelligence, Bratton concluded that the Japanese were preparing for the commencement of hostilities against America and her possessions. He galvanized the military into action. An army and navy alert order was sent out. Bratton theorized that the Japanese might launch surprise attacks against American bases in the Pacific the following weekend, November 29–30. When those days passed quietly, Bratton personally lost credibility, but no one doubted that the situation was still critical.

Meanwhile, Hull was also moved to action by the Japanese deadline. On November 26 he finally articulated the conditions under which the United States would consent to reopening trade. In essence, Hull seemed to state that the Japanese must withdraw from all of China, Indochina, and Manchuria and recognize the Chiang government in China. The Japanese assumed that Hull included Manchuria—or the Great Wall as the Japanese had renamed it—when he employed the noun China; Hull, however, meant to indicate only China proper, or those portions of the Chinese countryside south of the Great Wall.

The Japanese cabinet had concluded that withdrawal from any part of continental Asia was unacceptable as a prerequisite for the resumption of trade. American military planners were also skeptical of the usefulness of withdrawal. The Japanese feared that the Americans could simply cut off trade again after a Japanese retreat, while Americans feared that Japan would merely re-occupy conquered territories after a resumption of trade. News of Hull's statement was first known in Tokyo during a cabinet meeting late on the 27th, Japanese time. The cabinet was stunned. The ministers promptly labeled the document an ultimatum. It was not: an ultimatum is a specific set of demands with an exact time limit that threatens action if not accepted. Hull delivered no such document to the Japanese. But it is possible that even he did not realize how critical the problem of raw materials was for the Japanese, and how prophetic had been Ambassador Grew's warning that if the trade issue could not be settled peaceably, war might come "with daring and dramatic suddenness."

On December 2 fleet intelligence at Pearl Harbor learned that all Japanese naval radio ship call designations had been changed, the second such change within a month; this was the first time in anyone's memory that two such changes had been made in such rapid succession. Adm. Husband Kimmel, naval commander at Pearl, asked his fleet intelligence staff about the location of Japan's aircraft carriers. When Capt. Edwin Layton's reply did not fully satisfy Kimmel, he inquired, perhaps lightheartedly, "Do you mean to say they could be rounding Diamond Head [a volcano on southeastern Oahu only a few miles from Pearl Harbor] and you wouldn't know about it?" Layton, replying on the basis of the best information available to him stated, "I would hope they could be sighted before that."

In the next few days, Roosevelt was so sure that war was imminent that he informed the Australian and New Zealand governments that if British territory were attacked, the United States would join in the fight even if it had not been the victim of aggression itself, a pledge he never had to honor. Magic disclosed that Japanese troop transports were still headed south, evidently for Thailand or Malaya, with heavy naval escort. Japanese embassies abroad, including those in London and Washington, received orders to begin destroying codes and classified materials, and this last information was passed on to the naval authorities at Pearl. Secretary of War Henry Stimson decided to remain in Washington that coming weekend, rather than retreat to his Long Island estate, since, as he confided to his diary, the "atmosphere indicated that something was going to happen." Roosevelt was concerned enough that early on the evening of Saturday, December 6, he dispatched a personal telegram to the emperor, via Ambassador Grew. The president asked that negotiations begin again, requesting that the emperor act to preserve peace "for the sake of humanity."

During the afternoon of Saturday, December 6, the Tokyo–Washington telegraph circuit suddenly came to life when a message flashed from Togo to his ambassadors in Washington, advising them to stand by "for reception of a very long message in fourteen parts." Why send a message on Saturday afternoon when the embassy would normally not contact the U.S. government until Monday morning? Bratton and his naval opposite, Lt. Cdr. Alvin Kramer, were intrigued, and Bratton ordered the full staff of translators to be called back, most having left at noon. The incoming message was sent via both international telegraph agencies, RCA and Macay. The first thirteen parts of the message did not arrive in order, but as soon as the "purple" machine had decrypted them, they were discovered to be in English, needing no translation. This too was a first.

By 8:30 P.M. the Americans had typed up the first thirteen parts and readied them for distribution to all Magic recipients. Tokyo was holding the fourteenth part until morning. The document was a recapitulation of recent Japanese–American trade relations and was evidently going to reach a negative conclusion in its still missing final section. Kramer decided to make the rounds with it, incomplete though it was. He stopped first at the White House, dropping off a copy for the president. When Roosevelt read it, he remarked simply to his chief aide, Harry Hopkins, "This means war." Hopkins agreed, observing that America might strike the first blow. Roosevelt rejected this suggestion, stating: "No, we can't do that. We are a democracy and a peaceful people. But we have a good record." The other Magic recipients had less dramatic reactions, though all were disturbed. Gen. George Marshall, army chief of staff, had retired early and was not awakened.

The next morning the fourteenth part arrived, stating simply that further negotiations were useless. It was followed by a message ordering Nomura and Kurusu to present the document to Hull at precisely 1:00 P.M. Washington time same day. A further message ordered the embassy to destroy all remaining codes, ciphers, and confidential documents. Still later, Togo personally telegraphed his two ambassadors, congratulating them on their efforts to preserve peace and, in effect, relieving them of any responsibility for the fact that they had not succeeded.

Secretary of Navy Frank Knox was among the first to learn of the new messages. One of his staff suggested that he telephone Admiral Kimmel on Oahu and advise him that hostilities were about to commence. The 1:00 P.M. deadline would be 7:30 A.M. in Hawaii, or just after dawn. Stark reached for the phone but then thought better of the matter. Kimmel was not cleared to receive Magic. Worse, anyone could be a silent third partner to their conversation over a line protected only by a simple scrambler device. Stark attempted to call the White House instead, but could not reach the president, who was talking on the phone himself, after which he was closeted with his personal physician for sinus treatment.

Colonel Bratton meanwhile attempted to contact General Marshall, who still knew nothing of the fourteen-part message and subsequent documents. But Marshall, a habitual early riser, had left his quarters at Fort Myer near Washington to participate in his one recreation, horseback riding, and could not be reached. When he finally returned to his quarters, he learned that Bratton urgently desired to speak with him, so he showered and reached his office in Washington about 11:29 A.M. About twenty minutes passed while Marshall read the accumulated messages. The general, the most authoritative military figure in the capital, perceived that the fourteen-part message might well be, in effect, a substitute for a declaration of war. On a yellow legal pad, he swiftly composed a telegram for all army and navy commanders in the Pacific. It read:

> First Priority Secret. The Japanese are presenting at 1 P.M. Eastern Standard Time today what amounts to an ultimatum. Also they are under orders to destroy their code machine immediately. Just what significance the hour may have we do not know, but be on the alert accordingly. Inform naval authorities of this communication. Marshall

Within about forty minutes the message was well on its way to its intended recipients in Panama, San Francisco, and the Philippines. But the army message center failed to raise the army authorities at Fort Shafter on Oahu because of atmospheric conditions. A more powerful naval transmitter nearby was available, but rather than admit failure to the navy and risk further possible delay if that means failed as well, the army message center sent the encrypted message as a telegram to Gen. Walter Short, the army commander in Hawaii. The wire was not sent at the urgent rate, and until received and decrypted at Fort Shafter, those who processed it had no hint of the critical nature of its content. Western Union handled the wire and nonetheless sent it with a fair amount of dispatch. Relayed to San Francisco, it reached Honolulu several minutes before the attack but was delivered to Fort Shafter by an American boy of Japanese ancestry only after the attack was under way. Both Admiral Kimmel and General Short reacted with predictable anger when the delayed message finally reached them, but it actually was unlikely, as will be seen, that prompt delivery would have alerted them to the Japanese attack.

Suggestions for Further Reading

Scholarly studies of Japan's road to war during the 1930s provide a rich historiography. As might be expected, this list contains some dated, though not surpassed works, as well as newer scholarship. Robert Butow's *Tojo and the Coming of the War* (Stanford, CA: Stanford University Press, 1961) is still standard on the subject. Helpful studies focusing on the Showa period of Japanese history include Herbert Bix, *Hirohito and the Making of Modern Japan* (New York: HarperCollins, 2001); Takafusa Nakamura, *A History of Showa Japan, 1926–1989* (Tokyo: University of Tokyo Press, 1998); Peter Wetzler, *Hirohito and the War: Imperial Tradition and Military Decision Making in Prewar Japan* (Honolulu: University of Hawaii Press, 1998); and Tessa Morris-Suzuki, *Showa: An Inside History of Hirohito's Japan* (New York: Schocken Books, 1985), who follows the lives of three Japanese coming of age in prewar Japan. One of the most useful general texts detailing the prewar history of Japan is Kikiso Hane's *Modern Japan: A Historical Survey* (Boulder, CO: Westview Press, 1986). Herbert Feis, *The Road to Pearl Harbor* (Princeton, NJ: Princeton University Press, 1950) is a good factual account of the events culminating in the attack of December 7, 1941. Youli Sun's *China and the Origins of the Pacific War, 1931–1941* (New York: St. Martin's Press, 1993) portrays the prime factor for American–Japanese conflict arising over Chinese disputes. Jonathan G. Utley, *Going to War with Japan, 1937–1941* (Knoxville: University of Tennessee Press, 1985), gives very useful insights into the mechanics of diplomacy and military policy formulation during the last years of peace, especially the U.S. executive decision that unintentionally escalated to the point of freezing all Japanese assets in the United States in July of 1941. Jonathan Marshall challenges and expands Utley's thesis regarding the importance of resources in the coming of the war in *To Have and Have Not: Southeast Asian Raw Materials and the Origins of the Pacific War* (Los Angeles: University of California Press, 1995). Ambassador Grew's views are given in his *Ten Years in Japan* (New York: Simon and Schuster, 1944), and in *Turbulent Era*, 2 vols. (Boston: Houghton Mifflin, 1952). A good essay on Matsuoka, by Barbara Teters, "Matsuoka

Yosuke: The Diplomacy of Bluff and Gesture," is in *Diplomats in Crisis: United States–Chinese–Japanese Relations, 1919–1941*, ed. Richard D. Burns and Edward Bennet (Santa Barbara, CA: ABC-Clio Press, 1974), pp. 275–96. Diplomacy in the mid-1930s and the role of the Japanese navy are covered in Stephen E. Pelz, *Race to Pearl Harbor: The Failure of the Second London Naval Conference and the Onset of World War Two* (Cambridge, MA: Harvard University Press, 1974). Akira Iriye provides a more general survey of the origins of the war in *The Origins of the Second World War in Asia and the Pacific* (London: Longman, 1987), and *After Imperialism* (Chicago: Imprint Publications, 1990). Paul Haggie, *Britannia at Bay: The Defense of the British Empire Against Japan, 1931–1941* (New York: Oxford, 1981) is well researched from British primary sources, as is Peter Lowe, *Great Britain and the Origins of the Pacific War* (Oxford: Clarendon Press, 1977). Specific studies of Japanese–American trade relations, from opposite political viewpoints, are found in Michael A. Barnhart, *Japan Prepares for Total War: The Search for Economic Security, 1919–1941* (Ithaca, NY: Cornell University Press, 1987), and James R. Herzberg, *A Broken Bond: American Economic Policies Toward Japan, 1931–1941* (New York: Garland, 1988). The standard Japanese work on the origins of the conflict, translated into English, is *Japan's Road to the Pacific War*, 5 vols., ed. James Morley (New York: Columbia University Press, 1976–85). Lee Chong-tung, *Counterinsurgency in Manchuria: The Japanese Experience, 1931–1940* (Santa Monica, CA: The Rand Corporation, 1967), gives a unique view of the problems that the Japanese military faced in Manchuria. One of the best studies of America's naval preparations for war with Japan is contained in Edward S. Miller's *War Plan Orange: The U.S. Strategy to Defeat Japan, 1897–1945* (Annapolis, MD: Naval Institute Press, 1991). Finally, the first volume of S.E. Morrison's history of U.S. naval operations during the war, *The Rising Sun in the Pacific* (Boston: Little, Brown, 1947), remains a reliable, if brief, sketch of the origins of the conflict.

3

Planning Operation Hawaii

Yamamoto's Plan

Operation Hawaii, as the attack on the U.S. Pacific Fleet in Pearl Harbor was first code-named, was the conception and responsibility of one man—Adm. Yamamoto Isoroku, commander in chief of the Japanese combined fleet since August 1939. Paradoxically, Yamamoto had lived in the United States, admired American culture, and believed that Japan probably could not win a protracted conflict with the United States. Born in 1884, Yamamoto was a graduate of Eta Jima, Japan's naval academy. As a promising young naval officer, he had participated in the Battle of Tsushima in 1905, losing two fingers when one of the guns on his ship exploded. In the 1920s he attended Harvard for two years and also served an equal amount of time as Japan's naval attaché in Washington. He was an early and ardent advocate of naval air power and greatly admired Gen. William "Billy" Mitchell, although there is no evidence they ever met.

Yamamoto greatly respected American industrial potential and spoke English fluently. He also became an ardent poker player while he lived in Washington. Yamamoto became the master of the calculated risk; indeed, some American officers who rather consistently lost to him at cards were convinced that he cheated, so good was he at bluffing. Once, soon after the war had erupted, a fellow officer asked him what he intended to do after Japan won. After a thoughtful moment, he replied, perhaps only half jokingly, "Ideally, I would like to retire to Singapore and open a gambling casino, to repay the emperor the cost of the conflict."

A true leader in every sense of the word, Yamamoto seemed to inspire absolute confidence in those under his command. He represented Japan at several international naval conferences in the 1930s and then became naval vice-minister. He repeatedly cautioned against war with America, warning that the United States was not a decadent nation and that any enemy who wished to vanquish it would have to be able to literally occupy Washington and dictate peace terms in the White House. He opposed naval cooperation with the army and with Nazi Germany so vehemently that fellow officers felt his life was in danger. Some contend that a reward had actually been offered for his assassination; and, reportedly, fellow officers sometimes deemed it prudent not to accept a ride in his automobile. Hence he was posted to sea duty as commander in chief of the combined fleet in August 1939, where it would be impossible for any assassin, at least any member of the army, to reach him. Not long after Yamamoto assumed this post, the emperor summoned him and inquired about the possibility of winning a war with the United States. Yamamoto candidly replied: "For the first six months of a conflict I will run wild like a boar, and for the first two years we will prevail; but after that, I am not at all sure of events."

Since 1919 America had maintained a Pacific fleet at Pearl Harbor, with an alternate base at San Diego. Early in 1941 Roosevelt ordered the fleet to remain at Pearl to act as a deterrent to Japanese aggression on the western rim of the Pacific Ocean. Japanese naval planners had long talked of a surprise attack against the U.S. fleet at Pearl, but there were no specific plans. In the age of coal-burning ships, Pearl Harbor had been virtually unreachable. Long-range naval vessels and seaplanes brought the outpost within Japan's range. Even still, such an attack had to overcome serious technical and intellectual obstacles. The difficulties involved were formidable. Pearl Harbor lay 3,500 miles from Japan, and the Japanese did not view themselves as possessing a true deep-water navy. Technologically, the Japanese naval construction of recent decades had taken place under strict treaty limitations and self-imposed restrictions that resulted in a fleet designed to operate in close proximity to home bases. The fuel capacity of Japanese ships, as compared to those of the same type in the American navy, was slight—a damning shortcoming considering that an attack against Pearl would necessitate steaming 3,500 miles, undetected, to the world's strongest naval base, a seeming impossibility. Intellectually, Japan also faced challenges. Prior to 1941 every naval battle in Japanese history had been fought within 200 miles of one of the home islands. In the past, this had assured that Japan's enemies had traveled to them and suffered the inevitable attrition that accompanies a long voyage under wartime conditions. (The United States' primary justification for the insistence on the 10 : 10 : 6 ratio during the Washington Naval Conference, and a cardinal consideration of all subsequent "Orange" planning, was based on the assumption that in the event of war, it would be the Americans, and not the Japanese, who would advance across the Pacific to engage in decisive battle. This line of reasoning further assumed that attrition from such a campaign would almost certainly result in losses up to one-third of the advancing force before final engagement occurred.) If Japan were to risk the strike across the Pacific to attack the Americans at home, it had to consider the possibility of potentially staggering losses associated with such a bold venture.

Yamamoto, however, was never a man to be daunted by obstacles. He told the naval general staff in Tokyo that their battleships—particularly the forthcoming leviathans *Yamato* and *Musashi*, 70,000 tons each—were "about as useful as the Great Wall of China." The naval general staff disagreed; it did not share Yamamoto's enthusiasm for the aircraft carrier and aerial torpedo. The staff believed they had no cause for concern. As commander in chief of the combined fleet, Yamamoto was only their servant; the naval general staff was the fountainhead of all naval planning. Any innovative ideas Yamamoto might breed would theoretically be safely contained on the bridge of his own flagship at sea. However, they failed to reckon with the force of Yamamoto's personality.

In the late spring of 1940, after observing a demonstration of Japan's new aerial oxygen-driven torpedo (a variant of the submarine "long-lance" torpedo), which left no tell-tale stream of bubbles in the water after being dropped, Yamamoto wondered aloud to his chief of staff, Vice Adm. Fukudome Shigeru, whether a torpedo attack against U.S. ships in Pearl was now possible. Fukudome believed the thought had merely flickered through Yamamoto's mind randomly. Certainly the suggestion appeared impractical. Any aerial torpedo, upon being dropped, would dive to a depth of at least seventy-five feet before leveling off to its preset running depth. The deepest portion of Pearl Harbor, battleship row, was only forty-two feet deep. For the moment Yamamoto shelved the idea.

His interest revived suddenly early in November of 1940 when the British Mediterranean fleet executed a surprise dusk attack against the Italian fleet at Taranto. The British utilized twenty-one old Swordfish biplanes flying from the deck of aircraft carrier *Illustrious* in the attack. Three Italian battleships were sunk with aerial torpedoes, while only two British aircraft were lost. The British had used torpedoes that had run at a very shallow depth from the moment of release from their aircraft. Yamamoto was intrigued. If the British could overcome the difficulties involved, so could the Japanese navy. In December of 1940 he set portions of staff to planning a surprise attack against the Americans at Pearl Harbor.

Yamamoto ultimately chose Genda Minoru, the air commander of the carrier *Kaga*, Japan's leading naval ace and a veteran of the China conflict, to write the plan that would be used against the Americans. Genda warmed to the idea. He quickly produced a rough sketch of how such an attack should be carried out. The plan had some flaws but was basically quite sound. Next,

Yamamoto turned the plan over to another acquaintance famous for his thoroughness and good judgment. The real burden of editing thus fell to Capt. Kuroshima Kameto, a man who favored long working hours and preferred to live like a hermit in his cabin until any particular project was completed. Other hands as well worked to refine Genda's original concepts. Genda had no mere hit-and-run raid in mind. He called for massing six carriers for a decisive blow against the United States Navy at Pearl Harbor. He envisioned a devastating aerial attack, delivered by a fast-moving carrier task force. Battleships and cruisers had no essential role in the attack and were added to the Pearl Harbor task force largely to placate the naval general staff.

The problem now became gaining approval in Tokyo for so bold a plan. Yamamoto told his staff that Japan could not attempt to conquer the El Dorado of the South without securing its left flank. Since that meant the Philippines would have to be conquered, American intervention was assured. Yamamoto decided that only his attack plan to neutralize or sink outright the U.S. fleet in Hawaiian waters would allow Japan time needed to consolidate its empire. The war would have to begin with a massive blow against the U.S. Pacific Fleet. Note that the Japanese placed their emphasis on the attack against the Pacific Fleet and not against its shore installations on Oahu.

At no time did anyone realize in advance that an attack against the U.S. Pacific Fleet's oil supplies at Pearl, which were then still stored above ground in conventional "tank farms," would force the fleet to withdraw to San Diego, albeit intact. Nor did the Japanese fully realize how efficient the naval establishment ashore was. Yamamoto was well informed as to the productive capacity of American mainland facilities, but even he failed to fully appreciate the efficiency with which the United States Navy could rebuild itself if repair shops and supplies were readily available. The U.S. and Japanese navies differed in one very significant element in that each ship the Japanese produced was a unique creation and each captain was told not to lose his ship, for he would never receive another. Similarly, the Japanese were loath to separate crews from ships in fear of hurting morale (a practice that proved devastating later in the war). Not only could the United States out-produce the Japanese in new ship construction, but the existing U.S. fleet was far more standardized and amendable to wholesale overhaul and repair in case of emergency. A significant flaw of the Pearl Harbor attack plan was its failure even to target the vast machine shops, repair facilities, and fuel supply depots in the first two waves of attack. Only an optional third wave, which was never attempted, considered attacking the facilities that eventually allowed the United States Navy to rebuild as rapidly as it did and virtually negate the material losses of the strike within eighteen months. For all of his knowledge of America, Yamamoto failed to appreciate its true naval strength.

47

Certainly he had a more immediate concern: gaining approval in Tokyo for his daring Pearl Harbor plan. Here, Yamamoto decided on a drastic move. In July of 1941 he wrote a letter concerning Operation Hawaii to Adm. Nagano Osami, chief of the naval general staff, discussing the wisdom of the operation. The document was entrusted to Kuroshima, who was authorized to state that if Tokyo would not approve Operation Hawaii, Yamamoto and his entire staff would resign and undertake civilian pursuits. The naval general staff caved in and very reluctantly agreed to the operation, which they code-named Operation Z after the famous Z flag Admiral Togo had flown as his personal banner during the victorious battle in the Straits of Tsushima in 1905.

They gave Yamamoto his way in recognition of his forceful personality, the soundness of many of his basic strategic concepts, and the confidence in him that the emperor had often voiced. Hirohito treasured Yamamoto's opinions almost as much as he did Konoe's. He often remarked that Yamamoto and Konoe were the only two leaders who would speak to him with complete honesty and candor. Nonetheless, the naval general staff had the gravest reservations about Operation Z; if it failed Japan would lose the war on the first day. At least one member of that body planned to commit suicide if that should happen.

Yamamoto probably enjoyed making his superiors in Tokyo uneasy. He knew the risks involved in Operation Hawaii but never voiced the misgivings heard in Tokyo. Instead he strove to ensure the attacks in all but one respect. He had been willing to tell the naval general staff that he was better informed than they, particularly when it came to air power, but he was not willing to tell the same officers that he was their social equal. He let them choose the commander of the Pearl Harbor attack force, and their decision was not a fortuitous one. Vice Adm. Nagumo Chuichi was selected to command the task force of six carriers and assorted support vessels.

Nagumo was fifty-four years old at the time of his selection. He was a torpedo expert but of the submarine rather than the aerial variety. While Nagumo was courageous enough for the assignment, he had little faith in or understanding of naval air power. Hence, he viewed his assignment with trepidation. His colleagues in Tokyo made a somewhat more fortunate choice when they named Rear Adm. Kusaka Ryunosuke as Nagumo's chief of staff. Kusaka had previously skippered two different carriers. He had more faith in Yamamoto's plan than Nagumo had, and he gave Yamamoto more credit than did Nagumo; if Yamamoto desired Operation Hawaii, Kusaka reasoned that his faith in the plan had to be justified. Kusaka's one constant phrase of advice to his superior was "Don't worry"—a phrase for which he became justly famous well before his six carriers reached Hawaiian waters.

The Pearl Harbor task force was officially designated the First Air Fleet. Partially on Genda's advice, Cdr. Fuchida Mitsuo, a seemingly fearless and somewhat daredevil aviator, was selected to lead the 350-odd carrier-borne aircraft to their target. The plan called for launching only half of the aircraft at one time because no one had ever launched so large an aerial armada before and theoretically there was risk of confusion, midair collision, and the like. There would be two assault waves, thirty minutes apart. Technically, Fuchida would command only the first wave. That wave would be comprised of forty torpedo bombers, each bearing one long-lance torpedo, horizontal bombers, dive-bombers, and the new zero-type fighters for defense. The second wave would be similarly comprised, except that torpedo bombers would not be included, since they required too great an approach time to their targets once the element of surprise was lost. But whether surprise was achieved or not, Yamamoto meant for the attack to go forward. He warned the pilots that they might have to fight their way into the area, a fact that would scotch the stories that the First Air Fleet had orders to abort the mission if it was detected before launch.

The undersea phase of the attack, which scarcely materialized, was intended to reinforce the air attack. The Japanese dispatched fifteen *I*-class submarines to Hawaiian waters, where they arrived some days before the attack. Five of these craft carried midget, two-man subs on their decks that were to be launched prior to the attack so that they might penetrate the harbor itself once the attack had begun. Since radio reception is uncertain in an area at sea as close to the equator as Hawaii, and because the subs could transmit or receive only when on the surface, recalling them would have been difficult.

Nor would the attack have been canceled if the American fleet had moved to sea that fateful weekend. Contingency plans had been made for locating the American ships wherever they might be, and the Japanese fervently hoped that the U.S. Pacific Fleet would not be anchored in Pearl, but at the Lahaina anchorage, off the coast of Maui. Lahaina's far deeper waters would have ensured that any ship sunk there could not have been raised and salvaged. The Japanese were fairly certain that the American fleet would be in Pearl Harbor on a Sunday morning, however, because according to their sources, that is where it always was.

Japan had only one extraordinary source of intelligence concerning Hawaii and the security of America's Pacific Fleet. This was Yoshikawa Takeo. A former officer in the Japanese navy, Yoshikawa was officially removed from navy service because of poor health, and intelligence work was offered him. He arrived in Honolulu at the end of March 1941. At the Japanese consulate he used the name Morimura Tadashi. There is no evidence that he had been told of the Pearl Harbor attack. Nor, contrary to later claims, did he engage in romantic escapades of the spy thriller genre. He kept largely to himself, and most of his intelligence to Tokyo consisted of reporting things like which ships were in harbor at any particular moment. He never used a camera in his work and aroused no suspicions, at least none outside the Japanese consulate.

Yoshikawa was quietly repatriated with the rest of the Japanese diplomatic personnel posted to the United States when war came. Only after the cessation of hostilities did his true role become known. He did provide the Japanese with invaluable, if routine, information, though he probably never broke U.S. law. The Japanese obtained confirmation through him that the fleet was inevitably in port on weekends, not protected by anti-torpedo nets, and that barrage balloons had not been raised in the harbor. He was, in short, a small but vital cog in the Japanese machinery that enabled Japan to surprise the Americans on the morning of December 7, 1941.

American Attitudes on the Eve of the War

The U.S. army and navy leaders on Oahu were unaware of Japan's specific aggressive intent toward the fleet in their care. In part this was because many in Hawaii, and in Washington, deemed it suicide for Japan to initiate hostilities against a power with five times Japan's gross national product. Misunderstanding also played a crucial role in America's estimate of Japan's intentions. If the Japanese leadership thought the average American soft, dedicated to a materialistic life, and unwilling to fight on the other side of the Pacific, many American military leaders believed the Japanese were inferior warriors and particularly unsuitable as aviators. More than one American star or flag-grade officer was heard to observe that because of shoddy training, lack of first-rate aircraft, and the Mongolian fold in the ear (which was thought to severely impair the sense of balance), the Japanese aviator was simply not to be taken seriously. And, of course, the same arguments that dismayed the naval general staff in Tokyo lent comfort to Hawaii's defenders: Japan had never launched a surprise naval attack so far from home, and so on. Finally, the actual physical climate and the lush tropical vegetation that characterized the Hawaiian Islands almost automatically lulled one into a false sense of security. The "Tahiti syndrome," as some later called it, was no dream. One has to visit or live on the islands to appreciate fully the extent to which nature itself contributed to the Japanese success.

When the fleet lay at anchorage, as it did that Sunday morning, the United States Army on Oahu was responsible for protecting it. Lt. Gen. Walter Short had commanded the army on the Hawaiian Islands chain since February 1941. Having taken his officer's oath in 1902, he was due for retirement. He would have preferred to live out his final days in khaki stationed in his native Texas, but at George Marshall's specific request he was posted to Hawaii instead. Short's task was not easy, in that Oahu was traditionally a navy preserve. But he did discourage interservice rivalry and had a fair amount of both men and material to work with in executing his tasks. Short ultimately commanded the Hawaiian air force—the Army Air Corps contingent on Hawaii. (Officially, the air corps became the Army Air Force in March 1941.) He was also responsible for the only fixed or shore radar that might warn of approaching ships or planes. These, however, only operated from 4:00 A.M. until 7:00 A.M. each morning.

Although he unquestionably did his best, Short simply did not understand the nature of his ultimate task. He revealed later that he believed the danger of a Japanese air raid against Pearl was greatest when the fleet was not in port, betraying a misunderstanding not only of his mission but also of just which targets on Oahu the enemy might find most tempting. On at least one occasion he told his pilots that when war came they might find themselves shouldering rifles, a remark that could scarcely have encouraged air corps morale. And, perhaps above all, he was preoccupied by the possibility of sabotage.

It is true that over 140,000 Americans of Japanese ancestry lived on Oahu alone, although most were native-born U.S. citizens. Having been impressed with Nazi "fifth-column" actions in Europe, Short was convinced that anti-sabotage measures were his prime task. Unbeknownst to anyone in Washington, he instituted no less than three degrees of military alerts. Alert number one was against sabotage only; alert number two was against sabotage and an air raid; only alert number three was a true alert in that it contemplated dealing with anything the Japanese might attempt, including invasion.

Short did not reveal to Washington his retrograde system of alerts, which had no precedent in modern American military history. George Marshall later accepted blame for not having caught a phrase Short used in detailing the response to one of the war warnings he had received from Washington: Short notified Marshall that he had gone on alert one status. Marshall erred, but the primary blame must fall on Short's shoulders. Short was encouraged in his preoccupation with sabotage by the Honolulu office of the FBI, which was naturally concerned with such matters but overstressed sabotage in its liaison work with Short. Far worse, in the belief that segments of the local population might try to destroy his aircraft, Short ordered them parked together in the center of his airfields instead of dispersed around the apron of the fields, a standard precaution against enemy air raid. He also naively assumed that the navy was routinely conducting air patrols to detect enemy airplanes; this was not the case. And he did not give sufficient attention to his radar stations. To be sure, the radar at Short's disposal was not the sophisticated device it is today. It had a range of perhaps 150 miles, and there was no way to determine the altitude of a contact. But Short held it in far more contempt than did the army commanders in Panama or on the West Coast (although not those in Manila), as will be seen.

Short had his faults, but the navy demonstrated still greater unpreparedness. Adm. Husband Kimmel was as dedicated an Annapolis man as that institution has ever produced. A graduate in 1904, he had been thirteenth in his class. On February 1, 1941, he assumed the post of commander in chief, U.S. Fleet, which was a misnomer, and also his actual working title, commander in chief, Pacific Fleet (CINCPAC). Here, for the first time in his career, Kimmel may have been over his head. He routinely worked longer hours than any officer probably should, projected an arrogant image, and could not abide criticism even in the most muted form. He demonstrated little grasp of the potential of naval air power. Like many naval leaders of the day, he believed that, come the day of reckoning with Japan, he would lead his fleet across the Pacific to the vicinity of the Philippines. His fleet would then engage the Japanese in a classic battleship against battleship encounter that would decide the mastery of the Pacific.

Kimmel was an aggressive-minded leader who did not tolerate his word being questioned. He was greatly concerned by the undeclared naval war in the Atlantic, since his warships and tankers were being taken through the Panama Canal for convoy escort duty against Hitler's submarines. On one occasion he went directly to the White House to arrest further weakening of his fleet. But, as he himself privately admitted to his defense attorney during a subsequent investigation of the Pearl Harbor tragedy, he simply did not believe that the Japanese were capable of attacking his fleet while it was anchored at Pearl. He obviously knew nothing of Yamamoto. Like many leaders, Kimmel believed that the best defense was a good offense, a strategy that could not be expected to protect his fleet when the Japanese would obviously have the luxury of striking the first blow. Finally, Kimmel's selection of at least one key subordinate was a poor one.

Rear Adm. Claude Bloch, Kimmel's third in command, also held the title of commander of the fourteenth naval district. This gave him direct responsibility for coordinating the navy's air and sea patrols with the Army Air Corps in scouting the skies for Japanese intruders. Bloch took this task very lightly. He was in his last post before retirement, and evidently therefore viewed his position as something of a sinecure. The most damning testimony concerning his role in the tragedy came from his own mouth when, during the various investigations following the Japanese attack, he proved himself a master of the nonresponsive reply and outright evasion. His liaison work with the army had been particularly sloppy, and Kimmel should have removed him.

Hindsight is always twenty-twenty, but in Bloch's case, more than one army officer had been disturbed by his careless performance well before the Japanese attack.

The Attack on Pearl Harbor

In November of 1940, unknown to anyone at Pearl, Admiral Nagumo's First Air Fleet had begun quietly gathering at Hitokappu Bay, north of Hokkaido, in the Kurile Islands. Nagumo's task force included thirty-three ships. Nagumo would fly his flag from the carrier *Akagi*, roughly 40,000 tons and built from a converted battle cruiser hull, as was true of her sister carrier, *Kaga*. Two newer but smaller carriers, *Soryu* and *Hiryu*, dating from 1937, were also assigned to the operation, as were two brand new flattops. *Zuikaku* and *Shokaku* sailed to attack Pearl on what essentially were their maiden voyages. These last two carriers displaced roughly 30,000 tons each.

Two battleships, three cruisers, eleven destroyers, three submarines, and several tankers rounded out Nagumo's flotilla. At 6:00 A.M. on November 26, 1941, the task force sailed for Pearl Harbor. They stood out to sea undetected. Indeed, they could not have asked for more perfect weather for the purpose of sailing undetected. Nagumo and his officers and crews saw neither sun, moon, nor stars until the morning they launched their attack, which did make navigation difficult, although no one was lost overboard while refueling, as some contend. They took a course to Pearl following a northern route, which offered the least possible chance of detection. Several passenger liners belonging to the Japanese government had followed the identical route, and the area was generally vacant sea, devoid of any maritime traffic. They did not have permission to attack when they sailed, however. But on December 2 they received the message, "Yama Niitaka nobore"—climb Mount Niitaka, giving them authorization to attack their prey. Obviously, by that date the Japanese government was absolutely convinced that war was a necessity. Nagumo's fleet sailed in a complete communication blackout, in seas heavy with swells.

On December 7 they reached launch position, which was supposed to be 200 miles north of Pearl but was in actual fact 180 miles north—a minor error indicative of their excellent navigation given the weather. At 5:30 A.M. Nagumo launched two high-altitude scout planes, one to overfly Pearl itself, the other to fly over Lahaina anchorage. The army signal corps' Opana Point radar station, which covered the island's northwest approaches, tracked them. The radar information center at Fort Shafter assumed they were friendlies. No one could guess the planes' altitude. In addition, Hawaii was then almost exclusively a playground for the wealthy, no small number of whom had private planes that could and did produce blips that morning.

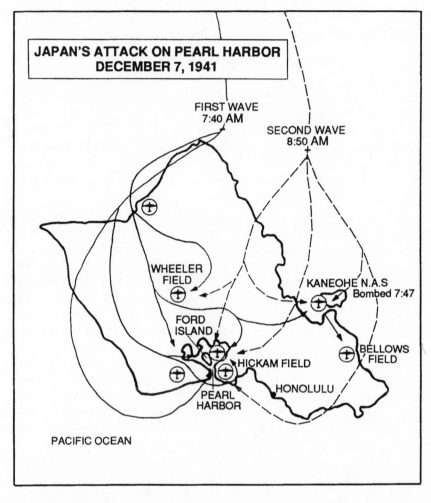

A little before 6:00 A.M., in extremely heavy seas, Nagumo turned his carriers into the wind and began launching his first assault wave. Normally, with a pitch of over 5 degrees, the launching would have been canceled. On the morning of December 7, the pitch was well above 10 degrees. At a 15-degree pitch, the carriers rode up and down on each successive swell, necessitating that each pilot begin his launch run as the carrier rode downward in order to clear the end of the carrier deck as it pitched upward. Worse, waves crashed over the carrier's decks. This was dangerous, and had water shorted out the circuits of the forward flight elevators, Nagumo could have launched no more aircraft. Of the 180-odd aircraft comprising the first wave, only one was lost in launch. The second wave, launched soon after the first, had no casualties. Nagumo now had 351 aircraft speeding toward Pearl, about ninety minutes due south.

It was almost, but not quite, a routine morning at Pearl Harbor. The Japanese *I*-class subs and their five midget sister craft had arrived in Hawaiian waters some days before. As the aviators had feared, the submariners were overzealous, for at 6:45 A.M. destroyer *Ward* had opened fire on one of the Japanese midgets, which had jumped the gun by attempting to enter the harbor's mouth. *Ward* promptly notified the fourteenth naval district, but its report met with initial skepticism, since earlier sightings had proven false. The report reached Bloch and then Kimmel. Kimmel admitted he was not certain what the report meant, but agreed to come to his office to await its verification. By the time he arrived there, war had erupted.

Similarly, the Opana Point radar station picked up both incoming waves of Japanese aircraft, but again Japanese luck held. The radar contact, reported just after 7:00 A.M. to the radar information center at Fort Shafter, was written off as routine because a flight of B-17s was due in that morning from the West Coast, and like the Japanese, they had orders to approach Oahu from the north. Indeed, whenever aircraft were due in from California, the military would pay one of Honolulu's two radio stations to remain on the air all night so that the incoming planes could home in on its signal. The Japanese did not know this in advance, but in their aircraft Fuchida and his men received last-minute weather reports from the American station and were able to make minor course corrections by using the station's signal. Still, Fuchida grew apprehensive as he approached his target, since the cloud cover began to thicken. If he overflew his target, the sound of his plane's engines would certainly alert Pearl's defenders. Then, suddenly the clouds parted and the island of Oahu was visible.

Japanese do not think in fortune-cookie English any more than Americans do. However, Yamamoto himself had selected the code word with which Fuchida was to signal Nagumo's ships that surprise had been achieved. Yamamoto had frequently employed the phrase, "If you wish the tiger's cubs, you must enter the tiger's lair," in discussing the wisdom of the Hawaii operation. So the code word, to be repeated three times, was *tora*—literally, tiger. Fuchida's radio man tapped out this phrase at 7:53 A.M.

Actually, the first bombs fell on the new Kaneohe Naval Air Station on the eastern coast of Oahu at 7:47 A.M., dropped by a group of aircraft that had left the main body of Fuchida's force some moments prior for that purpose. Fuchida was to signal to his men as to whether surprise had been achieved. He miscommunicated with a group of his bombers, and as a result the planes attacking Pearl believed that surprise had not been attained. Fuchida had planned that if it had been achieved, the torpedo bombers would attack first,

Pearl Harbor on a weekend morning in October 1941. In the center is Ford Island; just to its left is Battleship Row, which on this occasion included one aircraft carrier. (*National Archives*)

lest the smoke from bombs detonating on their targets should obscure Battleship Row.

Because of the confusion, all the pilots attacked their targets at the same time; some of the torpedo pilots complained that smoke made their bombing runs difficult, but there were no other practical difficulties. Only at the last moment had the Japanese discovered that they could prevent aerially dropped torpedoes from plunging into the mud at the bottom of Battleship Row by fixing wooden extensions onto the torpedo fins. The Japanese used their newly altered warheads with deadly efficiency.

The Results of the Attack

There were nine American battleships in Pearl Harbor that morning, counting the retired *Utah*, moored west of Ford Island and equipped with a wooden deck platform. Fuchida and his torpedo commander had warned the others to ignore *Utah*, but in the absence of any carriers in the harbor—and carriers were their priority targets—several Japanese pilots attacked her. There were eight serviceable battleships in port that morning, including the *Pennsylvania*, flagship of the fleet, which was in dry dock. Three of the seven battleships on Battleship Row were anchored alone, while *Tennessee* with *West Virginia*, and *Maryland* with *Oklahoma* were anchored in tandem. The inside ships in the pairs were invulnerable to torpedo attack and sustained the lightest damage. Since an aerial attack of this magnitude against heavily armored vessels was such a novel experience, the Japanese were forced to use innovative techniques. Because they did not possess a bomb capable of penetrating a battleship's gun turret, the Japanese placed fins on armor-piercing shells from the battleship *Nagato* and dropped them from their high-level bombers. These shells were responsible for the destruction of the battleship *Arizona*.

On December 6 the *Arizona* had reportedly received too large a supply of powder; rather than return the excess, it had been temporarily stored outside the forward magazine in passageway areas. Whatever the truth to this report, when an armor-piercing shell penetrated Arizona's number-two forward turret, it produced an explosion that detonated the forward magazine, lifting the ship out of the water and breaking it in two. The explosion was awesome. A huge fireball, flecked with bits of debris and exploding shells from *Arizona's* magazine, surmounted the ship. The blast actually snuffed out fires on the adjacent repair ship *Vestal*, littering its deck with bodies and wreckage. Windows in downtown Honolulu were reportedly shattered by the blast. *Arizona*, broken in two, settled into the mud of Battleship Row, fracturing the water mains that supplied Ford Island. A clock found later during the salvage operations aboard the ship had its hands fused to its face at 8:06 A.M. as a result, very

probably the exact moment of the ship's destruction. Over one thousand men died in that single moment. The ship's captain was cremated instantly on the bridge. A rescue party later found only a puddle of melted gold where he had been standing. It was his Annapolis class ring; all that remained except ashes.

As torpedoes tore into the neatly arranged ships on Battleship Row, diesel oil poured into the harbor, for in the American battleships the ship's fuel was stored between the inner and outer hulls, inviting a fire if any battleship ever took even one torpedo. The oil made swimming almost impossible for survivors. Its eventual ignition produced immense billows of jet-black smoke. Patches of burning oil drifted down to the harbor's mouth and literally out to sea with the tide. Many survivors remember the burning oil as the most frightening spectacle they have ever witnessed.

The Naval Air Station on Ford Island, Pearl Harbor, during the December 7, 1941, attack. (*United States Navy*)

Several ships' captains gave the signal "all ships sortie," although Kimmel eventually canceled it, suspecting correctly that Japanese submarines might be lurking outside the harbor's mouth. The largest ship to leave the harbor was the cruiser *St. Louis*. Very early on in the attack, the radio signal "air raid Pearl Harbor, this is no drill" had been flashed out from two separate sources at almost the same moment (it was later amended to "air raid Pearl Harbor, this is not drill"). But it was the announcement as first worded that forever woke most Americans from their long isolationist somnolence. Nonetheless, Honolulu's two radio stations continued for a time with their standard Sunday morning fare, although early on they did request all service personnel to return to their posts.

Kimmel arrived at his office during the attack but could only watch helplessly as great ships, albeit outdated dreadnoughts, died before him. In addition, the Japanese strafed the airfields and bombed planes, which were conveniently bunched together in the center of the fields. By 8:35 A.M., the first wave had finished its work and began winging its way back toward Nagumo's carriers. A lull of about twenty minutes ensued, during which Fuchida remained over the harbor.

By 9:00 A.M. the second wave, commanded by Lt. Cdr. Shimazaki Shigekazu, arrived. As Pearl came into view, the sight that greeted his fliers must have riveted their attention. The pride of the American Pacific fleet lay burning in the harbor: battleships *Maryland* and *Tennessee* damaged, *Arizona* destroyed, *Oklahoma* capsized, *California* and *West Virginia* resting on the bottom of the harbor, their superstructures still burning. *Nevada* was the only survivor capable of getting under way after the first attack, and it made a run for the mouth of the harbor.

Nevada had steam up on her gauges when the attack had commenced because the captain wished to test the ship's newly reconditioned boilers. It had taken a few hits from contact bombs, but retained sufficient watertight integrity to allow it to attempt to clear the harbor and enter the open seas, where it could maneuver freely. *Nevada* became the primary target of the second wave's attack. Fuchida and other Japanese pilots realized that if they could sink just one such ship in Pearl's narrow entrance, they could bottle up the entire harbor for months. F.W. Scanland, captain of the *Nevada*, realized this as well and opted to beach his ship after it took several more direct hits, rather than risk closing Pearl indefinitely.

By this time American anti-aircraft batteries were putting up a spirited defense. Admiral Kimmel, who placed great emphasis on rote training, had not realized that frequent handling of the delayed fuses in anti-aircraft shells would damage them. Moreover, storing ammunition at the ready, where it was subject to physical shock and the elements, caused it to deteriorate as well. Consequently, Kimmel's training program paid off in a rapid rate of fire but ineffective marksmanship. The army had not practiced such tactics and scored a much higher rate of accuracy, though fewer batteries actually engaged the enemy. In contrast, many of the naval shells actually plummeted to earth in downtown Honolulu, several miles away, where they caused substantial damage.

The final target of the Japanese attack was the flagship *Pennsylvania,* which received several hits from contact bombs before its dry dock was flooded in an attempt to control fires. Unfortunately, the water that rushed in from the harbor became covered by a heavy layer of diesel fuel from the ship's fractured fuel tanks. This oil ignited and caused the magazines of the destroyers *Cassin* and *Downes*, sharing the dry dock forward of the flagship, to explode. The intensity of the resulting fires actually buckled the armor plates of the *Pennsylvania.*

By 10:00 A.M. the attack had terminated, though few at Pearl realized it. The Japanese had lost only 29 of their 351 planes. Nagumo had been told he might expect to lose about one-third of his planes and ships, so he was all the more elated at this stunning victory. When Fuchida arrived back aboard the carrier *Akagi*, he urged that a third wave be immediately readied. Nagumo, however, was already planning to retire and return to Japan. Air Commander Genda, who had not taken part in the attack, argued together with Fuchida that one should press one's advantage to the utmost.

Fuchida also reported that he had seen a plane with carrier markings land at Pearl during the attack. This was correct. Carrier *Enterprise* was closing on Pearl; she was only 200 miles distant when the attack began. Genda volunteered to lead half the aircraft aloft to search for American carriers, while Fuchida would return to Pearl to bomb American shore installations and what remained of the American fleet. There was ample daylight left to accomplish all of these tasks and still retire safely with a total victory in hand, and most of the pilots stated they were not fatigued and were ready for the job. Nagumo argued that a great victory had already been won, and that he did not feel authorized to leave Japan's strike force in jeopardy any longer than absolutely necessary. Furthermore, he maintained that its supply of oil was low, and that American submarines might find them. Another attack, he continued, would be no surprise. Nagumo's authority, if not his arguments, ultimately held sway. The First Air Fleet, its location still undetected by the Americans, turned westward and steamed out of Hawaiian waters, its job only half done.

The U.S. military on Oahu had not located Nagumo's fleet, a failure that was in a sense greater than having been caught by surprise. Achieving surprise is always, to a degree, a measure of luck. The United States Navy was still capable of delivering a crippling blow to the Japanese force if they could locate and engage it, since Kimmel possessed numerous cruisers, destroyers, and submarines. But, by using *Enterprise*'s planes to search toward the south, the military authorities gave the Japanese both a tactical and a strategic victory, allowing Nagumo to slip away completely undetected.

But navy and army personnel at Pearl did not realize that the Japanese were retiring. Indeed, they began preparing for the worst. Many expected not only renewed air attacks, but an actual invasion. Having underestimated the Japanese for so many years, Hawaii's military authorities now reversed themselves and the Japanese navy was suddenly credited with far more offensive potential than it possessed. Many trained, seasoned observers later swore (under oath) that enemy air attacks continued until dusk. General Short mobilized the local militia and retired to the Aliamanu Crater, where he prepared to repulse the expected invasion. Families of naval officers boarded buses and moved "inland." Since there was very little actual inland, the drivers were instructed to continue driving until they received new orders. Soldiers were posted at defensive positions along the coastline and awaited the first waves of Japanese troops. Rumors also spread that the Japanese had poisoned the local drinking water supply. Thus, no few residents of Oahu resorted to bottled liquids of all varieties. One of the local residents, evidently noted for his sobriety, reported that he had spotted a dog on Ewa Beach barking, obviously in code to an offshore Japanese submarine. The report was actually checked out, although it is very doubtful that it was really taken seriously.

Less humorous was the naked vengeance some pilots exacted on the Japanese population of Hawaii. The local fishing fleet, staffed mainly by Japanese Americans and almost all without radios, were deliberately tagged as "unidentified" vessels. American planes shot them out of the water, some several days after the attack. When survivors complained to authorities, they were informed that Japanese aircraft were responsible. Many innocent people in uniform and out lost their lives during the next few nights as they were unable to respond with the proper code word or phrase when suddenly challenged by trigger-happy sentries.

The Japanese had succeeded in neutralizing the American battle fleet. They also killed nearly 4,000 Americans, if we count those who died later of infection and related causes. Of 231 United States Army planes on Pearl, 166 were reportedly repairable or untouched; of 250 naval aircraft, only 54 remained. But the American carriers, not in port that morning, were untouched, as were the shore installations, tank farms included. As for the battleships, they were in reality World War I–type dreadnoughts, which, when raised (all but two, excluding *Utah*, saw action again), were to prove valuable in bom-

A clock brought up from the battleship *Arizona*, showing the time of her destruction in the Pearl Harbor attack. *(U.S. Navy, courtesy of Mr. Michael Wenger)*

barding islands prior to an amphibious landing but played no other substantial role in the conflict.

The very fact of a surprise attack, begun before Japan's ambassadors in Washington could deliver notice of termination of diplomatic negotiations, united the American people against Japan as nothing else could have done. For all of these reasons, Yamamoto considered the attack to be but 50 percent successful. Some commentators have contended that the Pearl attack was virtual suicide for the Japanese in the long run. Even Yamamoto acknowledged the improbability of fighting a successful sustained war against the United States. But without removing the threat of the American fleet, Japan could not safely embark on the conquest of the El Dorado of the South. Hence, whatever the long-range consequences, the attack was a short-term strategy in every sense, undertaken, in the end, regardless of the risks or morality involved, to allow the opportunity for Japanese victory.

The success of the Japanese attack on the American fleet at Pearl Harbor on December 7, 1941, can be attributed to both the skill and the care that went into Japanese planning, as well as the mistakes and overconfidence of

American military leaders in both Hawaii and Washington. Congressional investigations into the Pearl debacle revealed a command structure that, while loose and sometimes negligent, was neither criminal nor completely culpable. Academics and amateurs alike have attempted to read sinister plots into the American side of the Pearl Harbor attack, suggesting that America's Allies, or even its own political leaders, knew of or incited the Japanese attack and failed to provide advance warning to U.S. forces. Aside from accusing American and Allied leaders of treachery or even outright murder, these allegations damn with faint praise the achievement of the Japanese navy. The Japanese successfully negotiated all of the obstacles discussed earlier and surprised the strongest American military installation in the Pacific at a time when even civilians realized the imminent threat of hostilities. That seasoned military commanders were caught unawares in this highly charged atmosphere should be seen not only as a testament to the Americans' relative overconfidence, but also to the magnitude of the Japanese accomplishment.

Kimmel, Bloch, and Short, in that order, must bear responsibility for being caught unprepared. Apologists claim that Washington withheld vital information from them. The extent to which U.S. intelligence had broken Japanese codes is a point of great contention among historians. Some point to the "winds execute" phrase (so-called by later congressional investigating committees)—"East, Wind, Rain"—as evidence that Washington deliberately denied Kimmel and Short vital information. Much ink has been spilled concerning this relatively minor matter. Briefly, several weeks before, anticipating that normal communications with embassies abroad might be ruptured, Tokyo had arranged to signal imminent danger of war with America by including the phrase "East, Wind, Rain" in commercial weather forecasts to alert the Washington embassy that war was near. No evidence can be found that the Japanese ever used this "winds execute" phrase. And why should they have? Normal communication remained intact throughout the attack. And even had they employed it, the phrase merely signaled imminent *danger* of war. Similarly unimportant was the fact that Magic staff decrypted several intercepts from the spy Yoshikawa in Honolulu detailing the position of Kimmel's warships and indicating the direction from which torpedo planes might best attack them.

After the event it is easy to pick out the relevant clues from a mass of raw "noise." Kimmel and Short knew nothing of the "winds execute" plan and they were not notified of Yoshikawa's telegrams. It seems scarcely likely that these clues would have made any difference. If an intruding enemy submarine, and a midget one at that, almost certainly operating from a mother craft, does not suffice to indicate that hostilities are imminent, it seems doubtful that knowledge of Yoshikawa's telegrams would have altered events. All diplomatic legations gather information of this sort, although it should have been transmitted to Kimmel and Short as a routine security precaution, since it did directly concern the potential security of the fleet. But in view of the fact that no one thought the Japanese capable of launching an attack at Pearl, Yoshikawa's telegrams are insignificant. Witness that when the marines at Kaneohe Naval Air Station phoned Kimmel's headquarters and indicated in language as strong and with as much urgency as could be mustered that they were under Japanese attack, they were told to knock off the nonsense and sober up. In the end, the very daring nature of the scheme ensured its success: the American commanders at Pearl can only be blamed to a degree for not anticipating what was considered by the best naval minds of the day to be impossible or very nearly so.

Suggestions for Further Reading

The definitive work on the planning of the Pearl Harbor attack is *At Dawn We Slept,* by Gordon Prange (New York: McGraw-Hill, 1980), from which the authors have taken many details of this narrative. The voluminous collections of Gordon Prange continue to provide valuable materials, some of which have been collected and edited in David M. Goldstein and Catherine V. Dillon's *The Pearl Harbor Papers: Inside the Japanese Plans* (Washington, DC: Brassey's, 1993). Hiroyuki Agawa's *The Reluctant Admiral: Yamamoto and the Imperial Navy* (New York: Kodansha, 1979) is the best biography of Yamamoto available. Roberta Wohlsetter's *Pearl Harbor: Warning and Decision* (Stanford, CA: Stanford University Press, 1962) gives the American background of the attack. In *Origins of the Pacific War and the Importance of "Magic"* (New York: St. Martin's Press, 1997), Keiichiro Komatsu attributes much of the success of the Japanese raid to misunderstandings and overreliance on poorly interpreted Magic data. A.A. Hoehling, *The Week Before Pearl Harbor* (New York: Norton, 1963), relates something of a personal view of the personalities in the nation's capital relevant to the Pearl Harbor saga. The definitive account of the Pearl Harbor attack itself is *December 7, 1941: The Day the Japanese Attacked Pearl Harbor*, by Gordon Prange (New York: McGraw-Hill, 1988), but see also: Edwin T. Layton, *And I Was There: Pearl Harbor and Midway—Breaking the Secrets* (New York: Morrow, 1985); Kazuo Sakamaki, *I Attacked Pearl Harbor* (New York: Associated Press, 1949); Andrew Lind, *Hawaii's Japanese: An Experiment in Democracy* (Princeton, NJ: Princeton University Press, 1946); Allen Gwenfread, *Hawaii's War Years* (Honolulu: University of Hawaii Press, 1950); and correspondents of *Time, Life*, and *Fortune* magazines, *December 7: The*

First Thirty Hours (New York: Knopf, 1942). Antony Best's *Britain, Japan and Pearl Harbor: Avoiding War in East Asia, 1936–1941* (London: Routledge, 1995) portrays the Japanese–American confrontation as a result of a much deeper and older conflict between the British and the Japanese. F.C. Jones, *Japan's New Order: Its Rise and Fall, 1937–1945* (London: Oxford University Press, 1954) is an outdated but still useful work. John Stefan, *Hawaii Under the Rising Sun: Japan's Plans for Conquest After Pearl Harbor* (Honolulu: University of Hawaii Press, 1984) is an interesting speculative piece.

4

From Pearl Harbor to the Java Sea

MacArthur and the Philippines

The failure of the U.S. military on Oahu to anticipate the Japanese attack on Pearl Harbor is perhaps understandable. No such excuse, however, can be proffered to explain the negligence of the United States Army command in the Philippines. Gen. Douglas MacArthur had less of an excuse than any other American commander on Pearl Harbor day. A graduate of West Point in 1903, MacArthur's first posting was to the Philippines, where he assisted his father, who was the military governor of the islands. MacArthur had observed the Russo–Japanese War in 1905. He had been received in audience by the emperor Meiji and was conversant with Japanese military strategy and tactics. Perhaps partially due to an overly doting mother (she had lived on post at the Point during his four years as a cadet), he was sadly involved with his own ego, and reliable evidence indicates that he was suicidal by the 1930s. MacArthur was tremendously unpopular with his fellow officers. Most saw him as vain and self-interested. He was a master of self-promotion and often slighted or ignored the contributions of others to his successes, a trait that would eventually make him quite unpopular with his troops in the Philippines. Forced in 1935 to resign as army chief of staff by President Franklin D. Roosevelt because he was discovered to have a Eurasian mistress, MacArthur resigned his commission as well and became field marshal of the newly forming Philippine army. The most revealing account of his personality was dispatched to London during the conflict by a British observer at his headquarters. It read in part:

He is shrewd, selfish, proud, remote, highly-strung and vastly vain. He has imagination, self-confidence, physical courage and charm, but no humor about himself, no regard for truth, and is unaware of these defects. He mistakes his emotions and ambitions for principles. With moral depth he would be a great man: as it is he is a near-miss, which may be worse than a mile.

MacArthur did his best to prepare the Filipinos to meet the Japanese on the beachheads. "War Plan Orange" called for a retreat from Manila and central Luzon to the Bataan peninsula and the island of Corrigedor once the Japanese landed, to await relief from the American navy. MacArthur discarded the plan as defeatist. MacArthur harbored little respect for the Japanese and intended to defeat them at the coastline should they attempt to invade. In matter of fact, however, he hoped it would never come to that. MacArthur harbored the unrealistic and incredible notion that should war come, if the Philippines did not directly engage the Japanese they might be allowed to remain neutral. This hope flew in the face of all evidence to the contrary available to American military sources. In July 1941 MacArthur regained his commission in the United States Army and was given charge of all forces in the Philippines. He was awakened early on the morning of December 8 and informed of the attack on Pearl Harbor.

He evidently panicked or else demonstrated nothing short of criminal stupidity by misinterpreting Japan's hostile intentions. With his talent for insulating himself from reality, MacArthur had not even heard of radar until the fall of 1941, when Adm. Thomas Hart explained to him the principles and benefits of the new technology. As soon as the attack on Pearl had been verified, Army Air Corps Gen. Lewis Brereton asked his permission for a preemptive strike against Japanese airfields on Formosa. MacArthur denied the request, evidently hoping not to incite Japanese retaliation; he even claimed Brereton had not made it, which is untrue and all the more damning, for as supreme commander for the Philippine area, *MacArthur should have ordered the strike himself.* As a direct result, nine hours after Pearl Harbor his air force was destroyed on the ground at Clark Field, north of Manila. The bulk of his planes was lost, including eighteen B-17s and fifty-three P-40s.

Somewhat in MacArthur's defense, the Philippines had always caused a problem in American Pacific war planning. War Plan Orange had gone through numerous adaptations since President Theodore Roosevelt had made the first call for serious war planning against the Japanese in 1906. A rift between branches of military planners had arisen almost immediately. From the start, the navy counseled writing off the islands as indefensible. The islands lay over 5,000 miles from Hawaii and over 7,000 miles from the U.S. West Coast.

They were less than 2,000 miles from the Japanese mainland. Any force committed to their permanent defense would be overrun in the initial onslaught of the war, and any force hurried to their defense before proper control was established of the intervening seas would almost surely suffer a similar fate. Army personnel were slightly more optimistic. They felt that with proper training and supply, a combined American and Filipino force could hold out almost indefinitely for the arrival of relief. For a time during the 1920s the navy had moved closer to this opinion and embraced a policy known as the "Through Ticket," which envisioned the immediate steaming of the fleet to the Philippines after the outbreak of hostilities. The navy, however, abandoned this plan as impractical by the early 1930s. But even if it had still been the navy's full intention, for obvious reasons it would not have been possible on December 8, 1941. Even before the attack, though, the navy believed that in the event of war it would have to eventually liberate the Philippines after a period of occupation by Japanese forces. The army was never totally reconciled to this position, though its opposition was mostly muted. Not only did MacArthur reject the "Orange" plans during the period before Pearl Harbor, but he also refused to establish a solid defensive position in its immediate aftermath. The Philippines were warned that Pearl had been attacked, and it had always been assumed that in the event of war, MacArthur's force would be a primary Japanese target.

MacArthur should have lost his command after the fiasco that claimed the bulk of his air defenses. However, the American people already had villains in the persons of Kimmel and Short, who could, to a degree, plead that an attack against Pearl could not have been anticipated. In the case of MacArthur, his most ardent followers to this day cannot explain his negligence. He was not relieved of command, as were Kimmel and Short, presumably because calling public attention to his errors would have made the entire American command structure in the Pacific seem incompetent.

All of this affected the leadership in Washington. President Roosevelt remained calm, despite telephone calls from congressmen urging that the West Coast be abandoned and that battle lines be established in the Rocky Mountains. The military wished to surround the White House with tanks, but this Roosevelt wisely rejected. On Monday, December 8, Roosevelt addressed Congress and asked for a declaration of war against Japan only, which was promptly approved. Roosevelt did not mention Germany or Italy, despite the fact that many in Washington evidently believed the Germans were behind the attack, and some even believed that Germans had piloted some of the attack aircraft at Pearl as well as the Philippines. (In fact, Germany had been told nothing of the Pearl attack plan, possibly in retaliation for having kept Operation Barbarossa, the attack on Soviet Russia, from the Japanese earlier that year.) Several days before the attack, Magic intercepts had indicated that Hitler had promised that Germany would unquestionably declare war against America should Japan do so. Three days later Hitler kept his promise, and Italy similarly followed with a declaration of war. (The United States declared war on Germany and Italy on December 11.) Roosevelt did ask that a state of war be declared to exist with Japan as of the moment of the attack, since the navy had already ordered the initiation of unrestricted submarine warfare against Japan.

The War Spreads

In London, Prime Minister Winston Churchill went to bed the evening after Pearl Harbor more relaxed than he had been since the war in Europe had begun. He was now certain of ultimate Anglo–American victory over Nazi Germany as well as Japan. But in a very few hours he began to experience reservations. Evidently, one or more members of the American embassy in London indicated that America might devote almost full military might to crushing Japan first. As early as January 1941, the Americans and British had discussed a "Germany-first" policy should the United States find itself at war. Roosevelt and Churchill had formally embraced the "Germany first" strategy during a meeting in August off the coast of Newfoundland. After the Pearl attack, however, Churchill wanted to reaffirm American commitment to Europe and quickly arranged to visit Washington that coming Christmas for a meeting to consider overall strategy. A full-dress conference ensued, code-named Arcadia.

On the evening of December 22, 1941, Churchill arrived in Washington and was billeted on the second floor of the executive mansion itself. Roosevelt and Churchill rather quickly reaffirmed the Germany-first policy, the details of which took several weeks to hammer out. At Roosevelt's suggestion they discussed the appointment of a supreme commander for all Allied forces in the Far East. The president himself suggested Gen. Archibald Wavell, former commander of the British eighth army in Egypt, then in India. When he was informed of his appointment, Wavell dryly remarked, "I have heard of men having to hold the baby, but this is twins." Wavell made haste to inspect his command.

Concomitant with the attack on Pearl Harbor, the Japanese struck other Allied territories as well. The U.S. possessions of Midway Atoll, Wake, and Guam Islands were bombarded on December 8, Japanese time. The island of Guam, a U.S. possession since the Spanish–American War, had never fully been absorbed into the U.S. Pacific commonwealth. Like the Philippines, Guam was removed by over 6,000 miles from the American mainland and in the event of hostilities would prove a tempting target far more than it would a viable forward outpost. Strategic, economic, and treaty considerations (the Washington agreements forbade reinforcing Guam, and the Great Depression had made military expenditures of any sort very difficult) led the U.S. military establishment to neither strengthen Guam's small garrison force nor to equip it with any defensive weapons larger than .30-caliber machine guns. After a brief struggle in which seventeen Americans and one Japanese soldier lost their lives, Guam fell to Japan on December 12, 1941.

Similarly, the American garrison of 250 marines and 100 civilian volunteers on Wake Island was forced to stage a futile defense against a far superior Japanese force from December 11 to 23. The Americans were able to rout the first invasion wave of 560 Japanese marines on December 11. Here, the Japanese learned a lesson that the Americans were bound to find out for themselves later in the war: Preliminary bombardment failed to fully reduce defensive positions. Insufficient air cover also failed to support the attempted landing and Wake's defenders greeted the invasion force with a spirited counterattack that resulted in the loss of two destroyers and several troop transports. The Japanese did not repeat their mistake twelve days later, when the garrison fell to a much larger force supported by battleships and aircraft carriers. The defense of Wake Island, however, proved to be the high point of America's initial resistance to the Japanese offensive of December 1941, accounting for less than 500 Japanese soldiers, 2 destroyers, and several landing vessels. These casualties were caused largely by the small air force delivered to Wake by the carrier *Lexington* just prior to the attack on Pearl, along with shore artillery batteries commanded by Maj. James Devereux. The Japanese executed most of Wake's garrison in October 1943 after forcing them to rebuild the runways and buildings destroyed during the pre-invasion bombardment.

The veteran Japanese Thirty-eighth Army Division besieged the thirty-two-square-mile British crown colony of Hong Kong on December 8. Retreating to the island portion of that colony, a small force of regulars and volunteers held out as long as the water supply lasted. Lack of water would have meant epidemics, and on Christmas Day they capitulated.

To the south, the British were much more confident, indeed even smug. The fortress of Singapore had been touted as impregnable by assault from the sea. It had been fortified during the 1920s at a cost of millions of pounds sterling. British plans called for the defenders to hold out until the United States Navy lifted the siege. Lt. Gen. Arthur Percival was in charge of the multinational garrison at Singapore. Eight- to fifteen-inch naval rifles defended the seaward approaches and it was generally assumed that the fortress could hold out against a siege for up to ninety days. In this instance it was the British who mistakenly relied on the most aggressive points of War Plan Orange. Some American strategists had recommended transferring the Pacific Fleet to Singapore before the war in hopes of discouraging Japanese plans. Roosevelt had rejected this, but the British held out hope that the Americans would share the view that Singapore was an invaluable fortress that must be preserved. Hoping for a "Through Ticket" drive to relieve Singapore as well as the American possessions in the Pacific, the defenders hoped to see a U.S. task force steam over the eastern horizon. No one had foreseen that the American fleet might be resting on the bottom of its anchorage by the end of the first day of the conflict.

At 5:45 A.M. Hawaiian time (11:45 P.M. local time) on December 7–8, Japanese forces commanded by Lt. Gen. Yamashita Tomoyuki landed at Kota Bharu on the eastern coast of the Malay peninsula. The Japanese plan of attack relied on capturing the British airstrips located along the peninsula and using these as bases for land-based attack planes. Yamashita's operation would not benefit from carrier-based aircraft and therefore had to operate swiftly to secure land bases to support its own advance. The initial invasion took place two hours before the air raid on Pearl Harbor. Originally the schedules were to coincide, but Yamamoto argued that adherence to this timetable, to which he initially agreed, would force his Pearl Harbor task force to launch its strike well before dawn, and he requested that the army delay its bombardment and landing by two hours. This was refused. As it turned out, Winston Churchill heard of the air raid on Pearl before news of the Malay invasion reached him.

Complacency was the order of the day in Singapore, despite the fact that its fortifications were seaward only and useless if the Japanese penetrated the Malay peninsula and attacked the city from the rear. When Percival telephoned the governor of the colony, Shenton Thomas, to inform him of the Japanese invasion, Thomas replied, "Well, I suppose you'll shove the little men off." There was some reason for optimism. Not only did British forces in Malaya outnumber the Japanese, but one of Britain's newest battleships, the *Prince of Wales*, accompanied by the battle cruiser *Repulse*, had recently anchored in Singapore harbor. And many in both the navy as well as the army regarded the peninsula as impenetrable. The route from Kota Bharu to Singapore is 600 miles long, transected north to south by a mountain range, and contains dense jungle and deep rivers.

The Japanese focused their initial attack on the airstrips in the northern portion of the peninsula and then used them to support their drive through the interior. British resistance, often in the form of Indian troops, crumbled before the Japanese onslaught, in many cases retreating faster than the advancing Japanese could follow. Eventually, the Japanese drove the British back to the island of Singapore itself, which is separated from the end of the peninsula by the narrow, shallow Straits of Johore.

British losses were not confined to the peninsula alone, however. After the Japanese had taken the airfields at Kota Bharu, they began shuttling planes to it from the bases in southern Indochina. It was during one of these transfers that the *Prince of Wales* and *Repulse* were discovered searching for the supply vessels of the Japanese army. The *Repulse* was an aging converted battle cruiser dating back to the Washington Naval Conference, but the *Prince of Wales* was one of Britain's newest and most powerful battleships, containing the latest radar and defensive weapons. Ironically, it was on the deck of this very ship that Roosevelt and Churchill had agreed that the primary threat to peace lay in Germany and not Japan, and, based upon that assumption, announced a "Europe first" strategy. The presence of this modern naval marvel was a great reassurance to the defenders of Singapore. Percival had ordered Vice Adm. Thomas Phillips to take his ships north and destroy the supply ships of the invasion force. Phillips protested on the grounds that he had no air cover. Percival could promise nothing to Phillips; however, a handful of antiquated Brewster Buffalo aircraft did attempt to support his sortie after news of a Japanese attack against them was received.

When the Japanese pilots first encountered the *Prince of Wales*, they were hesitant. They had studied American ship silhouettes, but not those of the Royal Navy. The *Prince of Wales* bore a striking resemblance to a Japanese *Kongo*-class battleship. Not until the pilots dropped to 1,500 feet were they sure of the identity of their target. In less that two hours both capital ships had been sunk, at the cost of four Japanese aircraft. More significant than the loss to the Singapore garrison was the fact that aircraft had sunk a fully operational modern battleship under full steam and with full freedom to maneuver. The results of the encounter stunned Yamamoto's critics in the naval ministry.

Percival had over 80,000 men to hold the peninsula and thus slightly outnumbered the Japanese. These he strung out thinly, to stop the three-pronged Japanese advance down the peninsula. Morale was at its nadir in the British divisions, particularly among the Indian troops, who resented being treated as inferiors. Morale took a further blow when it was learned that the government of Thailand, after little resistance, had agreed to surrender to the Japanese. (This was primarily the work of several pro-Japanese elements in the Thai government.) Malaya was now cut off from Burma. Percival gave uninspired leadership and very little guidance of any sort. Retreating to the island, he deployed his men around its perimeter to repulse a Japanese landing. On the night of February 8–9, 1942, the Japanese swarmed across the Straits of Johore and were soon ashore, for Percival had left no reserves for a counterattack.

A rallying poster issued just days after the attack which brought the United States into the Pacific War. *(National Archives)*

By February 13 the defenders had regrouped just north of the city and were evidently preparing to contest its possession block by block. Japanese aircraft flew over the city at will and Percival would not order a complete blackout lest the British residents of the city be overly offended; he ordered a "brownout" instead, which supposedly shielded the more tempting targets from Japanese bombsights. By the morning of February 15, when the city's last remaining water reservoir had fallen to the Japanese, they had not yet reached the city limit. Apprised by his commissioner of public health of the resultant danger of an epidemic, Percival requested a truce.

Yamashita was not sure of Percival's intent in calling for a cease-fire. His own army, which had advanced so rapidly down the peninsula (often using bicycles) that it had overreached its supply lines, was chronically short of ammunition. Also, his troops were using amphetamine sulfate to reduce the need for rest, and many were reaching the limit of their physical endurance. In particular, Yamashita feared that the British would contest the city piece-meal, which was in fact what Churchill had ordered. Great was Yamashita's relief when he learned that the British would capitulate outright. Fighting ceased at about 8:30 P.M. on February 15. The emperor proclaimed a special holiday, as he had for Pearl Harbor, but Singapore Day witnessed far greater celebrations. Even schoolchildren were sent on holiday, a very rare event in Japan, and the entire nation celebrated the fall of Britain's vaunted Gibraltar of the Pacific.

The Fall of the Philippines

The fall of Singapore caused dismay in the Philippines. The Japanese had entrusted the capture of the Philippines to General Homma Masaharu, with a combined force of 43,000 men. Gen. MacArthur had one American division of 15,000 men; his Filipino forces of 100,000 men, divided between scouts, constabulary, and territorial militia, were largely untrained, most having about eight to ten weeks worth of preparation. After some minor diversionary land-ings, the main Japanese force under Homma landed in Northern Lingayen Gulf, which MacArthur had anticipated as the landing area of choice. De-spite some interference by the remaining B-17s, Homma had little trouble securing his initial landings or in following them up with the disembarkation of supply train columns.

The very small American Asiatic Fleet, comprised primarily of subma-rines, but also including a few cruisers and destroyers, sank one troop ship, but nothing else. Some submarine skippers did little more than observe the Japanese approaching, submerge, and move out of the area, and then surface to radio their enemy contact. Submarine duty in the United States Navy at

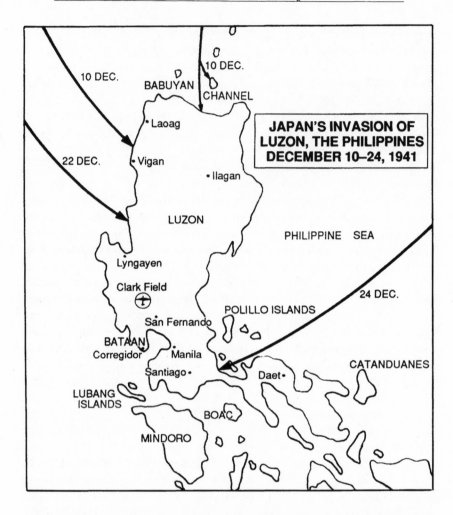

JAPAN'S INVASION OF LUZON, THE PHILIPPINES DECEMBER 10–24, 1941

10 DEC.

22 DEC.

10 DEC.

BABUYAN CHANNEL

Laoag

Vigan

Ilagan

LUZON

PHILIPPINE SEA

24 DEC.

Lyngayen

Clark Field

POLILLO ISLANDS

San Fernando

BATAAN

Corregidor · Manila

Santiago ·

Daet ·

CATANDUANES

LUBANG ISLANDS

BOAC

MINDORO

the beginning of the war was very discouraging. The rate of failure for torpedoes was extremely high, reasons for which will be discussed in a later chapter, and after firing several faulty "fish" many captains opted for discretion and chose to report their sightings to the air forces, whose ordnance was not so unreliable. The Japanese made a second, and much larger, landing on Christmas Eve at Lamon Bay, on the eastern littoral of Luzon. There they encountered varied resistance. Some Filipino units, at least initially, gave a good account of themselves, while others did very poorly, evidently owing to the varied quality of their prewar training.

MacArthur's plans to stop the Japanese at the waterline failed before the determined Japanese attack. Homma's main strike force was not confined to the beachhead, but was soon advancing southward along Highway Three toward Manila. The defenders abandoned the city and MacArthur declared it "open" on December 26. MacArthur had no choice but to admit tacitly that he had erred in attempting to stop the enemy at the beachheads. He now ordered War Plan Orange into effect. Evidently only then was the prior MacArthur order rescinded that had forbidden as defeatist the stockpiling of foodstuffs and munitions on Corregidor. The result would be disastrous. MacArthur's forces were spared immediate destruction, though, when Homma broke off his pursuit and instead focused on the capture of Manila. The Japanese general staff expected Homma to make as short work of the Americans as other generals had of other Allied forces, and the capture of the capital city would suggest that conquest of the Philippines was all but secure. But this diversion probably cost Homma a swift and total victory as it allowed most of MacArthur's men to reach the Bataan peninsula with much of their equipment.

In Washington, General Marshall strove to supply MacArthur with every sort of reinforcement, but his efforts were largely in vain. The Washington naval establishment, understandably shaken by the Pearl Harbor attack, was convinced that supplies could not be gotten further than Australia. Some freelance merchant marine "captains" refused at any price to move into Philippine waters, which had been mined and declared blockaded by the Japanese. And given the "Europe first" decision, any reinforcements sent would only have been destroyed or surrendered to the Japanese. This, MacArthur— perhaps understandably—would never accept, much less forgive.

On January 6, 1942, the last retreating American troops reached the Bataan peninsula, where they were now besieged. The total number on that rocky peninsula included 15,000 Americans and about 65,000 Filipino troops, with enough food for about a month. Also, there were over 25,000 civilians who had retreated with the armies, and they too had to be fed. At this juncture, the Japanese made another of their few errors. Homma had taken from his command the battle-seasoned Forty-eighth Division, which was now detailed for the conquest of Java. Its replacements were overaged garrison troops from Formosa with little battle experience. And Homma failed to recognize that the Allied forces were determined to fight, despite the severe shortage of foodstuffs. By early February, Homma realized he faced a far greater task than was at first apparent. He withdrew to consolidate, and until April 3 the Bataan front was relatively quiet.

Meanwhile, on February 23, 1942, Roosevelt ordered MacArthur to leave the Philippines for Australia. On March 12, MacArthur, accompanied by his wife and son, left Corregidor in a PT-boat. Upon his departure, MacArthur issued his famous declaration, "I will return." Many troops on the Bataan peninsula, which MacArthur had only left Corregidor to survey once during the siege, openly berated the general, referring to him as "Dugout Doug" and lamenting that he had not really been present for some time already. On March 17 MacArthur reached the vicinity of Port Darwin in Australia, during a Japanese raid on the harbor's facilities. Command on Bataan and Corregidor was left to Maj. Gen. Jonathan Wainwright. The defenders put up a strong fight but were doomed from the start. Troops were placed on half rations in January and reduced to quarter rations by April. Homma received reinforcements and continued his assault, including amphibious landings far behind the American and Filipino lines. On April 9 the defenders of Bataan surrendered unconditionally and the focus of the assault moved to Corregidor. After reducing the islands' defenses by naval and air bombardment, Japanese troops landed on May 5. That evening, Wainwright, pushed back to the tunnels in Corregidor and having only three days rations remaining, surrendered unconditionally. Homma demanded that Wainwright surrender not only his forces but also all forces remaining in the Philippines. This he did, though some individuals refused to be taken and retreated to the jungles to participate in guerrilla operations against the Japanese for the remainder of the war.

During both the Singapore and the Philippine campaigns the Japanese had encountered a situation that they were completely unprepared for—the surrender of tens of thousands of enemy troops. Japanese troops are instructed that surrender is not an option, and most are told to save their last bullet for themselves. The Japanese understand that not all nations believe or behave similarly, but they have little respect for soldiers who quit short of expending their last effort in battle. They expected that the defenders of the Western imperial possessions would fight as determinedly as they themselves, and failed to prepare for large numbers of prisoners of war. While they had anticipated several thousand prisoners, Japanese planning did not take into account the possibility of the surrender of entire garrisons and was therefore unprepared to deal with the large number of troops requiring food and shelter after many of their initial campaigns.

In the case of the Philippines, this unpreparedness was complicated by harsh feelings resulting from the severity of the resistance put up by the islands' defenders. The first of the "Bataan Death Marches" thus began on April 11. The surrendered defenders of the peninsula were forced to march as much as ninety miles to the camps the Japanese had prepared for them. The troops were often in horrible physical condition before the march started, owing to injuries and lack of food. About 600 Americans and several thousand Filipinos perished by deliberate Japanese cruelty. Besides the many troops who were physically unfit for the trip alone, other marchers were

American prisoners of war being led from the Bataan peninsula to prepared camps in the interior of Luzon. *(National Archives)*

robbed, beaten, or shot by their captors along the route. The conditions at the camps were similarly unequal to the task and many captives died of disease, malnutrition, and cruelty after having survived the grueling march. Mistreatment was neither systematic nor officially sanctioned though, as others following the same route were relatively well treated; evidently much depended on the personality of the officers commanding each individual march. These types of marches were repeated throughout the Co-Prosperity Sphere as the Japanese secured victory after victory in remarkably short order.

More Japanese Victories

Japan next advanced into British Borneo to seize its oil fields. Then a three-pronged attack was mounted against the Dutch East Indies. The great prize was the central island of Java. Here, the native population, who had suffered a great deal of oppression under Dutch rule, aided the Japanese. Small para-troop units were even used by the Japanese. On the night of February 28, 1942, the first Japanese landed on Java. This led to the Battle of the Java Sea, in which the Dutch confronted Japan. The Dutch had built a small but modern battle fleet in the late 1930s. After Hitler overran Holland, the Dutch fleet was posted to the East Indies and combined with remnants of American, British, and Australian naval forces to form the American–British–Dutch–Australian (ABDA) command. ABDA had almost no air cover, while the Japanese invasion force was supported by elements of Nagumo's First Air Fleet and its carriers. On the evening of January 27, under the command of Dutch admiral Karel Doorman, the ABDA sought out the Japanese in order to interdict their troop transports bound for Java. In three separate engagements, Koorman lost his ships. The Battle of the Java Sea resulted in the loss of two Dutch cruisers; five British destroyers were also sunk. In a later action, one American and one Australian cruiser and three destroyers were also lost. On March 8 all of Java capitulated to the Japanese.

Burma, bordering on British India, suffered a similar fate. It had first been attacked as early as December 11, when two key airfields in the southern-most portion of the country were seized. Having lived under British rule for scarcely two generations (the entire country had not been occupied by the British until 1885), the Burmese openly aided the Japanese. The seizure of Burma would threaten India, which was already ripe for revolt against British rule, deal a crippling blow to British pride in their *raj*, and cut the Burma road, leaving China completely isolated. Lt. Gen. Iida Shojiro jumped off from the northern Malay Peninsula on January 20. The only British hope was the monsoon rains, which would begin in late May. Iida quickly drove northward, as Burmese freely volunteered information on the location of

British and Indian troops and supplied other intelligence as well. Some Burmese refused to side with either the British or the Japanese, however, and fought for Burmese independence against both their old and new masters. On March 8, Iida occupied the capital, Rangoon, which the British had abandoned. Using the captured port as a supply base, Iida now received reinforcements and opened an offensive on March 19 to seize the remainder of the nation.

Iida now opposed a new enemy, a Chinese army under U.S. lieutenant general Joseph Stilwell. Roosevelt and Marshall had dispatched Stilwell to reassure Chiang that the Americans really did consider China a vital member of the Allies, and to see if there was any way to encourage the Chinese to engage the Japanese a little more vigorously. Stilwell entered the fighting in Burma hoping to reassure the retreating British and employ Chinese forces to delay the Japanese advance until the monsoon rains rendered the countryside impassable. This he could not do, however. Though Chiang released nominal control of three divisions to him, Stilwell complained, often with justification, that he could not coax the Chinese to fight unless victory was assured. The generalissimo had instructed his generals not to lose their armies, causing them to countermand or ignore many of Stilwell's orders. Chiang feared risking his best troops in engagements with the Japanese when he believed that the Americans could defeat Japan and his own worst enemies were the indigenous Chinese Communist forces he would face after both the Americans and Japanese had departed. Chiang also resisted committing troops to the defense of India as he feared that the British might push to have them participate in the suppression of what appeared to be an imminent Indian revolt. However, even if the Chinese had cooperated fully with Stilwell, Burma would almost surely have been lost anyway. The British had all but given up on holding the Japanese back and were in the process of retreating to the relative safety of India. By May 20 the British had completed the longest retreat in their military history. The monsoon rains came on schedule in 1942, but too late to save Burma. Stilwell also retreated with his Chinese forces, still convinced that, properly led, they were a match for the Japanese. Despite the defeat, he maintained a fervent desire to launch a new campaign to retake Burma as a first step to liberating China and preparing the way for the eventual invasion of Japan.

The Japanese had meanwhile moved to codify and round out their new empire. Northern New Guinea, the Gilbert Islands, and the Solomon Island group were added to the list of conquests. By May 1942 the Great East Asia Co-Prosperity Sphere, which Konoe had reluctantly proclaimed, was a reality.

Emperor Hirohito awoke one morning to read a report from Kido informing him that he had just acquired over 400 million new subjects. "The fruits of victory are falling into our mouths perhaps too quickly," he promptly observed. The Japanese had done the seemingly impossible. Inhabitants of the conquered regions would soon label the area the "Co-Poverty Sphere," but no one could doubt that Japan had gained her El Dorado of the South with dispatch. The American holdout on Bataan and Corregidor notwithstanding, the Japanese had exceeded their timetables for conquest by nearly 20 percent.

All this dismayed the American navy: It also disturbed Yamamoto, for the emperor proceeded to proclaim that the conflict was at an end, while Yamamoto's chief Pearl Harbor targets, the American aircraft carriers, still roamed the Pacific. In mid-March 1942 General Wavell lost his position as Allied Commander, Far East. MacArthur, now headquartered in Australia, assumed direct responsibility for the Southwest Pacific area, which initially included the Solomon Islands. Most of the remainder of the Pacific fell under the command of Adm. Chester Nimitz, who had succeeded Kimmel at Pearl. But there were to be many exceptions to the demarcated zones of command. Adm. Ernest King, who had succeeded Stark as chief of naval operations in Washington, never permitted a fleet carrier to be placed under MacArthur's command, for example. King also proved to be very distrustful of the British and never revealed America's Pacific strategy to them; he also contested the Europe-first decision at every turn, often in a highly abrasive fashion.

A New Kind of War

The war in the Pacific was fought in a manner the world had never before witnessed. The advent of new weapons of war led to new strategies and tactics as well. For the first time, control of the skies as well as the battlefields would weigh heavily in the outcome of the struggles. Some farsighted commanders had foreseen this and had adapted their thinking to accommodate this new reality. The most notable of these was Admiral Yamamoto, whose strategies flew in the face of accepted naval thinking by insisting that the future of the Japanese Imperial Navy lay not in its ability to engage in surface combat but rather in its potential to launch devastating long-range aerial attacks.

In 1921 Brig. Gen. William (Billy) Mitchell had tried to prove to the American joint chiefs and the world that an aircraft with contact bombs could sink a man-of-war at sea. Using the decommissioned German battleship *Ostfriesland* along with some aged American ships, Mitchell and his airmen demonstrated how properly administered aerial bombs could negate the superiority of large naval guns. Since the ships were anchored during the demonstration, some of the witnesses argued that if the ships were mobile, they could easily defend themselves. Mitchell found few supporters among the naval planners, who still adhered firmly to the battleship theories promulgated by Alfred T. Mahan half a century earlier. The prevailing thought among American naval planners, encompassed in the "Orange" plans, remained the same: the American navy, at the sign of imminent war, would sortie out from either Norfolk or San Diego and engage the enemy in a major surface action. This remained the predominant strategy up to the beginning of the Pacific War in 1941, though it was renamed "Rainbow" planning with the inclusion of multiple allies and enemies.

The United States initiated a carrier force as early as 1922, when the superstructure of an old collier was removed and it was refitted with a wooden deck instead. The result was the United States's first aircraft carrier, USS *Langley* (Carrier Vehicle-1). Five years later, the carriers *Lexington* (CV-2) and *Saratoga* (CV-3) were built on the reconverted hulls of two battle cruisers and were far and away better equipped for duty than *Langley* had been. For the United States Navy, however, the aircraft carriers continued to represent an advanced reconnaissance vehicle until the mid-1930s. Then, in 1934, the first U.S. carrier that was laid down as such, *Ranger* (CV-4), was commissioned and stationed at Norfolk. Improvements in aircraft and weaponry led the navy to reexamine its focus on the role of carriers. Their potential as offensive weapons in the American arsenal was researched, and naval aviators became increasingly important to America's defense strategy.

Meanwhile, the Japanese had realized the potential striking power of an advanced air force during the Manchurian and subsequent Chinese campaigns. Superior aircraft and close support tactics had given them a decided advantage over their industrially backward foe. At sea as well, the Japanese had advanced. By 1941 they boasted one of the most modern and capable striking forces in existence, often utilizing their carriers off the China coast to lend tactical support to the army. In Japan as in the United States, though, some doubt remained about the practical limitations of carrier-based warfare. Japan's most famous naval hero, Admiral Togo, had defeated the Russians in two major surface battles without the benefit of any aerial support. Many senior naval officers failed to see the need for a change in their thinking. Apparently attempting to appeal to all elements within the naval establishment, the Japanese naval-building programs of the 1920s and 1930s aimed at building dreadnought-style superships in every class that could either outgun or outrun any foe. This resulted in not only an impressive carrier program, but also the construction of super battleships like *Yamato*, *Musashi*, and *Shinano*. Ultimately this division of precious resources proved disastrous and the super battleships were as worthless as Yamamoto had predicted, but old habits (and viewpoints) die hard, and young naval officers in Japan were consistently forced to confront the old-time battleship strategists in the naval ministry when considering the empire's future.

The real break came in 1941, when the navy itself confronted the limits on its fuel supply brought about by the U.S. embargo. This forced decisions on how to progress pursuant to American strength in the Pacific. Conventional wisdom would have dictated a repeat of the Tsushima victory, including luring the Americans into home waters where attrition by distance and constant harassment would leave a weakened U.S. force to be destroyed by the Japanese surface fleet. But Japan could not afford to gamble on the Americans walking into their trap and were forced to resort to alternative measures. It is a testament both to the influence of Yamamoto and to the desperate situation in which Japan found itself that the leaders decided to support the strike on the fleet at Pearl Harbor.

In 1941 the American navy boasted seven active-duty carriers, of which three were stationed in the Pacific. Each carrier contained approximately seventy aircraft divided nearly equally between fighter, bomber, and torpedo planes. Before 1940, naval aviators had been required to qualify in all types of aircraft so that they could alternate between them if necessary. The relatively small number of aviators who chose to remain in the service rather than opting for the more lucrative civilian jobs available to trained pilots made this diverse training necessary. An increased emphasis on the need for trained flyers, however, drove the navy to offer better pay and opportunity for advancement to their aviators and stimulated an increase in recruitment as well. This in turn led to a greater flexibility on the part of the navy, which could now afford to allow its pilots to specialize in only one aircraft. Consequently, the length of training decreased. By December 1941 the United States had a very impressive group of aviators manning its carrier forces. Yamamoto's fears would be justified as subsequent battles in the central and south Pacific graphically demonstrated that Japan's inability to deal a death blow to this carrier force at Pearl Harbor would hurt the imperial cause more than anyone could have known at the time.

Suggestions for Further Reading

The best recent work on Douglas MacArthur is Michael Schaller's *Douglas MacArthur: The Far Eastern General* (New York: Oxford University Press, 1989); also helpful is D. Clayton James, *The Years of MacArthur*, 2 vols. (New York: Houghton Mifflin, 1972–75). For MacArthur's negative personality traits, see Joseph C. Goulden, *Korea: The Untold Story of the War* (New York: McGraw-Hill, 1982), esp. pp. xxii–xxiii. The story of the Wake defenders is well recounted in Gregory Urwin's *Facing Fearful Odds: The Siege of Wake Island* (Lincoln: University of Nebraska Press, 1997). Thomas David, *The Battle of the Java Sea* (New York: Stein and Day, 1969) is a useful study of this neglected battle, but see also F.C. Van Osten, *The Battle of Java Sea* (Annapolis, MD: Naval Institute Press, 1976). Much of the technical detail on aviator training and carrier operations has been drawn from John Lundstrom's seminal, if little-known, study, *The First Team: Pacific Naval Air Combat from Pearl Harbor to Midway* (Annapolis, MD: Naval Institute Press, 1984). Bruce E. Reynolds tells the story of Japan's sweeping early successes in *Thailand and Japan's Southern Advance, 1940–1945* (New York: St. Martin's Press, 1994).

5

Coral Sea and Midway

The Doolittle Raid

In the weeks after Pearl Harbor, the U.S. Fleet carriers engaged in harassment operations against the Japanese in the Central and South Pacific. Nimitz used his carriers to conduct harassment raids in the vicinity of the Marshall Islands and around Jaluit. The carriers were rarely exposed to substantial counter attack, and scored only a few modest victories against shore installations and reconnaissance aircraft. These raids provided valuable combat experience to the American crews, but they also demonstrated the obsolescence of many of the U.S. carrier-based aircraft. Most of the carriers received improved pursuit and fighter aircraft by mid-1942. Unfortunately for American combat crews, though, the woeful state of the U.S. torpedo bombers and ordnance was yet to be fully demonstrated, and rectified. However, while these raids kept up navy morale to a degree and did minor damage to the enemy, they may also have served to demonstrate to Yamamoto that the sooner the American carriers were destroyed, the better. In January of 1942 the United States had only two operative carriers in the Pacific—*Enterprise* and *Lexington*. *Saratoga* was in dry dock in the Puget Sound from a submarine hit on January 11, 1942. The last two operative U.S. fleet carriers extant—*Yorktown* and the newly completed *Hornet*—were transferred from the Atlantic quickly enough, but they still only marginally offset the substantial Japanese advantage in carrier vehicles. The United States needed a resounding victory, either militarily or psychologically, to redress the balance.

In the spring of 1942, President Roosevelt, in conjunction with Admiral King and Gen. Henry (Hap) Arnold of the Army Air Corps, conceived of just such a psychological boost with the idea of bombing Tokyo using planes flying from an aircraft carrier. This was a grave risk, as it would entail the use of two of the four operative carriers, since one would be needed to supply air cover for the attack carrier. The plan seemed hopelessly risky until an officer on King's staff observed that the Army Air Corp's longer-range B-25 twin-engine bomber might launch the attack from the deck of a carrier, which then could be further out at sea than otherwise possible. The 500 feet of runway afforded by a fleet carrier deck might well prove sufficient to launch such aircraft. However, the carrier's flight elevators would never suffice to stow them on the hangar deck below, hence they would be exposed to the elements and leave the carrier unable to provide its own combat air patrols. But the potential boost to morale was deemed worthy of the risk and with the explicit backing of Roosevelt, pilots were selected, and training began.

Sixteen B-25s would comprise the assault team, the planes being lashed down to the decks of carrier *Hornet* at Alameda Naval Air Station in San Francisco Bay. The bombers were to be led by Lt. Col. James Doolittle. *Hornet* rendezvoused with Halsey aboard *Enterprise* north of Pearl on April 13, 1942. After launch, Doolittle's fliers would bomb Tokyo and several smaller targets. Each would approach its target at a different altitude, from a different direction (relatively), and no two bombers would, theoretically, drop their loads at exactly the same moment, so that the Japanese would have maximum difficulty pinpointing their exact time and place of launch. They were then to transit the Sea of Japan and land behind Chiang Kai-shek's lines in northern China, adding to Chennault's forces. Launch was to take place 400 miles from the Japanese coastline.

The Japanese may well have detected Halsey's task force without his knowledge, but it made no difference—they did not know he carried twin-engine bombers, which had a longer effective range than any existing single-engine carrier bombers in either navy. But when Halsey visually sited a contact (two Japanese fishing boats, with radio masts) on April 18, at a distance of approximately 650 miles from the Japanese coastline, he felt he had no choice but to launch his aircraft prematurely. All were successfully airborne. Halsey did not, however, signal Washington or Chiang Kai-shek's regime in Chungking that his planes were airborne, as per his specific orders. In the end, it probably mattered little. A Doolittle description of the raid is worth quoting in full:

> We approached our objectives just over the housetops, but bombed at 1,500 feet. The target for one plane was a portion of the navy yard south of Tokyo, in reaching which we passed over what apparently was a flying school, as there were a number of planes in the air. One salvo made a direct hit on a new cruiser or battleship under construction. They left it in flames.
> After releasing our bombs we dived again to the treetops and went to

One of Col. Jimmy Doolittle's B-25s clears the deck of the USS *Hornet* enroute to its rendezvous with history in the skies over Tokyo. (*National Archives*)

the coast at that altitude to avoid antiaircraft fire. Along the coastline we observed several squadrons of destroyers and cruisers and battleships. About 25 or 30 miles to sea, the rear gunners reported seeing columns of smoke rising thousands of feet into the air.

One of our bombardiers strewed bombs along a quarter of a mile of aircraft factory near Nagoya. Another illuminated a tank farm. However flying at such low altitudes made it very difficult to observe the result following the impact of the bombs. We could see the strike, but our field of vision was greatly restricted by the speed of the plane and the low altitude at which we were flying. Even so, one of our party observed a ball game in progress. The players and spectators did not start their run for cover until just as the field passed out of sight.

Pilots, bombardiers, and all members of the crew performed their duties with great calmness and remarkable precision. It appeared to us that practically every bomb reached the target for which it was intended. We would like to have tarried and watched the later developments of fire and explosion, but even so we were fortunate to receive a fairly detailed report from the excited Japanese broadcasts. It took them several hours to calm down to deception and accusation.

During the attack, one of the bombers passed so close to an American-made Japanese passenger plane that the pilot could recognize the nationality of the B-25's crew. The plane was carrying Premier Tojo, who was evidently on his way to inspect an army flying school. The potential import of this brush with death was not lost on Tojo, who may well have been affected by the incident for the rest of his term in office. The navy had assured him it would be safe to go aloft that day, an error for which he never forgave the naval general staff. In fact, the premier recalled elements of the navy and increased the size of air defense for the home islands after the raid. These reductions of potential frontline power may not have significantly altered the outcome of the war, but as the fighting dragged on, every scrap of material would become precious to the Japanese war machine and the dedication of this equipment to home defense meant that much less at the front.

For Doolittle's flyers, the plans for proceeding after the strike on Tokyo began to break down very quickly. None of the planes ever joined Chiang's air force. Lacking enough fuel to reach nationalist Chinese lines, one plane turned toward Vladivostok, where its crew was interned by the Russians, although they were later allowed to escape via Iran and India. The remainder of the crews evidently bailed out, most over Chinese soil. Of eighty crewmen who participated in the raid, seventy-one eventually returned home. Three were killed, and eight were captured and brought to Tokyo and tried. In the grim words of Yamamoto's chief of staff, Vice Adm. Ugaki Matome, the captured airmen were "made to tell the truth" (very likely they were tortured) and revealed that they had flown from the carrier *Hornet*. The Japanese executed three of the flyers on the grounds that they had bombed schools. Yamamoto was mortified by the raid, but no one could now doubt that the American carriers indeed constituted a threat to the Japanese home islands. The Japanese army was similarly embarrassed. In China it took vengeance on villages that had received Doolittle's flyers, executing 250,000 civilians in reprisal.

The Battle of the Coral Sea and Its Consequences

Since the Pearl Harbor attack, the Japanese First Air Fleet had returned to Japan and then turned southward. Four of its carriers assisted in the conquest of the Bismarck Archipelego and a portion of the Solomon Islands. Port Darwin, Australia, was raided on February 19, 1942. Afterward, Nagumo sailed into the Indian Ocean and attacked two ports, Trincomalee and Colombo, on the island of Ceylon. The British cruisers *Dorsetshire* and *Cornwall*, the light carrier *Hermes*, and the destroyer *Vampire* fell prey to Nagumo's aviators. Nagumo, however, lost forty skilled pilots in the Indian Ocean operations. His carriers then headed for home, with the exception of *Zuikaku* and *Shokaku*, which were detached for duty in the upcoming Coral Sea campaign.

A constant source of trouble for all military establishments is interservice rivalry. Competition between ground, sea, and air forces arises from differences of tactics, objectives, and even jealousy. Every military structure in the war faced these problems, but they seemed to be endemic in the Japanese command structure. After the successes of early 1942, the Japanese navy and army had split over future strategic aims. The army, while not unaggressive, favored a holding action and consolidation of gains already made. Also, on grounds that Hitler might defeat the Russians, they wished to adopt a "wait and see" attitude toward the Soviet Union. Yamamoto believed he could not afford this attitude, reasoning that the American carriers might take the initiative against Japan. His staff had planned for a major operation against the tiny atoll of Midway, part of the Hawaiian chain but 1,200 miles west of Pearl. He envisioned a major engagement that would capture the atoll and then destroy the American carriers when they sortied out to dislodge Japanese forces from the area. He then planned to move against the Hawaiian Islands, and some staff hoped the Americans might then accept something of an armistice with Japan. However, Yamamoto had his way because of the force of his personality, although the Coral Sea operation, designed to conquer the southern half of New Guinea and thus further isolate Australia from the United States, would have to come first.

This time the Japanese would not enjoy the advantage of surprise. Yamamoto confided his most secret communications from his new flagship, *Yamato*, to and from Tokyo, using the JN-25 fleet code. This was the American name for the cipher, for it represented the twenty-fifth major version or variation of that code since the American navy had been monitoring it (JN stood simply for Japanese navy). Intelligence staffs in both Washington and Pearl kept a record of the cipher and attempted to probe its secrets, but it had not been sufficiently penetrated before December 7, 1941, to give warning of the attack.

At Pearl, Cdr. Joseph Rochefort held the title of combat intelligence officer. Utilizing, in part, men taken from the crew of battleship *California* and information passed on from British code-breaking experts, bits and pieces of the JN-25 code could be read by early 1942. Since the Americans were not capable of producing complete, exact translations of each decrypt, the officers in Pearl and in Washington often came up with differing explanations of the content and import of the same messages. By April, Rochefort had been able to deduce that a major Japanese operation was about to take place in or around Port Moresby, on the southeastern flank of the island of New Guinea.

New Guinea is the world's second largest island. The Japanese had invaded the northern half early in their initial offensive, securing the coastal areas. The inhabitants of the island, which the Australians regarded as something of a colony, included about 600 tribes and a very few white *copra* (coconut) traders. Almost half of the globe's 1,200 languages are spoken on New Guinea, so dense is the jungle that isolates its tribes. The only means by which the Japanese could cross from the coastal areas of the north to Port Moresby in the south was by traversing the formidable Owen Stanley mountain range by using the Kokoda Trail, a native passageway that could be crossed only with extreme difficulty. The Japanese opted to launch a seaborne invasion instead.

Operation MO was to be led by Admiral Inoue Shigeyoshi, sailing from Rabaul on New Britain in the Bismarcks, and was to contain three fleet carriers for air support. The light carrier *Shoho*, which was part of the South Seas Fleet, was to be joined by *Shokaku* and *Zuikaku* from the First Air Fleet, as they returned from duty in the Indian Ocean. The force would escort Japanese invasion troops from the north around the southeastern tip of New Guinea through the Jomard Passage and into Port Moresby. Although the Japanese felt certain that the Americans had one carrier operating in the vicinity, they thought three fleet carriers more than sufficient to deal with it.

In fact, the Americans had two carriers, *Yorktown* and *Lexington*, operating together as Task Force Seventeen under the command of Rear Adm. Frank

Jack Fletcher, in the waters east of Australia. Admiral Nimitz instructed Fletcher to interdict the Japanese operation but gave no further tactical instructions. After gaining antiquated maps of the area from the British admiralty, some dating from the eighteenth century, Fletcher proceeded to a point from which he believed he could intercept the Japanese invasion fleet.

The waters off the southeastern coast of New Guinea are treacherous. Indeed, there were only three safe routes for the Japanese to select. The first ran dangerously close to shore and threatened the fleet with the possibility of running aground. The second was quite safe but required a great deal of time, and the Japanese were not that patient. The final option was the Jomard Passage, a narrow corridor in the coral reefs where the ships could round the cape in good order and proceed rapidly to Moresby. This was the choice that Inoue made and that Fletcher had anticipated.

Each admiral was cautious and maintained constant aerial search patterns attempting to determine the location of his adversary. On the morning of May 7, 1942, the two forces spotted each other almost simultaneously. A Japanese scout plane sighted what it reported to be an aircraft carrier and escort that was in reality the oiler *Neosho* and destroyer *Sims*. The mistake was not discovered until Inoue had sent an attack force, which crippled *Neosho*, a survivor of the Pearl Harbor attack, and sank *Sims*.

American scouts inadvertently reported spotting several Japanese aircraft carriers when they had actually discovered an escort of destroyers and cruisers enroute to the main task force. Fletcher launched a full strike by both of his carriers against the target before realizing the mistake. Luck was with the Americans though, because as the strike force returned to their ships they spotted light carrier *Shoho*, which was operating independently from the *Shokaku* and *Zuikaku*. *Shoho* avoided the first wave of American planes, but soon the U.S. flyers were able to report America's greatest victory at sea since the sinking of a Japanese destroyer at Wake. "Scratch one flattop" was the message received by Fletcher aboard his flagship, *Lexington*.

The next morning the two forces closed on each other again. The American forces concentrated their attack on carrier *Shokaku*, as *Zuikaku* found refuge in a convenient rain squall. Several bombs found their mark but did not mortally cripple *Shokaku*, and Inoue ordered it to retreat to the north for repairs.

The Japanese found the Americans in open water and attacked both carriers. *Lexington* took two torpedoes on her port side and also suffered two hits from divebombers. *Yorktown* received one hit from a divebomber and escaped the action, but her fuel tanks were fractured. *Lexington* was on fire but was still afloat several hours after the attacks ceased. Initially fire control teams were able to control the damage, but *Lexington* suffered fatal damage when sparks from an electric generator motor, which had accidentally been left running, ignited gasoline fumes traveling through the ship's ventilating system. This critical error in judgment cost the American fleet one of its desperately needed carriers, as the fires that resulted were beyond control. Rear Adm. Aubrey Fitch was forced to order *Lexington* be abandoned.

Thus, the battle, which had been fought primarily in the Solomon Sea, was quite costly to both sides. The Japanese navy lost 77 aircraft, 1,074 men killed and wounded, and 1 light carrier sunk. Admiral Inoue, in something like a state of controlled panic after the loss of the carrier and aircrews, called off the Port Moresby invasion force, and so for the time being the Japanese army abandoned its designs on New Guinea. The Americans had lost 66 aircraft, 543 men killed and wounded, and 1 fleet carrier sunk. But they had managed a strategic victory. Thus ended the first naval battle in history in which the opposing naval vessels had not actually seen one another.

The most significant development in this battle may not have been what was lost, however, but what was damaged. Admiral Yamamoto chose to scratch the carriers *Shokaku* and *Zuikaku* from his pending Midway Operation AF plans to allow them time to expedite repairs and train new flight crews. He could have kept one ready for the Midway battle by taking aircrews from the other, but chose not to. The Japanese navy was wedded to the concept of operating ships, especially carriers, in pairs, and Yamamoto may have made a very costly mistake in his decision. The presence of even one of those two carriers might well have swung the balance in Japan's favor at the forthcoming battle of Midway.

Conversely, Admiral Nimitz ordered the estimated ninety days of repairs slated for *Yorktown* to be accomplished in seventy-two hours and sent it along to Midway. Once again the failure to achieve total success during the attack on Pearl Harbor came back to plague the Japanese. For if the third strike force commander Fuchida had called for had struck the fuel storage and repair facilities, *Yorktown* (and the entire American fleet for that matter) would have been forced to retreat to the West Coast. It could not then have responded rapidly, or in strength, to the coming Japanese threat. As it was, *Yorktown*'s repairs were accomplished with dispatch and its presence at Midway allowed the Americans to achieve a victory that might otherwise have been beyond their grasp.

Faulty intelligence was also a problem for the Japanese navy on the eve of its most ambitious campaign. Yamamoto was confident that he could annihilate the American carrier forces because his intelligence had reported that there were only three American carriers in the Pacific before Coral Sea. Japanese participants in that battle had reported sinking two American carriers, leaving only one more for the First Air Fleet to deal with. Even without

Shokaku and *Zuikaku* First Air Fleet still boasted four flattops. Also, Japanese air forces had scored some major victories over mobile naval forces near Singapore and in the Indian Ocean.

Even though the Coral Sea fight had not been planned as a major surface-to-air conflict through which naval hegemony could be achieved, it had great impact on the way naval conflict would take place in the future. Throughout the war the Japanese remained wedded to a modified form of the Mahanian Doctrine of a decisive naval engagement that would determine the fate of the opposing sides. Midway would be the closest the Americans ever came to committing a critical mass of their naval forces to a single engagement. At Midway the Japanese sought a decisive naval action to eliminate American carrier strength before it could recover, but that victory would never come.

In this combat environment trained pilots and air crews became a precious commodity as a single wave of airplanes could realign the balance of power with a well-delivered strike. The aviators were more important than the planes, and both navies went to great lengths to secure safe return of their pilots, often running great risks to their vessels and their crews in attempting to retrieve pilots returning after dark. The Japanese, however, made the critical error of not securing a seed crop of these experienced pilots to provide for the training and equipping of future fliers. This was done out of fear that breaking up a carrier's flight team would lower morale. The Americans realized the potential danger of depleting their experienced aviator stockpile and took pains to provide for the future of their naval aviation. In the upcoming battle of Midway, had either side had more carriers and aircraft, it would not have been able to man the additional planes. Prewar training programs had not been sufficiently expanded or accelerated to keep pace with the heavy battle losses experienced in the war to date, let alone provide a surplus of trained, not to mention experienced, flyers. The single exception to the shortfall was one Japanese carrier, *Shokaku*, which was sent back to Japan with many of its aviators, the ship itself intact but damaged. As stated above, aviators could have been taken from it and given to its sister ship, *Zuikaku*, which was undamaged but had suffered heavy losses of aviators.

The entire face of naval warfare changed after the Battle of the Coral Sea. The once mighty battleships became mere screening vessels for the precious carrier forces, which were the true offensive weapons of any task force. The operational tactic employed in sea battles would be to close to a range of approximately 100 miles and fly off waves of bombers and fighters to destroy the enemy's force while attempting to defend one's own from counterstrikes. Attacks would center on the carriers. Only after they had been destroyed would the bombers turn their attention to the supporting vessels. Torpedo bombers would launch their strikes from all points of the compass, assuring that the captain of the ship would not be able to evade all of the deadly "fish." Dive bombers would plummet down on their prey and attempt to hole the flight deck, or better, knock out the elevators that brought the planes up from the hangar decks. Fighters would accompany the bombers and attempt to clear the skies of enemy combat air patrols (CAP) that might disrupt the attacks. Luck and timing would have a lot to do with the success of these strikes, as will be seen, but the patterns always remained the same.

Midway

Considerable disagreement erupted between the naval intelligence structures at Pearl and in Washington. Capt. Joseph Redman and Cdr. John Redman, then the de facto gurus of naval intelligence in the capitol, did not believe that Commander Rochefort's analysis of Japanese intent was correct. They informed Admiral King that the next Japanese target was not Midway, as Rochefort believed, but Pearl itself. Nimitz, however, believed Rochefort's staff had made the correct estimate. The United States had acquired Midway Atoll in 1867 as a communications relay station for the telegraph cable that ran from Hawaii to the Philippines. The atoll is composed of two small land masses, Sand and Eastern Islands, and is surrounded by a coral reef. The atoll represented the westernmost extent of American-held territory in the Central Pacific in summer 1942. The United States had reinforced the atoll following the Japanese attack on Pearl, and built three runways on Eastern Island in a triangular configuration.

Rochefort compiled an impressive array of Japanese decrypts that referred to a forthcoming attack against an objective named simply "target AF." Both Rochefort and the Redman brothers were aware that on at least three separate occasions since December 7, 1941, long-range search planes flown from Japanese forward bases and refueled by submarines had reconnoitered Pearl Harbor. On March 4, 1942, Pearl was actually subject to a second, if much smaller, Japanese air raid. Two high-altitude Japanese scout planes, flying from the Marshall Islands and refueled at French Frigate Shoals by tanker submarine, proceeded to scout the harbor and dropped small bomb loads in the process. The bombs caused no damage, but greatly embarrassed Nimitz. His staff, after much study, concluded that Japanese planes were using French Frigate Shoals as a refueling point. Henceforth, Nimitz began garrisoning it with such American warships as he could spare. These facts led naval intelligence in Washington, however, to conclude that target AF was most probably Pearl itself.

Rochefort disagreed, although he subsequently suggested a means of testing his conclusion. Knowing that Midway obtained its fresh water supply by distilling sea water, he planned to have that garrison send a message in its routine housekeeping reports to Pearl stating that its fresh water condenser was malfunctioning. If this were the case, the Japanese would be interested, assuming that target AF was indeed Midway Atoll, and would almost certainly relay such information to Yamamoto himself. Rochefort received permission from Nimitz to implement his plan. He used the cable as a means of communication with Midway, knowing that the Japanese could not have tapped it. Via this route, Midway received orders to report in the clear that its fresh water condenser was malfunctioning. On May 12, two days after Midway sent the fake message, Rochefort's intelligence unit monitored a transmission from a Japanese listening post in Kwajalein Atoll notifying Yamamoto that objective AF was short of fresh water.

On May 14, 1942, Nimitz, siding with Rochefort, put the fourteenth naval district into a state of readiness to oppose the Japanese invasion of Midway. Rochefort intercepted a message on May 25 detailing the make-up, courses, and probable dates of the invasion forces. His best estimate was that the invasion of Midway would commence on the third of June. Naval intelligence in Washington still believed that Pearl or possibly the West Coast was the real Japanese target but allowed Nimitz to proceed.

To placate Admiral King, a separate force of two heavy cruisers, three light cruisers, and thirteen destroyers under the command of Rear Adm. Thomas Theobald was sent north to protect Dutch Harbor in the Aleutians. Rochefort's staff correctly believed the Aleutians to be a secondary, diversionary Japanese target, scheduled for bombing by a small Japanese carrier force. Theobold believed that the Japanese meant to invade Dutch Harbor, so he positioned his fleet 500 miles south and west of Dutch Harbor, near Kodiak, to intercept the Japanese. Hence, he failed to see any action, while leaving Dutch Harbor unprotected from an air raid. And the Japanese were able to follow up by occupying the islands of Attu and Kiska, westward in the Aleutian chain.

The Japanese Midway plan was as follows: a diversionary force under Vice Adm. Hosogaya Hoshiro would attack Dutch Harbor in the Aleutians by air the day before the planned assault on Midway. That same day, a small force of midget submarines would also penetrate Port Darwin and attempt to divert attention from the Central Pacific. This would attract American attention away from Midway Atoll, which was to be neutralized and then occupied by the Japanese. Yamamoto had specified that neutralization of Midway's defenses was to be accomplished by the First Air Fleet alone. He had been chagrined by the lack of respect his carriers still engendered in Tokyo (among other annoyances, the naval general staff still credited one of the midget submarines with the destruction of *Arizona*). He was determined to demonstrate that alone they could soften up the atoll preparatory to actual invasion. Therefore he split his forces further. On the day after the diversionary attacks, the First Air Fleet was to launch an air strike that would obliterate Midway's defenses. The First Air Fleet would be comprised of four carriers—*Akagi*, *Kaga*, *Soryu*, and *Hiryu*—with a total of 261 aircraft, and 2 battleships, 2 heavy cruisers, 1 light cruiser, 11 destroyers, and assorted support vessels.

The next day, Yamamoto's force (which Nimitz did not know about) would arrive 300 miles behind the First Air Fleet. This force contained seven battleships, including Yamamoto's flagship, the super battleship *Yamato*, two light cruisers, twenty-one destroyers, one light carrier, and two seaplane carriers filled with midget submarines, as well as the usual support craft. At the same time, the Midway invasion force under Adm. Kondo Nobutaki would arrive. It was to have sortied from Truk Island in the Carolines and would approach Midway from the south. It contained one light carrier, two battleships, eight heavy cruisers, two light cruisers, eleven destroyers, and twelve transports that contained the Midway invasion troops. Kondo's force also contained various support ships including two seaplane carriers and three converted destroyers carrying a force of marines.

As insurance that the American carriers would not be in the Midway area when Nagumo launched his air strike against the atoll, Yamamoto ordered one final force to American waters. A group of *I*-class submarines was to patrol the waters between Pearl and Midway. Unfortunately these submarines did not receive correct orders (an error in encrypting was evidently responsible) and arrived two days late at their patrol stations, after the American carrier force had sailed past on its way to Midway. Finally, Yamamoto had authorized a second reconnaissance of Pearl Harbor to make certain that the American carriers were still in port. This plan, known as Operation K, was aborted when the Japanese tanker submarine failed to make its appointed rendezvous with the two high-altitude seaplanes at French Frigate Shoals because a small American warship was anchored there. Admiral Nagumo did not know that *Operation K* had to be canceled. His task force was sailing through a storm front at the time of the report, and his radio receivers were not capable of penetrating the static. Yamamoto mistakenly assumed that if he himself had heard the report, Nagumo had heard it also. Consequently, he did not break radio silence to relay the message. Had they received the report, Nagumo's staff might have been a bit less confident and more wary.

Admiral Nimitz was aware of the strength of the Japanese forces opposing him. He knew that the Japanese expected that he would sortie his carriers to oppose the strike after Midway had been taken, and that they intended to destroy America's remaining naval strength in the Pacific and hopefully force

Washington to sue for peace. With the carriers removed, Hawaii and the West Coast would be left exposed and Roosevelt, already committed to aiding the allies in Europe, would have little choice but to negotiate with Japan. Therefore, Nimitz determined to strike the Japanese carriers before Midway was invaded, a scenario the Japanese had barely considered possible. His major problem was that he had only three carriers to oppose the enemy forces. Further, Admiral Halsey could not command the American carriers. On the return voyage from the Doolittle Tokyo raid he had contracted neurodermatitis, a skin disease severe enough to require hospitalization. Nimitz chose Halsey's cruiser commander, the elegant Adm. Raymond Spruance, as his successor. Admiral Fletcher was also detailed to the forthcoming operation and would function as overall American commander.

Spruance, flying his flag from *Enterprise*, sortied from Pearl on May 28, 1942, in command of Task Force Sixteen, which also included *Hornet*, six cruisers, and nine destroyers; Fletcher, commanding Task Force Seventeen and using *Yorktown* as his flagship, cleared Pearl Harbor two days later, accompanied by two cruisers. Between the 3 carriers, 228 aircraft were available, while on Midway itself were 19 B-17s, 32 Catalina flying boats, 16 Dauntless dive bombers, 6 Avenger torpedo bombers, and some hopelessly outdated fighters.

Nagumo, who had sortied from the Inland Sea on May 27, seemed little happier over the upcoming Midway operation than he had been when he sailed for Pearl Harbor six months before. But unlike the Pearl operation, he was embarked on an operation in which the authors rather blithely assumed that surprise would almost automatically be achieved. Since sailing for Pearl, Nagumo had navigated his fleet over 50,000 miles, and he did not like the condition of many of his aviators. Like Rochefort's combat intelligence team at Pearl, they were using amphetamines to maintain their alertness, and many evidently did so to excess, for more than a few actually reported encountering ghosts of dead relatives, among other oddities, to their flight surgeons. The same physicians often noted low red blood cell counts and elevated white blood cell counts as well among the flyers. There can be no doubt that Nagumo's aviators were suffering from exhaustion.

Further, Nagumo's trusted right-hand man on the voyage to Pearl, Kusaka, had been eclipsed in influence by Genda, who now gave indispensable advice on air operations, so much so that some wags referred to the First Air Fleet simply as "Genda's Fleet." But Nagumo also had very practical reasons for concern. The entire Japanese military and naval establishment was suffering from what was later termed "victory fever." Overconfidence seemed pandemic. Against all odds in the book, the Japanese had conquered the El Dorado of the South in record time, and despite a strategic defeat at Coral

Sea, they seemed unstoppable. This led to overconfidence, which worried Nagumo. Also, his two most experienced commanders would probably not be available at Midway. Fuchida, who had for several days been ignoring abdominal pain, reported to the flight surgeon on May 27 and was promptly diagnosed as suffering from appendicitis and prepped for surgery. And on the first of June, Genda reported to the sick bay; his temperature indicated a viral infection, either pneumonia or influenza.

First Air Fleet sailed into heavy seas and storms and on one occasion had to break radio silence to indicate a course change to all vessels. Contrary to the popular version of events found in Hollywood movies, Nagumo did *not* decide to fight the battle as if the Americans had anticipated his battle plan, but he was determined to leave nothing to chance. At the last moment, early on the morning of June 4, Genda discharged himself from sick bay and participated in a conference that decided that as the Midway-bound aircraft were launched, scout planes would also be sent aloft to seek out any enemy vessels in the vicinity. They were to search in particular to the north of Midway, which was exactly where the three American carriers were lying in wait.

Although Nimitz remained at Pearl, he also left nothing to chance. As of May 30 he instituted aerial reconnaissance out of Midway by PBY Catalina flying boats. Each day twenty-two of these aircraft flew in a spoke pattern 700 miles out from Midway to the northwest, alert for the Japanese. On June 3 one PBY sighted Kondo's invasion fleet rapidly closing on Midway from the south. But the pilot did not know which force he had sighted; he radioed Midway that he had sighted Nagumo's "main body" of ships, which had to mean the First Air Fleet. For the first and only time during the Midway operation, Nimitz gave his commanders at sea tactical instructions. He sent them an urgent message, assuring them the PBY had sighted Kondo's invasion fleet, stating Nagumo would strike from the northwest the next day, as anticipated. Fletcher and Spruance closed to a position almost exactly 200 miles north of Midway Atoll.

At 4:30 A.M., June 4, 1942, Nagumo began launching his Midway attack force. In fifteen minutes the entire attack force was in the air, led by Lt. Tomonaga Joichi. Tomonaga's force did not contain First Air Fleet's best pilots, however. Those flyers had been held in reserve unless the American carriers were spotted. Nagumo also launched the scout planes to hunt for American warships. Three of the Japanese scout planes left on schedule, but four were delayed for reasons that are still not evident. In particular, the cruiser *Tone* was delayed in catapulting off both of its scouts, which were coded as Scouts Three and Four. Both were delayed by precious minutes, and number four was launched only at 5:00 A.M. Nagumo had no choice but to wait.

At 5:45 A.M. a PBY (flying boat) radioed in the clear "many planes heading Midway." Nimitz was finally absolutely certain that he had been correct and Washington mistaken concerning the ultimate objective of Operation AF. Midway launched its fighters to stop the oncoming Japanese. Midway's Wildcats did their best, but they could not match the Japanese Zeroes, and the antiquated Brewster Buffaloes did not fare all that well either. At 6:30 A.M. Tomonaga's planes began bombing Midway. Despite the fact that Midway's airfield was on Eastern Island, Sand Island received much more Japanese attention. The oil storage tanks were set on fire, and many buildings were completely gutted. About twenty men on the ground were killed in the raid. Nagumo lost eight aircraft, while the Americans lost seventeen. The inexperience and poorer quality of Tomonaga's attackers was costly though, for the airstrips remained intact, as did numerous anti-aircraft guns. Thus, at exactly 7:05 A.M. Tomonaga radioed *Akagi* that "a second attack wave is needed over the target."

Meanwhile, at 5:20 A.M., the Americans had learned the position of Nagumo's carriers. Spruance decided to attack the carriers roughly two hours earlier than he had initially planned, in hope that he might catch Nagumo's flattops while they were refueling their Midway attack force. He was at maximum range, and began launching his aircraft piecemeal at 7:02 A.M. Spruance believed that a Nagumo scout plane had sighted his force, but he did not know his luck. *Chikuma*'s Number Five scout plane evidently flew directly over the American carriers, but somehow did not observe them. Scout Four, the longest delayed in launching, sighted the American ships initially at 7:28 A.M., but only at 8:20 A.M. was he able to report that a carrier was among the American vessels.

Nagumo had been in a quandary since he had received Tomonaga's request for another strike. Initially, half of the remaining aircraft had been brought on deck on two of his four carriers, which were armed with torpedoes and manned by the most experienced pilots in Nagumo's fleet in case American warships suddenly appeared. But at 7:15 A.M. Nagumo ordered all planes to switch to contact bombs; then, at 7:45 A.M., he ordered torpedoes left on those planes so equipped. Meanwhile, attacks against the Japanese carriers had begun at 7:08 A.M. Midway-based aircraft executed the first attacks, and while the attacks failed to score any hits, they did convince Nagumo that the airfields and installations on Midway constituted a serious threat and had to be neutralized.

At a little past 8:30 A.M. Tomonaga requested permission to land his returning Midway strike force. Genda made the decision: land the Midway strike force, rearm it with torpedoes, and dispatch all aircraft to the just-sighted American carrier. At 8:37 A.M. *Akagi* began landing Tomonaga's planes. But Rear Adm. Yamaguchi Tamon, in command of *Hiryu* and *Soryu*, argued that all remaining aircraft, however they were armed, should be launched at once against the American carrier, which would have meant letting Tomonaga's 100-odd planes fall into the sea for lack of fuel. Nagumo refused Yamaguchi's request. On Genda's advice, he made a more humane decision, albeit, as will be seen, an incorrect one.

It had been an exceedingly hectic morning for Nagumo'a hangar crews. The frequent changes of ordnance for the planes had been ordered in language that did not allow for delay, and they had complied. As a result, after Tomonaga's Midway strike force had returned, they were equipped primarily with long-lance torpedoes, as were most of the remaining aircraft.

Nagumo now turned to close distance with the sighted American carrier. He first came under attack from carrier-based Devastator torpedo planes, flying from *Hornet*, a moment or two after his course change, at about 9:18 A.M. The slow-moving aircrafts were equipped with antiquated steam-driven torpedoes little different from the Whitehead models of World War I. They did have magnetic detonators, but these tended to malfunction, and in any event they usually ran deeper than their preset running depth. Several American torpedo squadrons attacked Nagumo's force that morning, but not one American torpedo exploded against the hull of a Japanese ship. They did, however, draw Nagumo's Zero fighter umbrella to low patrol altitude, where they temporarily remained. Then, at 10:20 A.M., Nagumo received word that all his aircraft had been refitted with torpedoes and were nearly ready to attack the American carrier. He ordered his carriers to turn into the wind and commence launching at once. Seconds after the first plane left *Akagi*'s flight deck, American dive-bombers found the Japanese. A carrier at sea with freedom to maneuver would ordinarily least fear a dive-bomber attack, but Nagumo's carriers had no fighter protection left to cover them. The prior American air attacks had drawn the Zeroes down to wavetop level.

Further, Nagumo's flight decks were filled with fully armed and fueled aircraft, while the hangar decks of all four carriers were littered with contact bombs, left in the rush that allowed no time for them to be returned to ships' magazines. At 10:24 A.M. the divebombers swarmed in. Someone on the deck of *Akagi* cried "Helldivers!" as a warning (the Japanese had used this English term since a 1931 Hollywood production had glorified such pilots), but Nagumo's carriers could only engage in violent evasive maneuvers as protection.

Within six minutes, three of his four carriers were stricken. *Kaga* was hit first, then *Akagi*, and finally *Soryu*. Induced explosions followed the initial impact by American contact bombs on the flight decks, as flaming gasoline reached ordnance scattered on the hangar deck floors. Only *Hiryu* escaped. Nagumo barely managed to escape the bridge of *Akagi*, transferring his flag to the cruiser *Nagara*.

Yamaguchi, a Princeton graduate noted for his aggressiveness and also for a penchant for theatrics, struck back as soon as he was able. At 10:54 A.M., as a warning, carrier *Hiryu* still unscathed, he launched twenty-four aircraft against the sighted American carrier. At noon the aircraft found *Yorktown* and put several contact bombs into it. The returning pilots assured Yamaguchi they had sunk one American carrier. Yamaguchi now learned from a scout that a total of three American carriers were north of Midway. Hoping his pilots had already reduced this number by one, he launched his planes again, assuming they would damage or sink a second American carrier and even the odds. Instead they found *Yorktown* again and put two torpedoes into it. At 2:55 P.M., Capt. Elliot Buckmaster of the *Yorktown* was forced to abandon ship. Then, settling the score, American carrier planes found *Hiryu* just after 5:00 P.M. and left it ablaze. Yamaguchi delayed ordering his men to abandon ship, however, indulging his penchant for the dramatic by performing the traditional samurai ceremony. As a result, the captain went down with his ship.

The remainder of the combat action was incidental. At about 3:00 A.M., after receiving reconnaissance photographs of what was left of the First Air Fleet, Yamamoto ordered it sunk by its own destroyers. He then ordered a general withdrawal, admitting defeat. On June 6, a Japanese *I*-class submarine penetrated a protective destroyer screen and sank the slowly retreating *Yorktown*, whose damage was under repair. Finally, two of Kondo's retiring cruisers, *Mogami* and *Mikuma*, collided, and Spruance's planes sunk the latter. There was no further action of consequence.

At Midway, the scoring punch of the Japanese navy had been blunted: 4 carriers and 1 cruiser sunk, 5,000 Japanese had lost their lives, and 322 planes were lost. Worse, the pilots who were lost—many of whom had a thousand hours in combat experience over the skies of China, not to mention that gained since—were irreplaceable. American losses comprised ninety-nine carrier-based aircraft, thirty-eight Midway-based planes, and the *Yorktown*. As it was, if Nimitz had had *Saratoga* available, he would have experienced difficulty in rounding out their squadrons, and after the battle many of the remaining pilots were in a state of acute fatigue. Nimitz and King realized that something had to be done to ensure that there would be properly trained and experienced pilots on all American carriers. They decided to break up the veteran crews of *Yorktown*, *Enterprise*, and *Hornet*, and reassign them. Some veteran pilots were transferred to new squadrons to act as leavening while others became instructors. More to the point, steps were taken to ensure an increased flow of new pilots, particularly from San Diego. No such steps were taken by the Japanese, who stoically endured their losses as part of the cost of war, and evidently gave no thought to ensuring a flow of new pilots for what was sure to be a protracted conflict. They made no prognosis for the future, as Nimitz and King did. The results would be disastrous for the imperial forces.

The Japanese lost at Midway for reasons as complex as the Japanese order of battle for the action. They were overconfident of victory and, although it had no effect on the battle's outcome, security had been very lax. Japan's pilots were probably even more exhausted than their American counterparts, and the Japanese failed to anticipate that the United States would substantially penetrate their JN-25 fleet code cipher. (Later they assumed that the United States had probably known their intent via a chance submarine sighting of the First Air Fleet.) Yamamoto's plan hinged on surprise, even more than was the case at Pearl Harbor. Obviously, the American carriers could be drawn out for battle successfully only if they were at Pearl, or heading northward toward Dutch Harbor, when Nagumo made his first air strike against Midway. Failure to search properly for the U.S. fleet with a significant number of planes at the outset played its role in the disaster.

Yamamoto has also frequently been criticized for splitting his fleet. There is merit to this observation, but Yamamoto had his reasons. First, he wished the battleship admirals in Tokyo to appreciate properly the value of carriers in neutralizing a shore target. Second, he did not wish his presence in the immediate vicinity to hinder command structure. Third, his older battleships would have impeded the mobility of First Air Fleet. And finally, because of faulty intelligence, the Japanese estimate was that no more than two American carriers could be called upon to retaliate, which still gave Nagumo a 2 : 1 advantage.

Still, the basic Japanese plan, while overly complicated, was sound. If Rochefort and his staff had not read and correctly interpreted the JN-25 fleet code, Midway probably would have fallen, and the American carriers would probably have been drawn into a battle fought more on Japanese terms than it was. Yamamoto was certainly aware that American shipyards would be rushing out new vessels in the near future and that Japan's advantages lay in pressing the fight and forcing the Americans to fight before they were ready and in a place not to their favor. Both navies had assumed before the war that the decisive naval battle would be fought in waters closer to Japan's home islands, but there was little chance of luring the Americans into the heart of the Japanese-held Pacific in the summer of 1942. Midway offered a good location for mounting a threat against Hawaii, and Japan certainly had a decided advantage in terms of naval tonnage at this point. Nearly all signs pointed to a victory, if not total destruction of the American carrier fleet as a result of the planned Midway operation. The fact that Plan Midway did not fit in with the classic rule for sea engagement as outlined by Alfred T. Mahan means little. (Mahan himself was the son of a West Point instructor.) Mahan did not write in the age of naval air power. And of course, hindsight is twenty-twenty as usual.

The point is that Japan did lose at Midway, and from this battle to the end of the conflict, it reacted to American advances, rather than the opposite. Midway was the turn of the tide, and Yamamoto knew it.

However, the average Japanese, and indeed the emperor himself, did not know this. Premier Tojo was actually pleased that the Imperial Navy had lost at Midway. But rather than admit a national defeat, Tojo announced a victory, although his announcement gave no details. But all the rhetoric in the world could not restore Japan's four lost carriers, or their pilots. Midway belongs to that very small group of truly decisive military engagements.

Suggestions for Further Reading

There are several recent studies of Doolittle's exploit, including Carroll Glines, *The Doolittle Raid* (New York: Orion Books, 1988), and James M. Merrill, *Target Tokyo: The Halsey–Doolittle Raid* (New York, 1964). The best study of the Coral Sea campaign is John B. Lundstrom, *The First South Pacific Campaign: Pacific Fleet Strategy, December 1941–June 1942* (Annapolis, MD: Naval Institute Press, 1976), but see also Bernard Millot, *The Battle of the Coral Sea* (Annapolis, MD: Naval Institute Press, 1974). For the Midway engagement, we have relied on the following: H.P. Wilmott, *The Barrier and the Javelin: Japanese and Allied Pacific Strategies, February to June 1942* (Annapolis, MD: Naval Institute Press, 1983); Gordon W. Prange, *Miracle at Midway* (New York: McGraw-Hill, 1982); Mitsuo Fuchida and Masatake Okumiya, *Midway: The Battle That Doomed Japan* (Annapolis, MD: Naval Institute Press, 1955), written by Japan's Pearl Harbor hero; William W. Smith, *Midway: Turning Point of the Pacific* (New York: Crowell, 1966); Department of the Navy, *The Japanese Story of the Battle of Midway* (Washington, DC: U.S. Government Printing Office, 1947); George H. Gay, who wrote *Sole Survivor* (Naples, FL: Naples Graphics Services, 1979), survived a torpedo squadron at Midway; S.E. Morison, *History of the United States Naval Operations of World War Two*, vol. 4, *Coral Sea, Midway and Submarine Actions* (Boston: Little, Brown, 1949); Pat Frank and Joseph Harrington, *Rendezvous at Midway: USS Yorktown and the Japanese Carrier Fleet* (New York: John Day, 1967); Edmund Forrestal, *Admiral Raymond A. Spruance, USN: A Study in Command* (Washington, DC: U.S. Government Printing Office, 1966); Tameichi Hara, *Japanese Destroyer Captain* (New York: Ballantine Books, 1961); Robert Heinl, *Marines at Midway* (Washington, DC: Historical Section, USMC, 1948); and Thomas Buell, *The Quiet Warrior: A Biography of Admiral Raymond Spruance* (Boston: Little, Brown, 1974). The best overall study of this period is H.P. Wilmott, *Empires in the Balance: Japanese and Allied Pacific Strategies to April 1942* (Annapolis, MD: Naval Institute Press, 1982).

6

First Allied Land Victories

While the American victory at Midway may have been miraculous and monumental, it did not immediately alleviate the Japanese threat in the Central and South Pacific, nor did it win back one foot of conquered soil. The success of Japan's first six months of campaigning in the Pacific would be difficult to reverse, and the situation would only become more difficult if the Japanese were allowed to consolidate and properly defend their hard-won gains. Both Japanese and Allied planners set about accomplishing the same task during the summer of 1942: to devise a strategy that would allow them to secure control of the enormous central and southern Pacific basin and transform it into a defensible staging area for operations against the enemy.

The very nature of the terrain, or lack thereof, in the middle of the Pacific Ocean became the foremost determining factor of how the war proceeded after 1942. Literally thousands of islands dot the Pacific Ocean, some several hundred square miles in size, others only a few hundred square feet. Many of these islands are totally uninhabited and nearly uninhabitable. There is little "modern" civilization between Manila in the Philippines and Darwin in Australia. Therefore, nearly all of the materials of existence, let alone warfare, for a modern army had to be trundled along with the invading forces as the indigenous resources of the area were generally inadequate, if not openly hostile, to a modern military force. The great highway that allowed these resources to flow was the Pacific itself and so control of the seas became imperative. Midway, however, had proven that naval firepower alone was no guaranty of success on the seas. Both sides realized airpower was the key to success on land and at sea, and control of the air would depend on reliable, well-stocked, adequately defended landing sites. While Midway had decimated the First Air Fleet, it had not destroyed the entire Japanese carrier force, many of which would now be detailed to supplying and defending the newly established island bases of the South Pacific. Similarly for the Allies, the three operational American carriers in the Pacific were indispensable elements of the reduction and conquest of Japan's nascent empire.

The islands of the South Pacific became as valuable as the remaining carrier forces in the role of providing potentially unsinkable, if also immobile, air bases. Consequently, possession of the territory of an island became less crucial than possession of any runways located on that island. Ground troops were crucial insofar as they could secure and protect suitable territory for air support facilities. Conquest of large quantities of land was secondary to possession of strategic positions. Given this situation, the Japanese failed to adequately appreciate and pursue a policy that supported these necessities, choosing to garrison powerful but ultimately vulnerable fortresses with large numbers of troops, while at the same time incrementally sacrificing control of the skies and seas. The result, as historian Eric Bergerud has pointed out, was to transform many of these island fortresses into large prisoner of war camps as the war eventually passed these strongholds by.

As the Japanese expansionist phase of the war ended and the Allies began planning for their eventual advance toward the home islands, tremendous battles occurred at unlikely locations. It became increasingly evident to both the Japanese and the Allies that possession of specific islands was less significant than the ability to project air and naval power over an entire region. Both sides found that success was dependent on the ability to operate under a sufficient air umbrella of both attack and defense aircraft. Operations without such support were generally doomed to failure. The ability to create such a protective canopy was also an interlocking one relying on strategic outposts to maintain the integrity of the whole operation. Therefore, loss of even a seemingly insignificant base could spell doom for the whole network. For these reasons as well as others, the Japanese and the Allies both staked a great deal on several early and, on the surface, apparently inconsequential locations in the South Pacific. Cracking or defending the shell of Japanese defense became the highest priority for both of the belligerents by the fall of 1942.

Fighting on New Guinea

The initial landings on Guadalcanal and New Guinea in 1942 were, like Midway, reactions to Japan's attempts to secure outer bases from which to defend its empire. After MacArthur escaped from Corregidor, he sought refuge in Australia, where he believed he would find an American army with which he would soon return to liberate the Philippines. When he arrived, he found the Australians in a state of acute anxiety, with virtually no

American troops in the country. MacArthur had to convince Prime Minister John Curtin and Gen. Thomas Blamey, commander of the Australian army, to forsake the Brisbane Line, a line of defense for the continent intended to abandon the lightly populated northern portion of the continent in favor of supporting the large cities of the southeast. Australians, like many Americans who had advocated a policy of abandoning the West Coast for a defense line beginning at the Rocky Mountains in the days immediately following Pearl Harbor, were overestimating the threat posed by Japanese power. While there were some Japanese leaders advocating strikes on northern Australia and even dreaming of one day occupying or rendering the subcontinent a tributary, cooler heads, even in Tokyo, realized the difficulties inherent in such a scenario given Japan's resource limitations and did not seriously consider invasion. Army and navy planners did, however, consider New Guinea crucial to the Japanese empire and revisited plans to secure the valuable harbor at Port Moresby.

MacArthur convinced Curtin and Blamey that the defense of Australia should in effect be in New Guinea. American as well as Australian troops would be employed. It was agreed that MacArthur would command Australian units so long as they operated south of the equator. The arrangement worked well, but the occasional difficulties were not insignificant. At one point, disembarking American troops at Brisbane told their Australian counterparts, who were embarking, of their intentions toward Australian women when they received leave. More than words were exchanged. In this "Battle of Brisbane," gunfire ensued and several dozen lives were lost. For the sake of Allied unity the matter was quickly hushed up.

The Japanese army on New Guinea had decided to attempt to force the Kokoda Trail and proceed to Port Moresby without the aid of the navy. The disastrous episode in the Coral Sea had convinced army planners that they would be better served by relying on their own resources and not counting on the navy for significant support. Maj. Gen. Horii Tomitaro took command of a dual offensive aimed first at capturing the coastal city of Buna for its aerial support value, after which he was to cross the Owen Stanley mountain range and capture Port Moresby, the colonial capital of the island. The second feat would indeed have been impressive, for the New Guinea jungles, located directly south of the equator, are very probably the most dense, impenetrable jungles on the planet. The Kokoda Trail itself is hardly a readily passable route, and the Owen Stanley range has peaks as high as 15,000 feet. Even the local inhabitants thought the Japanese foolish to attempt so challenging an undertaking.

Meanwhile, MacArthur had begun to commit the remaining Australian forces to Port Moresby and the defense of New Guinea. The Australian Seventh Division was the first to arrive, and was eventually joined by the American Thirty-second, or Red Arrow Division, from Wisconsin and Michigan. The Australians had deployed troops along the Kokoda Trail as delaying or skirmish forces. None of the groups was large enough to stop the Japanese advance, but they could buy the defenders of the port enough time to establish a line of defense that would hold. The Australians also built airfields around Port Moresby and were supplied with sufficient aircraft to cut Japanese supply lines and interdict the advance. This last became crucial as the Japanese proceeded without the standard air cover that had marked earlier successful campaigns. The failure of Japanese air support proceeded from several factors. Foremost among these, and a source of difficulty throughout the war, was the nonexistence in the Japanese military of an equivalent to the Army Corps of Engineers. This absence assured that all construction projects undertaken by the Japanese would be slow, inefficient, and often of inferior quality. The two proper air bases used by the Japanese in the Central and South Pacific at Clark Air Field in the Philippines and Rabaul in the Bismarck Islands were already in place when the Japanese captured the islands. Many of the fields built by the Japanese were of inferior quality and were plagued by recurrent problems with repair and serviceability. The Japanese were also, at this early date, already beginning to feel the pinch of decreased numbers of trained and experienced pilots to fly close support and other combat missions.

General Horii pressed his men on after the rapid fall of Buna on the southeastern coast of New Guinea and began pushing back the Australians in an attempt to cross the mountains before the onset of the rainy season. The Japanese pressed to within twenty-five miles of Moresby. They could actually see the port before the Australian defenders were able to turn them back on September 24, 1942. Because they had intended to take the city and subsist on supplies garnered there, the Japanese found themselves forced to retreat short on food, medicine, and ammunition, and with no prospect of resupply. Consequently, attrition due to natural factors, particularly climate and disease, was as great as that caused by fighting. Tropical diseases exacerbated by malnutrition and climate decimated the Japanese ranks. The retreat became horrific as Japanese losses to wounds and disease mounted. The Kokoda Trail was literally lined with the bodies of soldiers too sick and weak to proceed and doomed to reside in unmarked graves. As the rainy season began in the mountains, what had been small streams during the Japanese advance became raging torrents, each of which posed a different obstacle to the Japanese retreat. It was while attempting to cross one such swollen river that General Horii drowned when his makeshift raft overturned. The

Australians were able to push the Japanese back to their defensive positions at Buna while inflicting heavy casualties on them as well.

Guadalcanal and Related Actions

On July 3, 1942, an Allied reconnaissance aircraft, while on routine patrol, had discovered an airfield under construction on the small island of Guadalcanal, in the Solomon Island chain. Until this time the island had little significance, other than having served as the location of a Lever Brothers copra plantation. The Americans, aware that Guadalcanal had been part of the British empire, again turned to antiquated British admiralty maps and Australian charts to plan their landings. Obviously the Japanese were building a landing strip to provide fighter and bomber strength to augment the reconnaissance plane base already established at nearby Tulagi, on Florida Island. With these, they could interdict U.S. shipping to Australia and deny the Allied forces "down under" much-needed supplies.

The First Marine Division, which had trained at Quantico for service in Europe, was hastily dispatched to San Diego, where its men embarked for the Solomons via New Zealand. On August 7, 1942, the marines landed on Guadalcanal virtually unopposed. The only Japanese troops present, about 2,200 (probably Korean) construction workers, evidently unarmed, fled into the interior as the leathernecks approached. Later the Japanese sent in regular army troops. The Americans quickly secured and began improving the airfield and renamed it for Maj. Lofton Henderson, a marine dive bomber who had lost his life in the Battle of Midway. The ice manufacturing facility, also captured intact, was rechristened the Tojo Ice Plant (under new management). Nineteen thousand marines under the command of Maj. Gen. Alexander Vandegrift landed during the initial invasion and took up defensive positions around the perimeter of the airstrip.

Vice Adm. Frank J. Fletcher gained permission to withdraw his carriers from the vicinity late on the afternoon of August 8 in order to refuel. He commanded two of America's remaining three carriers in the Pacific. Evidently Fletcher did not wish to place them in undue jeopardy. The marines thought very poorly of this decision, however, and some commented aloud they believed Fletcher wished to add a fourth color to the American flag. His decision delayed the landing of much needed supplies and probably cost marine lives by depriving them of naval air cover.

Rear Adm. Richmond Turner was posted to the straits off Savo Island, north of Guadalcanal, to intercept any Japanese resupply or surprise attack efforts. Early on the morning of August 9, 1942, the Japanese sent a force of five heavy cruisers, two light cruisers, and a destroyer under Rear Adm. Mikawa Gunichi to engage the American forces at Guadalcanal and destroy their transport and supply vessels if possible. At 1:00 A.M. the Japanese met a force of five heavy cruisers and several destroyers, commanded by British Rear Adm. V.A.C. Crutchley, which was guarding the northern passage to Guadalcanal.

Although the Americans actually had some prior warning, including unidentified radar contacts, it was not credited and so the attack came as a complete surprise. Within thirty minutes, the Japanese inflicted on the combined Australian and American forces the worst defeat they had ever suffered in a conventional, "textbook" fight. The Allies lost four of their five heavy cruisers, including the Australian cruiser *Canberra*, and a destroyer, along with 1,270 officers and men killed and 900 more wounded. After the action ended, Capt. Howard D. Bode, commander of the cruiser *Chicago*, committed suicide, even though his ship had survived, albeit seriously damaged, the night's fighting.

In return, Mikawa lost thirty-seven men and fifty-seven wounded. Mikawa, afraid of American carrier plane strikes, withdrew unaware that Fletcher's carriers had already left the area. By withdrawing, Mikawa failed to engage the American transport vessels that had been left unprotected off the coast of the marine landing site. At his base at Rabaul, Admiral Yamamoto's chief of staff, Vice Adm. Ugaki Matome, observed that Japan had now made up for the losses at Coral Sea and Midway, and ordered Mikawa to finish off the Allied naval forces in the vicinity. Mikawa lost one of his heavy cruisers, *Kako*, to a submarine during the withdrawal but still achieved a stunning victory. He had failed, however, in his primary mission to destroy the transports and supplies destined for the marines at Guadalcanal. The battle set a precedent for future action in the Solomons. The Japanese increasingly, and with great success, relied on night actions to offset growing Allied air superiority. And while able to deal grievous wounds to the Allies in these surface engagements, they were less successful in other ways. Ugaki and other naval commanders became increasingly impatient with the surface fleet's apparent ability to successfully confront the Allied battle fleets, while rarely being able to seriously threaten the supply line to the troops ashore.

The Battle of Savo Island was only the first in a series of colorful and bloody naval actions that took place in the waters around Guadalcanal. The United States Navy enjoyed the advantage of radar, albeit quite primitive, while hardly any of the Japanese ships were so equipped. But the Imperial Navy ensured that the men who served aboard its ships had night vision, the ability to see extraordinarily well in the dark. The Japanese relied more and more heavily on their ability to surprise the American fleet at night as the

Guadalcanal campaign progressed. For several months the difference of power in the Solomons was as clear as night and day. American air power ruled the daylight hours, but Japanese tactics and bravado controlled the nights. As radar grew more sophisticated and the Allies learned how to use its findings better, however, the balance shifted to the American side, but only after many costly attempts to engage the enemy in night combat where the latter's reliance on their men's ability gave them the edge.

In subsequent encounters the Japanese and the Americans both suffered substantial losses. The enormous cost in lives and vessels led the narrow body of water separating Guadalcanal from Florida Island to be christened unofficially Ironbottom Sound. The American carrier *Wasp*, recently transferred from the Atlantic, and the Japanese light carrier *Ryujo* were sunk, along with numerous other vessels of all sizes and classes. Probably the greatest loss for the Japanese was the battleship *Kirishima*, sunk by the battleships *Washington* and *South Dakota* on November 12, 1942, in the sort of "Orange Plan" surface engagement between battleships that had been anticipated before Pearl Harbor by both the American and Japanese naval establishments. Both sides had determined that Guadalcanal was to be a significant, highly publicized campaign. The victor would at the least have a significant propaganda advantage. Guadalcanal came to be the Japanese military's priority as they increasingly diverted resources from other sectors into the conflict. However, the Japanese fought the battle in a piecemeal fashion, both from a naval standpoint and in reinforcing the garrison on Guadalcanal. They often failed to coordinate their attacks between various branches of the same service, let alone between the various services. The primary reason for this was the difficulty they had in providing even the basic necessities of men and material to the island. Ugaki commented often on the frustrating inability of the Japanese navy to provide adequate tools to its soldiers, while the Americans seemed to reinforce at will. While this may well have been the Japanese take on the situation, the Marines on Guadalcanal would most likely have disagreed; in any case, it was not the situation strictly through chance. American forces concentrated on stopping the supply convoys and disrupting reinforcing efforts above all else, often risking the last strength of the navy's precious carrier forces in pitched battles.

The last significant naval battle was that of Tassafaranga Point, fought on November 30, after which the Japanese imperial command determined that Guadalcanal was no longer worth the great expense required to hold it. They did not, however, convey this message to the ground soldiers on the island. All told, the Americans had lost one carrier, seven cruisers, and five destroyers; the Japanese had lined Ironbottom Sound with one carrier, two battleships, one cruiser, and six destroyers. Ugaki commented that the Allies were willing to sacrifice much of their heavy shipping to buy time for the troops ashore and that Japan did not have this luxury.

The Americans had failed to press the advantages that radar gave them, while the Japanese navy had used its night training to great effectiveness. Though the precise numbers are uncertain, another factor contributing to Allied success was the tremendous attrition forced on Japanese army and naval aviation. The air war over the South Pacific was fierce and costly. Again, Japan lost an irreplaceable multitude of trained pilots, not to mention their aircraft. In numbers it was a tactical draw, but it was a strategic victory for the Americans, who had started the rollback of the Japanese empire. The hard shell of imperial defense had been cracked and the Allies could now choose the time and place of their next advance. Although the Japanese had lost the battle at sea, the struggle on the ground continued for several more months.

In the interim, the aggressive Halsey replaced Adm. Robert Ghormley as overall commander in the South Pacific, Rear Adm. Thomas Kinkaid relieved Fletcher, and Maj. Gen. Alexander Patch, commanding the so-called American Division, replaced Vandegrift and his exhausted First Marine Division. Life on Guadalcanal was putrid in every sense for both sides. In part because Fletcher had pulled out before all the necessary supplies were landed, shortages were endemic. Many nights the "Tokyo Express" would proceed down "the Slot," the channel between the northern and southern Solomons, essentially unopposed, and shell the marine positions and Henderson field. Although these attacks did not kill a substantial number of marines, they had considerable harassment value and were quite effective as a psychological weapon. Every marine on the island came to dread twilight.

The marines subsisted on rations that had been condemned but saved as an economy measure in 1931. Vile as these foodstuffs were, they were a virtual feast compared to the Japanese soldiers' diet of roots, berries, and the occasional insect. And on rare occasions individual Japanese actually practiced cannibalism. The average marine on Guadalcanal lost eighteen pounds; the average Japanese lost forty. For both sides disease was as deadly as the opposing enemy. Dysentery, severe malaria—including the cerebral variety, which was much harder to prevent or to treat since it resulted in convulsions—and beri beri took a heavy toll on the troops. The Japanese suffered more because they received virtually no supplies and had little means of combating illness, but even the marines were forced to remain in line positions unless they ran a fever of over 102 degrees. Guadalcanal was a supreme test of will for all involved.

The Japanese attempted numerous methods of supplying their forces, including rapid destroyer or transport runs, submarines, and even tying half-

Japanese war dead on Guadalcanal, August 1942. (*National Archives*)

filled drums of supplies together and towing them behind destroyers, then cutting them loose as they approached the coastline in the hope that the tide would wash them ashore. American forces successfully interdicted or at least disrupted most surface efforts, and the subs could not provide enough supplies even when they could get through. As for the towed drums, the Japanese did not anticipate the irregular neap and dodging tides that bathed the Solomons. These unpredictable currents often washed the supplies back out to sea or, on more than one occasion, down to the marines near Henderson Field. The only thing the Japanese were able to pour into Guadalcanal with regularity was reinforcements. While a total of 39,000 Japanese fought there, they never could muster at any one time a numerical advantage over the Americans, who committed 24,000 men to the island.

During the first week of February 1943, 13,000 Japanese soldiers were evacuated from Guadalcanal after being promised that they were being transported for a direct amphibious assault against Henderson Field. The evacuation was handled extremely well and was unknown to the marines until after its completion. It did not, however, conform to the warrior code of *bushido*, which dictated that one should die rather than withdraw (or surrender). Most of the soldiers evacuated were never again fit for front-line duty.

The marines had now surmounted the first obstacle in the reconquest of the Solomon chain. The ensuing battles would be fought against an enemy instructed to stand with the materials available or die in the service of the emperor. The U.S. naval strategy of island hopping was first executed, albeit on a relatively minor scale, in the Solomons, though the pattern became that of subsequent campaigns throughout the Pacific. Allied forces would invade sparsely defended islands and capture or develop airfields from which they could provide land-based air support for further invasions. The key to success was never to travel out from under the protective umbrella of land- and carrier-based air power. The enemy did not have to be defeated in all of its strongholds either. The ocean and the jungle would render landlocked Japanese garrisons useless once bypassed by Allied forces and deprived of contact with the empire. The marines only assaulted the vital islands in the Solomon chain, including New Georgia (June 21–August 27, 1943), Rendova (June 30–August 27), Choiseul (Augst 27–28), and Shortland (August 27), until they reached the final link in the chain, Bougainville.

The first manifestation of this strategy became Operation Cartwheel, which dealt only with the Solomon Islands and New Guinea. The goal of Cartwheel was to conquer the small enemy positions on the islands surrounding the Bismarck archipelago, thereby isolating the major base of Rabaul, located on the northeast tip of the island of New Britain. The navy had gained permission to execute this strategy over the complaints of Douglas MacArthur,

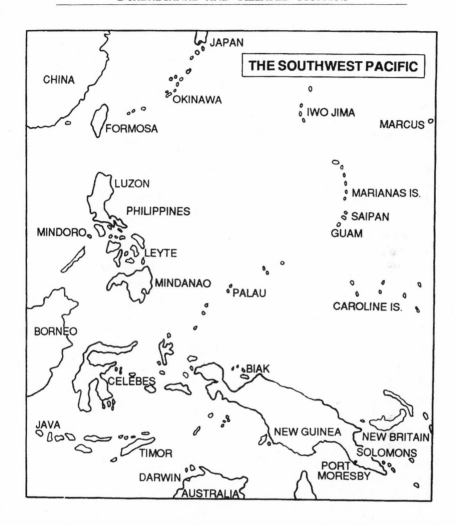

THE SOUTHWEST PACIFIC

who argued that in order to win one must fight the enemy wherever he is found, which would in effect have meant an invasion of every Japanese stronghold. In addition to avoiding potentially brutal campaigns, the navy's strategy offered the unanticipated opportunity to remove one of Japan's greatest leaders from the conflict.

After Midway, Cdr. Joseph Rochefort was dispatched to Washington to be decorated for his contribution to the Midway victory. But there he fell afoul of the Redman brothers and was not decorated. Instead, Rochefort finished his wartime years in command of a dry dock on the West Coast. Apparently his superiors were embarrassed and/or envious of his stellar performance, and since the navy then regarded intelligence work as far inferior to sea duty, this decision, in a sense, should not have been surprising. Luckily, though, even with Rochefort gone the decrypting staff at Pearl, which he had assembled, was still functioning well. In early April of 1943 a message was intercepted revealing that Admiral Yamamoto intended to visit aviators on Bouganville as part of a series of front-line inspections undertaken to raise morale. This message, with its precise timetable, was passed on to Washington, where Admiral King read it and realized its potential import. Had the message concerned any other commander, probably nothing would have been done. But knowing Yamamoto's penchant for promptness, and realizing how important he was to Japan's war effort, Washington decided that an attempt should be made to eliminate him.

On April 18, 1943, Cactus air group, as the marine and army air corps air arm on Guadalcanal was code-named, dispatched a squadron of American P-38 Lightning fighters to intercept and ambush Yamamoto and his entourage. The Lightnings caught Yamamoto's two transport bombers just after their Zero escort had turned away. Capt. Thomas Lanphier found himself the only pilot within range of the lead bomber, which was at treetop level about to land at Bouganville. Lanphier, who was approaching from the rear at an oblique angle, believed his target would escape, but since he had not yet tested his guns, he fired a burst into the bomber. Like all other Japanese planes, the bomber did not have self-sealing wing tanks. It burst into flames, then fell into the jungle. In it was Yamamoto, who probably never even realized what had happened, since two bullets were found in his body—one in the skull, the other in the base of the spine.

Yamamoto's staff, who always traveled in a separate plane, crashed into the surf just offshore but survived the attack. Cdr. Watanabe Kaysuji, perhaps Yamamoto's closest friend, retrieved the admiral's body, which was cremated in the jungle. The ashes were transported back to Japan. After a full state funeral, they were buried next to Admiral Togo and the emperor Taisho.

The Japanese navy now faced a crisis in its leadership structure and a blow to morale from which it would never fully recover. Yamamoto was replaced by Adm. Koga Mineichi, one of his ardent disciples. Like Yamamoto, Koga was loath to cooperate with the army but fervently believed in the primacy of naval aviation over battleships. However, he lacked Yamamoto's forceful personality, and while he commanded the combined fleet, little initiative against the Americans was taken.

Roosevelt, always the consummate politician, insisted that the next American offensive action take place in the northern Pacific. Here, actual U.S. territory was under Japanese occupation. During the Midway operation, a subscript of Yamamoto's plan had been to capture several of the outermost islands of the Aleutian chain and establish outposts there to use as air bases for raids on Dutch Harbor. The islands of Attu and Kiska had been taken without opposition on the 6th and 7th of June 1942. The Japanese had established garrisons there and used them as their northern- and westernmost outposts. While the Aleutians, like the Solomons, had been written off as too costly to retain if the Americans seriously contested their occupation, they still constituted something of a prestige item. Tokyo had in effect told the commanders involved to stand with what they had at their disposal.

This had come on the heels of a naval battle off the Komondorski Islands on March 26, 1943, in which a small American cruiser force engaged a Japanese supply force attempting to reach the Aleutians. In a long-range gun battle, the Americans damaged the Japanese cruiser *Nachi* while an old cruiser, *Salt Lake City*, was crippled. After that, the Japanese resorted to submarines to supply the outposts. When the Americans invaded on May 11, 1943, the Japanese put up a stiff but doomed defense. On May 29, after losing 516 men killed and 1,136 wounded, the Americans once again flew their flag over Attu. Of the 2,150-man Japanese force, all but 19 perished. When a joint Canadian–American force landed on Kiska on August 15, they found the island deserted, much to their embarrassment. In less than one hour on July 28 the Japanese had executed a textbook withdrawal of their 5,000-man garrison.

The Japanese Are Driven from New Guinea

Much to the delight of the Australians, the New Guinea campaign had been going well for the Allies during 1942. By November the Australian Seventh and the American Thirty-second Infantry Divisions had driven the Japanese back within their defensive positions around the coastal villages of Gona and Buna. Their progress had stalled, however, due to lack of proper supplies and the effects of tropical/jungle illness. MacArthur and his headquarters a thousand miles away had no concept of the difficulties involved. But MacArthur did place Lt. Gen. Robert Eichelberger in charge of the combined force, and Eichelberger immediately set about correcting the logistical and morale problems that had been inherent in the command. The Allied offensive progressed again. Gona and Buna fell to the Allies by January 21, 1943, at a cost of more than 8,000 Australians and Americans killed and wounded. This victory opened the way for an expanded campaign on the northern coast of New Guinea. While Midway had been the first decisive victory over the Imperial Japanese Navy, Gona and Buna had proven that the Imperial Japanese Army was vulnerable as well in the jungle milieu.

While MacArthur was massing troops in Australia for a series of amphibious assaults on the northern coast of New Guinea, a battle was raging for air supremacy. The air bases established by the Allies at Port Moresby and by the Japanese in the northern villages were in constant aerial combat, high-lighted by bombing raids on each other's fields. The Japanese flew not only from air bases on New Guinea but from the fortress of Rabaul as well. During the battle fought March 2–4, 1943, the air forces of the Allies discovered and destroyed a force of destroyers and transports steaming in the Bismarck Sea from Rabaul to New Guinea. Using a tactic known as skip bombing, medium U.S. bombers flew in at masthead level and released their bomb loads short of the target. The effect was the same as skipping stones across a pond. The bombs bounced across the water and slammed into the sides of the support vessels at water level, with devastating effect. During the ongoing battle, the Japanese lost seven transports and four destroyers. The Americans also managed to shoot down twenty-five Japanese planes, while themselves losing only three bombers and two fighters.

In an attempt to regain air superiority in the Solomons and New Guinea, Admiral Yamamoto had stripped the South Seas Fleet in Truk of its remaining planes and pilots and sent them to Rabaul. He was not, however, able to supply Rabaul with properly trained replacement aircrews. As previously mentioned, the Japanese had made no effort to husband their trained pilots to use as instructors and leaven for the raw recruits. The results were devastating to the Japanese, who lost almost 3,000 planes from November 1942 through December 1943. The Japanese were unable to sustain losses at this rate, and so the Allies were able to establish air superiority by mid-spring 1944.

By June 1943 MacArthur was ready to launch amphibious assaults along the coast of New Guinea. The pattern these landings followed became a recurring theme. First, American fighters and bombers would soften up the intended landing sight and provide sufficient cover for the Allied troops to come ashore. Next, army engineers and navy Seabees would build airstrips or repair existing facilities to allow aircraft to operate from them on advance missions against future assault locations. This procedure was then repeated. This tactic not only avoided confronting Japanese forces directly, but also forced them to abandon their fortifications if they hoped to engage the Allied troops. By March 1944 the Allies had reached what would be the decisive battle for control of New Guinea.

Japan hoped to place insurmountable obstacles at strategic points along the Allies' path. Chief among these was at Rabaul. They also concentrated large numbers of troops at locations along the coast of New Guinea. This strategy not only failed, but showed a marked failure to appreciate the nature of island warfare and resulted in the isolation and loss of many of Japan's finest fighting forces. The Japanese Eighteenth Army, among other Japanese units, had amassed nearly 65,000 battle-ready troops at the twin villages of

Wewak and Madang. MacArthur wisely opted to bypass that stronghold. He proceeded to the strategically important city of Hollandia, to the rear of the Eighteenth Army. In order to be successful, though, MacArthur needed air support, which his land-based aircraft would not be able to supply. Thus, Nimitz agreed to allow MacArthur to use his fast carrier fleet to provide the necessary air cover, while the engineers and Seabees carved out airstrips on several nearby islands that MacArthur intended to secure.

On March 30, 1944, the Allies began their preliminary bombardment. Two days later the Australians engaged a portion of the Eighteenth Army near Madang. On April 22, MacArthur surprised the Japanese by attacking Hollandia and taking the village of Aitape, in the rear of their lines. Airfields were constructed at Aitape. Within two days the Allies were conducting air attacks on the Japanese force from both sides. Nearly all Japanese air power had been destroyed as a result of the preliminary invasion bombardments, and the Eighteenth Army was forced to retreat into the jungle. The Eighteenth Army did launch an offensive against Allied positions in Wewak in late June, but suffered heavy losses and was pushed back once again into the interior. The Allies easily overran Hollandia and proceeded northward. In hard fought battles, the Allies took the islands of Wakde and Biak in mid-May. When Noenfoor and Sansapor were taken at the end of July, Japanese strength in New Guinea had effectively been destroyed.

The battle for the island of Biak, May 27–July 29, 1944, was a turning point in Japanese military strategy. Up to this time, it had been the practice of Japanese forces to meet the invaders on the beachhead, and if unsuccessful, proceed to launch suicidal *banzai* charges at the enemy's position in an attempt to drive him back into the sea. At Biak, the Japanese commander opted to withdraw his forces inland and set up a defensive network that would exact a heavy cost in Allied lives, which the suicide charges had failed to do. This would frequently be the pattern for further land engagements during the war. By early August 1944, MacArthur could state that New Guinea had been secured.

MacArthur benefited from lessons learned by the navy in the Solomons campaign. The advantage lay with the attacker in island warfare because defenders simply could not be everywhere at once. So long as the Allies could capture seemingly insignificant islands and quickly develop and supply airfields on them, the Japanese would have almost no chance of responding in strength and with coordination of effort. The true genius of "island hopping" was its ability to keep the Japanese off balance and constantly responding to Allied initiatives. That, combined with the flood of new and improved weapons at the Allies' disposal, virtually guaranteed the outcome, if not the timetable, of the war's conclusion.

American Strength and the New Technology of War

Admiral Yamamoto had voiced concern long before the war began about America's overwhelming industrial potential. Even then he had realized that in a conflict with America victory must be achieved before full use could be made of the military construction capacity of Detroit, the Brooklyn navy yard, and countless other industrial complexes he had personally inspected during his sojourn in the United States. Indeed, the Sparrow's Point plant of Bethlehem Steel Company in Baltimore, working around the clock, produced more steel during the conflict than Japan, Germany, and Italy combined.

The pendulum swing of military advantage became complete by late 1943 as a result of newly developed technologies. The new weapons that were introduced placed the Allies in a position of superior power that they never relinquished. First proposed and blueprinted in 1939, *Essex*-class aircraft carriers were introduced en masse in 1943. These carriers were larger, faster, and had greater aircraft capacity that anything built before. The new carriers displaced 36,380 tons fully loaded and were 880 feet long. The *Essex*-class carrier typically carried eighty-seven aircraft and could make well over thirty knots. Twenty-four of these carriers were built. Only in 1970 were the final two of this class, *Hornet* and *Bennington*, retired from active sea duty. (As of the original publication of this book, the carrier *Lexington*, although extensively rebuilt from its original *Essex*-class design specification, still served the Naval Air Station at Pensacola as the navy's only permanent training carrier.)

New subclasses of aircraft carriers were also introduced in 1943. The use of light carriers and escort carriers helped turn the tide of war. The *Independence*-class light carrier was smaller and faster than the old *Lexington*, *Yorktown*, and *Hornet*, although it could carry only half the aircraft of the *Essex* class. Finally, the escort, or jeep, carriers, constructed partially of plywood, were lighter still and provided efficient, rapid, and inexpensive transport of aircraft. Their ability to supply a nearly constant flow of aircraft to forward airfields ensured that Allied control of the skies was never in doubt. The jeep carriers were nearly disposable because they could be built so quickly, but they rendered invaluable service in, for example, Leyte Gulf.

Also developed in 1943 was the Grumman F6F Hellcat. The Americans had always suffered because of the inferior quality of their aircraft, especially the fighters. When the Americans retook the Aleutians, however, they managed to capture intact a Japanese A6M3-type Zero. Lord of the skies, the Zero had devastated American fighters. It could only be bested when American pilots used "hit and run" tactics (sometimes known as the "Thatch Weave"), or enjoyed numerical superiority. The American designers tested and almost literally dissected the Zero, designing and building a plane that would outperform it in almost every respect: the F6F Hellcat. Faster, nearly as maneuverable, and much more heavily armored, the Hellcat was for the most part a superior plane. Rugged and durable, it became the staple carrier-based fighter of the United States Navy. This, coupled with the fact that after Midway Nimitz and King had provided for a cadre of properly trained combat pilots—which the Japanese had not—made the Hellcat a true killing machine. The Hellcat was not alone, however, in types of fighter design. Along with the F6F were introduced the F4U Corsairs, the workhorses of marine aviation; P-38 Lightnings; and P-51 Mustangs, as well as a host of other superior new-generation fighters, none of which the Japanese could match.

The development of new aircraft was not limited to fighters alone. Although its potential would not be recognized for many months, a new aircraft made its appearance in early 1944, courtesy of the Boeing Corporation. The B-29, or "Superfortress" as it came to be known, was the largest plane ever built. It had fuel-injected engines and a pressurized cabin that, in part, allowed it to fly much higher than any of its Japanese counterparts. Its cruise speed was approximately 290 miles per hour and it was capable of traveling up to 3,000 miles. It had a payload of 20,000 pounds and was heavily armored. For self-defense, the B-29 was armed with twelve .50-caliber machine guns and a 20-mm cannon. The first of these planes was given to bomber command in China to be used against the Japanese home islands, but they did not work out when employed from Chinese bases, as will be seen. When eventually stationed on the Mariana Islands and used for attacks on the home islands, the B-29's became a devastating weapon in the American arsenal. The Japanese came to regard the B-29 with a mixture of fear and awe, especially after they saw several at close hand. Particularly impressive was the strength of its basic air frame and its payload capacity, and the Japanese were also puzzled by the extent to which the Americans took steps to protect their aircrews. But the war in the Pacific was not going to be won strictly through airpower.

Americans also developed the tools necessary to support a new type of ground warfare, one that some experts claimed could not be carried out as desired. Amphibious assaults called for special vehicles to ensure success. The Marine Corps, the navy's specially trained assault troops, were assigned to lead the island-hopping campaign as it reclaimed the vital islands of the Central Pacific. Yet in 1941 they did not possess any special sort of boat or craft that would allow them to travel from their home vessels to the shore and launch an invasion.

The navy's marine architects reputedly proclaimed themselves incapable of producing a boat the sort the Corps desired: lightweight, so it would draw no more than four feet of water and thus be able to cross coral reefs; equipped with a landing ramp, which would allow its occupants to step out onto the beach itself; reasonably spacious, if open to the weather, capable of carrying several dozen men and some equipment. When the navy responded, in effect, that such a vessel could not be built, a reputed one-time Louisiana bootlegger and highly skilled shipbuilder produced the Higgins Boat, which the marines waggishly claimed had been used by its builder to elude Federal Revenue agents. Regardless of the truth of this claim, the Higgins Boat, although without armor, was the Corp's workhorse landing craft for the better part of the Pacific War (almost all other landing craft used in the Pacific were of British design). Officially designated as an LCPL, the Higgins Boat, constructed of wood, was thirty-six feet long, ten feet wide, weighed 18,000 pounds fully loaded, and drew three and one-half feet of water. It could carry, at the most, thirty-six fully loaded marines.

Finally, the American submarine warfare effort underwent dramatic changes in late 1943. American skippers had complained from the outset of the war that there were problems with the torpedoes carried by both the American submarines and torpedo planes. The torpedoes tended to run too deep, or detonate too early, or not detonate at all. Torpedo improvements, particularly in the form of the Mark XVI electricity-driven torpedo, as well as new tactics like operating submarines in wolf-packs to prey on Japanese convoys caused a dramatic increase in submarine effectiveness. The submarine campaign will be dealt with in greater depth in Chapter 8.

The Debate over the Theaterwide American Strategy of Island Hopping

By late 1943, Washington had witnessed a heated debate over strategy between the army and the navy, with mixed results. MacArthur, who originally had the Solomons in his bailiwick, had at first opposed the bypassing of Rabaul, but his public relations staff now claimed that island hopping was a MacArthur invention. The effect in Washington in general and in the naval establishment in particular of his fraudulent claim can be imagined. While both the army and the navy agreed that island hopping was the strategy of choice for the reconquest of the Pacific, two very distinct and different ideas began to form about how best to accomplish this advance. General MacArthur proposed a direct route of attack from New Guinea through the Philippines to the Japanese home islands. If he were given control of the naval forces in the Pacific, he felt this drive well within his abilities. Pointing out that his plan left the Allies' flanks open to attack, the navy proposed an equally direct route to the home islands

From left to right: General MacArthur, President Roosevelt, Admiral Nimitz, and Admiral Leahy on board the cruiser *Baltimore*, July 26, 1944, in Pearl Harbor. *(United States Navy)*

that called for skirting the center of the Japanese empire and advancing northward through the Marshall, Gilbert, and Mariana island chains.

The two sides had reached an impasse. Largely by default, it emerged that both strategies would be implemented. But no one at first knew this would be so, for many believed that given the overall "Europe first" commitment of the war effort, such could not be the case. Ironically, though, until November 1943 the United States had committed more personnel and supplies to the Pacific campaign than it had to Europe. It was only America's industrial strength, which was at first unrealized, that permitted the twin-pronged Asian strategy, as it came to be called, to be implemented. Thus, MacArthur was given enough naval support to initiate his plan while the navy was to use the marines and proceed with its strategy. The two would link up at the base of the home islands in a joint assault on Okinawa, sometime in the future. All told, six marine and twenty army divisions would participate in the Pacific conflict.

Some have claimed that the two prongs supported one another and kept the Japanese off balance. Perhaps they did. But had Japanese intelligence ever been capable of breaking American ciphers and determining how unco-ordinated the two advances were, the Japanese could have concentrated their strength first on one prong and then could have shifted to the other, thereby possibly lengthening the conflict, though in all probability not changing its eventual outcome. This is the primary danger when commanders divide their forces. As it was, Halsey and the navy far outpaced MacArthur, who became bogged down with the New Guinea campaign. The Japanese were never ca-pable of predicting the Allies' next move, though. They were forced to rush to countermeasures and never had the initiative. By maintaining the element of surprise, the Allies were able to keep the Japanese guessing and always had the numerical advantage when and where they chose to fight.

Had the United States chosen to name a single supreme commander in the Pacific, rather than relying on the considered opinion of divergent personali-ties, the chance of Japanese intelligence surprising the Allied forces could have been reduced to practically nil. One overall military leader, such as Admiral Nimitz, perhaps the most gifted and talented admiral in the nation's history, could have kept the advance through the Pacific on an even keel and perfectly organized. This was not possible, though, because of the personali-ties involved. The painful fact is that Douglas MacArthur had many enemies in Washington because he treated both army and navy staff officers there as if *they* were his enemies: in doing so, he gave life to what was at first true only in his imagination. He even claimed that while chief of staff in the early 1930s, he had uncovered secret navy plans to isolate the army commanders in the Pacific and win the war unaided. MacArthur himself did not under-stand, at least at first, the basic principles of island hopping, and no one in the naval establishment from Washington to Pearl would have tolerated serv-ing under him had he been made Pacific commander in chief. If a joint com-mand was possible in Europe, where different nationalities were present, it should have been possible at least among American forces in the Pacific. But it was not to be. As Army Chief of Staff George Marshall remarked after the conflict, the personalities involved, especially MacArthur and Claire Chennault (who will be profiled in Chapter 8), made a single commander neither possible nor practical.

Implementing Island Hopping in the Central Pacific

In November 1943 Admiral Nimitz was prepared to take the next step in his planned reconquest of the island chains leading to Japan. The first of these landings, code-named Operation Galvanic, was to take place in the Gilbert Island chain, a former New Zealand colony. The islands of Betio in the Tarawa

Atoll as well as Makin were designated as necessary to control the Gilberts, which stood directly athwart the American supply route to Australia.

Galvanic was to be the first of the navy's Central Pacific drives. But the Japanese had begun reinforcement of the islands long before the evacuation of Guadalcanal in February 1943. In order to relieve pressure on the Solomons, Lt. Col. Evans Carlson's Second Marine Raider Battalion had staged a raid in the Gilberts in mid-August 1942, which caused the Japanese to strengthen their defenses. Nimitz spent the greater portion of the year 1943 husbanding his strength for Galvanic in Oahu, the Fijis, and the New Hebrides.

Makin Atoll, in particular Butaritari, was the first American target. Very early on the morning of November 20, 1943, the 165th Infantry Regiment of the army's Twenty-seventh Division landed on Makin, where they were opposed by 250 Japanese and some construction workers, many of whom were Korean and could have had little love for the Japanese. Whatever the case, Makin was secured by twilight of November 23, 1943.

Tarawa Atoll was another matter. Like many of the islands the navy would have to seize, Tarawa was surrounded by a coral reef. Betio (pronounced Bashio), the selected target island, is a little less that 300 acres in area, but has caves: the island's neap and dodging tides, which are irregular and almost impossible to predict, complicated the landings. The Japanese had also placed there a few of the eight-inch guns captured when Singapore surrendered, although these did little to help or hinder either side. Several British advisers warned that the marines' Higgins Boats would not be able to cross the reef at high tide, as did a native, who risked his life to inform the Americans that the tides would not permit an invasion the next day, November 21.

Obviously believing they had better information, the navy proceeded on schedule. Many marines had to wade in chest-deep water when their boats grounded on the coral reef, which was 400 to 500 yards offshore. Betio's defenders were largely Japanese marines, commanded by Rear Adm. Shibasaki Keiji. Indeed, many of his men were positioned in deep, if damp, underground caves that even naval shells had not penetrated. And although the Japanese did contest the beach landing, they chose to wait inland to inflict maximum casualties on the Americans. The marines' answer to this was to pour or pump gasoline into caves or very heavily fortified pillboxes and then ignite it. The island was declared secure on November 23, but pockets of enemy resistance continued for many days. Well over 900 marines died capturing the island, while about 4,200 Japanese combat troops perished defending it. Several days later, other islands in the atoll chain were seized to negate the threat of air strikes that might cut the great circle (shortest) route from the U.S. West Coast to Australia and New Zealand.

Several lessons were evident. A longer naval and air bombardment was

American war dead on Tarawa, November 1943. Photographs like this one caused widespread shock and outrage in the United States. *(National Archives)*

needed, along with greater aerial reconnaissance to pinpoint enemy strong-holds. But the United States had gained an excellent base from which to build up strength for its next objective, the Marshalls.

In January 1944, as MacArthur continued his campaign in New Guinea, the navy was readying itself for forthcoming operations in the Central Pacific. Admiral Halsey had acquired a well-coordinated, fast carrier force of six heavy and six light carriers, with fast battleship, cruiser, and destroyer escorts. Designated Task Force Thirty-eight and commanded by Vice Adm. Marc Mitscher, the force employed lightning strikes against Japanese strong-holds. This carrier force was called upon to establish air superiority over the Marshalls before the invasion force arrived.

Nimitz made a bold gesture by insisting that the marines take only the Kwajalein and Eniwetok atolls, bypassing the numerous other Japanese strongholds in the chain. Kwajalein was a key Japanese communications center, and Nimitz evidently perceived it as a priority target. After Mitscher's force had reduced the Japanese air power in the vicinity, the big ships approached and initiated a three-day saturation bombardment of the atoll. The Japanese had 8,000 men on Kwajalein under Rear Adm. Akiyama Monzo. When the Seventh Infantry landed on Kwajalein, they found the Japanese dug in as they had been at Tarawa, but the Americans put their experience with this style of warfare to good use and suffered comparatively light losses. In the meantime, the Marine Fourth Division had landed on the nearby islands of Roi and Namur. In all, the United States used some 41,000 men to take the atoll and lost 372 killed and 1,000 wounded. The Japanese, in comparison, had lost all but 130 of their original force. By February 7 the atoll was declared secure; the Americans had denied the Japanese an important communications center.

On February 17, 1944, Mitscher's fast task force was used once again, this time in a raid on the redoubtable Japanese garrison at Truk. Knowing that the Japanese had a sizable force on the island, and that the true importance of Truk was its port facility, Halsey opted to launch an air strike in order to neutralize the base. Admiral Koga, commander of the Japanese combined fleet stationed at Truk, managed to get his warships out intact. Mitscher's pilots did sink fifty merchant vessels in the harbor while destroying 275 aircraft as well. Later, while patrolling the waters around Truk, Admiral Spruance managed to sink a light cruiser and a destroyer. The myth of Truk's invincibility had been destroyed, as had its usefulness as a Japanese staging area.

At the same time that Mitscher was attacking the base at Truk, the United States Army and Marines were reducing the Japanese garrison at Eniwetok. The three main islands of the Eniwetok Atoll were defended by 2,200 men of the Japanese First Amphibious Battalion. All three islands were secured by

February 21, at the cost of 339 American dead. The entire Japanese garrison was wiped out in brutal hand-to-hand warfare, supplemented by the Americans' extensive use of flamethrowers. With the fall of Eniwetok the way was open for the American advance to the Marianas.

From the standpoint of the average Japanese soldier, it may have been just as well that so few of them survived. The code of *bushido* held that the highest disgrace for a soldier was capture. "Save the last bullet for yourself," read the opening statement of most training manuals for enlisted personnel in the Japanese army. If a soldier was captured, the Red Cross would report that fact to the Japanese government, and the soldier's family, friends, and neighbors would very probably literally pretend that he had never existed.

The few Japanese taken prisoner were captured under unusual circumstances. Some were rendered unconscious by bursting shells, only to regain consciousness in an American medical facility. Seeking information on enemy dispositions, American commanders would occasionally call for prisoner capture. In any event, Japanese captives usually gave false names, or pleaded that their families not be told of their captivity. The Japanese occasionally took prisoners for the same reasons. But essentially, for the man actually on the front line, the war was one of racial extinction, similar to many of the campaigns against the American Plains Indians. No quarter was ever asked. Only rarely was any given.

By the end of 1943 the Japanese were in a very different posture and position than in 1941. Their navy especially lacked key personnel, particularly aviators. Many had perished by the end of the year. True, the Japanese had accumulated an impressive cadre of naval aces. The greatest was Lt. Nishizawa Hiroyoshi, who accounted for at least eighty-seven aircraft before perishing in 1944. (His record makes him the most prodigious ace of the Pacific theater of the war.) But the later aces tended to have less impressive records and were professionally short-lived, as a recent Japanese study indicates (see the reading list below). Star- or flag-grade commanders had also been lost, and veteran soldiers as well as pilots who could remember the first combat actions were now the exception. The impressive aggressive posture of the imperial forces was depleted. Morale remained high, but the resources necessary to maintain the war machine were growing scarcer with the passing of every day.

On the other hand, the United States had mobilized impressive military and naval might that dwarfed what Japan had marshaled in 1941. At least 110,000 Japanese fighting men had been bypassed on islands, left to spend the remainder of the conflict squinting at the horizon for a relief fleet that would never arrive. The decisive battle between the battleships anticipated by the Japanese Naval General Staff had not come, but the tide of war had turned. Japan's outpost sentinels were gone and there was no hope of recapturing them.

The Americans, with their new technology, manpower, and industrial resources, had gained the upper hand. The conflict would now be fought largely on American terms. Time was also now an American ally. The Japanese leaders in Tokyo could only watch and wait for the time and location of the next American blow.

Suggestions for Further Reading

The Allied counteroffensive in the Pacific is also an area rich in scholarly studies and has seen several beneficial additions recently. Eric Bergerud's *Touched with Fire: The Land War in the South Pacific* (New York: Penguin Books, 1996) is very good, as is the same author's *Fire in the Sky: The Air War in the South Pacific* (Boulder, CO: Westview Press, 2000). Walter Lord's *Lonely Vigil: Coastwatchers of the Solomons* (New York: Viking Press, 1977) is a very worthwhile history of the Australians who stayed behind after the Japanese conquest as unknown observers; a second good study on the same topic is Eric Feldt, *The Coastwatchers* (New York: Oxford University Press, 1978). Dudley McCarthy, *South-West Pacific Area—First Year, Kokoda to Wau* (Canberra: Australian War Memorial, 1956) is one of a series of official Australian histories of the war south of the equator. John Miller Jr., *Cartwheel: The Reduction of Rabaul* (Washington, DC: Army Historical Office, 1959), and Samuel Miller, *Victory in Papua* (Washington, DC: Army Historical Office, 1957), are two useful official United States Army studies. Brian Garfield, *The Thousand Mile War: World War II in Alaska and the Aleutians* (Garden City, NY: Doubleday, 1969) is the best study so far of the war in the Aleutians; John Lorelli, *The Battle of the Komandorski Islands* (Annapolis, MD: Naval Institute Press, 1984) is an account of that relatively neglected engagement. A good account of MacArthur during this period appears in Chapter 8 of Ronald Lewin, *The American Magic: Codes, Ciphers, and the Defeat of Japan* (New York: Farrar Straus Giroux, 1982). For amphibious warfare, see Danial Barbey, *MacArthur's Amphibious Force Operations, 1943–1945* (Annapolis, MD: Naval Institute Press, 1969), especially useful for the development of landing craft and interservice rivalry; James Ladd, *Assault from the Sea: The Craft, the Landings, the Men* (New York: Hippocrene Books, 1976); and Peter Isley and Philip Crowl, *The U.S. Marines and Amphibious War: Its Theory and Its Practices in the Pacific* (Princeton, NJ: Princeton University Press, 1951). The historiography on the Guadalcanal campaigns is very good, including Richard Frank's *Guadalcanal* (New York:

Random House, 1990); Jack Coggins, *The Campaign for Guadalcanal* (Garden City, NY: Doubleday, 1972); and Eric Hammel, *Guadalcanal: The Carrier Battles* (New York: Crown Publishers, 1987). Thomas Miller, *The Cactus Air Force* (New York: Harper and Row, 1969) explores the adventures of the marine aviators on Guadalcanal. The definitive work on the "black sheep" squadron is Frank Walton, *Once They Were Eagles: The Men of the Black Sheep Squadron* (Lexington: University Press of Kentucky, 1986). Stanley Smith, *The Battle of Savo* (New York: Macfadden-Bartell, 1962) is a passable account of the naval action. Peter Phinney, *The Barbarians: A Soldier's New Guinea Diary* (St. Lucia: University of Queensland Press, 1989), an Australian's diary, is joined by John Crawford's *Kia Kaha: New Zealand in the Second World War* (Aukland: Oxford University Press, 2000) and David Day, *Reluctant Nation: Australia and the Allied Defeat of Japan, 1942–45* (Melbourne: Oxford University Press, 1992) in revealing a little-known side of the war fought "down under." Similarly, *To Kokoda and Beyond: The Story of the 39th Battalion* (Melbourne: Melbourne University Press, 1988), ed. by Victor Austin, includes Japanese as well as Australian materials on a "scratch" unit that suddenly found itself in the first line of defense after Pearl Harbor. For Tarawa, see Joseph Alexander, *Utmost Savagery: The Three Days of Tarawa* (Annapolis, MD: Naval Institute Press, 1995), and Eric Hammel and John Lane, *Seventy-six Hours: The Invasion of Tarawa* (New York: Tower Books, 1980), which is in part a study via oral history. The definitive Japanese account of naval aviator aces is Ikuhiko Hata and Yasuho Izawa, *Japanese Naval Aces and Fighter Units in World War Two* (Annapolis, MD: Naval Institute Press, 1989); on the same topic see Rene J. Francillon, *Japanese Aircraft of the Pacific War* (New York: Funk and Wagnalls, 1970); and Jiro Hirokoshi, *Eagles of Mitsubishi: The Story of the Zero Fighter* (Seattle: University of Washington Press, 1981), which speak to the matter of Japanese aircraft production and performance. For American aces, see Edward Sims, *The Greatest Aces* (New York: Harper and Row, 1967).

7

The Marianas and
the Philippines

The loss of the Solomons, the increasing isolation and marginalization of Rabaul, along with the devastation of Truk meant that the outer perimeter of the Japanese defenses had successfully been pierced. In the same manner that the results of Midway removed the capacity of the Imperial Japanese Navy (IJN) to launch offensives, the decimation of Japan's forward defensive bases meant that the Allies would be determining the location and timing of future operations in the Central Pacific. While Japanese military might was far from destroyed, the truth was that the Japanese could no longer hope for the quick, decisive victory that would force Washington, London, and the rest of the Allies to the bargaining table. The unavoidable truth was that American industrial capacity would indeed now be able to come fully into play and time was on the side of the Allies. Japan's only hope, and that far from sure, was to make the Allies pay such an enormous price for the conquest of the empire that they would tire of the expense and choose to negotiate a peace settlement. Even this possibility faded as 1944 witnessed the rolling back of the Axis powers across both Asia and Europe. At a conference in North Africa in early 1943, Winston Churchill and Franklin D. Roosevelt had pledged their nations to the pursuit of the unconditional surrender of the Axis powers. The campaigns of 1944 were prosecuted with that reality in the minds of both the Japanese and the Allies. For the Allies, nothing short of total victory would suffice. For Japan, defeat meant utter destruction. With that as the backdrop, we turn our attention to the desperate and brutal struggles of 1944.

The Marianas

Having secured the Marshall and Caroline Island chains, the United States Navy prepared to climb the next rung of the ladder leading to the Japanese home islands. The Mariana Island group contained three significant islands: Saipan, Tinian, and Guam. Saipan had been mandated to Japan under the Versailles Treaty in 1919 as reward for its nominal participation in World War I. The Japanese had intended eventually to annex the island and had initiated a rather substantial colonization effort on it. Thus, for the first time Japanese civilians would be eyewitnesses to the American conquest of an island.

Tinian, a sister island to Saipan, was the site of a large Japanese air facility. From the runways on Tinian, the Japanese could venture as far south as Truk, or, conversely, as far north as Tokyo. These runways were a primary target of the Allied advance. The remnants of the IJN relied on them for air cover since the destruction of much of the Naval Air Fleet. Tinian was the hub of the second layer of the Japanese empire's defense. Just as capture of the Solomons and New Guinea had opened up the frontiers of the Japanese empire to attack, the capture of Tinian would open the way to the home islands themselves. Possession of them would place the heart of the Japanese empire well within range of the new B-29 bomber. Finally, the southernmost island of the chain, Guam, had been a U.S. possession since 1898. Although the Americans had never effectively developed Guam in a commercial sense, its inhabitants were fiercely proud American citizens. Thus, it was both psychologically and politically important that Guam be liberated at an early date as a token of faith to other captive indigenous populations to demonstrate American good will—most especially to the Filipinos.

Though Japan's tenacity and self-sacrificing dedication seem to belie a stoic resignation to its national fate, many naval planners still held out hope for victory over the Allies in one last decisive surface engagement. The "Orange" style plan that Japan had pursued since the war's origin called for a major surface battle in home waters. It also assumed that the American fleet arriving to do battle would have suffered significant attrition as a result of submarine, destroyer, and air harassment. Even allowing for a substantial productive capacity (though the Japanese never expected the kind of productivity that actually occurred), the fleet would be stretched to the end of its substantial supply line, fighting under an umbrella of Japanese aircraft, and facing a combined force of Japanese naval fire power. Japanese battle reports beginning with Coral Sea and continuing through the end of the war consistently included damage claims that were, being generous, overly optimistic (or, being less kind, pure fabrication). Submariners, destroyer and cruiser captains, and aviators routinely submitted reports with grossly bloated destruction totals. These reports were generally accepted at face value and became the basis for future plans. Given this environment, even Tojo's claim that Midway was a victory does not seem so outrageous. More importantly however, the attrition that naval planners were desperately hoping for seemed to be taking place. For them it was justification for their optimism regarding a final decisive battle with the American fleet. They could not be sure where this battle would take place, and therefore created contingency plans based on several locations. Army and navy planners alike, though, agreed that the Marianas and the Philippines must not fall.

The Marianas were essential to the maintenance of the Japanese empire for the same strategic military reasons that the Americans desired them. Therefore, the military leaders in Tokyo determined to pursue an all-out effort to ensure that the Marianas remained in Japanese hands. On the first of April 1944, Admiral Koga, commander of the Japanese combined fleet, perished when his plane was lost at sea. His successor, Adm. Toyoda Soemu, was both more aggressive and more persuasive. He initiated Operation A-Go in an effort to deal a crippling blow to the United States Navy. He set his staff planners to work almost as soon as he took command, but the battle may have come sooner and in a different location than he had anticipated. Unaware of the divided Allied command, the Japanese assumed that the thrust through New Guinea was the main Allied offensive front and that they would continue to approach the home islands along that line through the Palau Islands and the Philippines. The A-Go plans attempted to anticipate action along this front. The arrival of an American fleet off of Saipan changed the location, but not the expected outcome for Japanese planners.

Saipan would be a difficult objective for the Allies. Twelve miles long, it had a curving mountainous spine and was located 100 miles north of Guam. Nimitz and King both regarded Saipan as the key to the Marianas, and so the Guamanians would have to wait until Saipan fell for their own liberation from the Japanese. Saipan is honeycombed with caves, perhaps more per square mile than any other island of its approximate size in the Pacific. Lt. Gen. Saito Yoshitsugu commanded the island's garrison. Technically, though, the Japanese command structure was unique on Saipan, for Admiral Nagumo had requested a land command. Nagumo was allegedly in charge of the overall defense of the island, which was to be coordinated with the navy. In actual fact, however, Nagumo was just a bystander, which was as he wished. With no hope of avenging his losses at Midway—only two of the six original carriers of the First Air Fleet (*Zuikaku* and *Shokaku*) and very few of its veteran aviators remained—Nagumo had undertaken a mission from which he did not wish to return.

Beginning on June 11, 1944, Mitscher's fast carrier task force had begun neutralizing the island's defenses. Along with Saipan, though, the Americans anticipated A-Go's reliance on land-based aircraft to support naval operations and launched strikes on air bases on Taiwan, Chichi Jima, and other surrounding islands. The resultant destruction denied the IJN nearly 900 air-craft they had counted on to protect their sortie. As if the devastation of so much air power were not enough, the IJN also had to deal with disastrously incorrect reports from the fliers based at Saipan and Tinian. Inexplicably, the Japanese commander assured IJN that he was well supplied with planes and pilots and that his fliers were effecting devastating losses on the Americans with numerous carriers sunk and many other vessels destroyed or neutral-ized. Thus, the naval forces that approached Saipan did so with a misguided notion of the resistance they should expect. The battle fleet accompanying the American invasion force pounded Saipan for several days before the ac-tual landings, intending to soften up the Japanese defenses. Though it almost certainly produced some reduction in Japanese strength, it failed to produce a significant result. The Japanese garrison numbered 30,000 men—two full divisions, in effect. Saito contested the islands at the waterline, as the Sec-ond and Fourth Marine Divisions discovered when they landed on June 15. Resistance was more than even the marines had bargained for, and the only reinforcement to be had was the Twenty-seventh Army Division, a National Guard unit recruited from the New England states. There is no doubt that the Twenty-seventh performed below par, probably because of the attitude of some of its senior officers, who had enlisted in peacetime and evidently took their duties too lightly. Individual men fought bravely, but their leadership was sometimes lacking. The Twenty-seventh's contributions on Saipan were negligible and its commander, Maj. Gen. Ralph Smith, was relieved at ma-rine insistence.

Nagumo lived long enough to witness several of the ships his aviators had sunk at Pearl Harbor bombard targets on the island of Saipan. Fighting was hand to hand, especially after the five days it took the marines to get beyond the beachheads. When the Americans had clearly triumphed, Saito and Nagumo committed *seppuku*, ritual suicide, with the usual wartime twist of having an officer stand behind the suicide to put a bullet into the dying man's head, lest he be captured, sutured, transfused, and made a prisoner of war by the enemy. Before his death, Saito, acting in Nagumo's name, had ordered what would be the biggest *banzai*—suicide charge—of the war, to be ex-ecuted the next morning. Marines and soldiers of the Twenty-seventh Divi-sion knew what was coming long before. Saito's remaining troops consumed large quantities of the Japanese rice wine, sake, that evening, on the grounds that it was a vasodilator that would facilitate bleeding, thus ensuring a more rapid death in battle.

At dawn well over 3,000 drunken Japanese swarmed into a gap that had opened in the Twenty-seventh's lines. The Japanese poured through, bearing down upon amazed marine artillery groups, which had to fuse their shells to fire literal muzzle bursts to stop them. The charge was as colorful, and perhaps frightening, as it was futile. American losses were 3,100 killed, 13,160 wounded; Japanese military losses were staggering: 27,000 killed. This latter figure does not include some 22,000 civilians who took their own lives, evidently believing Japanese army propaganda concerning the American forces about to occupy their homes. They had been told that civilians would be torn to pieces by gorillas brought from the United States for that purpose. Whether they accepted such propaganda as literal truth or not, many chose to jump from cliffs rather than submit to life under the American flag. In a morbid way, these suicides fueled the national spirit of *bushido* that grasped the country. Ugaki reflected in his diary that he and his sailors could never face the spirits of those brave women and children who had been willing to die rather than surrender unless they too pursued destruction before dishonor. At home, the Japanese government made plans for a national defense force that would call upon the entire population to prepare for death before defeat.

Even though the slaughter seemed one-sided, it was not accomplished easily or without price by Allied forces. The marines on Saipan had complained of the lack of proper air support, and with good reason. Upon learning of the presence of an American invasion force in the Marianas, Vice Adm. Ozawa Jisaburo had promptly executed Toyoda's plan to destroy Allied air and naval power. Utilizing all of Japan's remaining available carrier strength, he marshaled a force that carried out four attacks, the first on June 19. He had over 420 aircraft, plus 100-odd land-based aircraft from adjacent islands, including Guam, technically under his command. He hoped to double that number with support from Saipan, Tinian, and surrounding bases, and had even been assured of their assistance, though it never materialized. Counting on the truth of reports sent in from area commanders regarding the punishment already inflicted on the enemy force, Ozawa sailed to meet the Americans confident that he could deliver a powerful *coup de grace*.

Unknown to Ozawa, the virtually untouched force under Admiral Spruance contained seven fleet and eight light carriers, giving him almost double the planes available to the Japanese. Here, the Hellcat fighter made its most impressive showing against the Zero; during the first attack 330 Japanese planes were shot down while the United States lost a mere 30 planes. Further, American submarines *Albacore* and *Cavallo* found Ozawa's carrier force and put their new, improved torpedoes into two of his carriers: the new 34,000-ton *Taiho*, which was serving as Ozawa's flagship, and the veteran carrier *Shokaku* were thus both lost. *Taiho* especially was a devastating loss, demonstrating not only the effectiveness of the American submarine campaign, but also the decline in IJN training and efficiency, as well as the increased burden on the military to make due with inferior materials. *Taiho* was hit by a single torpedo, and was capable of maintaining full speed and operation. However, as a result of American submarines effectively strangling Japan's access to the rich oil fields of the East Indies, the IJN had to burn lower-grade fuel oil that gave off a noxious odor. *Taiho's* commander unwisely chose to leave ventilation shafts open to clear the air. This measure also succeeded in filling the ship with highly flammable fumes, which ignited and literally tore the ship apart from the inside. Mitscher pursued the enemy, inflicting further losses; Japan lost the carrier *Hiyo* (29,000 tons), and 65 more aircraft, while 100 U.S. aircraft were lost, the bulk because they ran out of fuel and ditched in the ocean.

In addition to the advantage in carriers and aircraft, the Americans had adopted new methods and equipment to protect them. Preceding the carrier task forces was a powerful battle line composed of battleships, refitted and new, cruisers, and destroyers, all copiously equipped with anti-aircraft (AA) weapons. The battle line would throw up a curtain of AA miles before attacking planes reached the vulnerable carriers. It would also act as a decoy to lure inexperienced Japanese pilots who might waste their lethal loads on the inviting, but much tougher, hulls of the battleships and cruisers. The guns on these ships were deadly accurate as the Americans had begun incorporating radar targeting into them, resulting in a dramatic rise in effectiveness for ship-based AA fire. The combination of the battle line and a large and materially superior combat air patrol meant that few of Ozawa's attackers actually had the opportunity to threaten the American carriers. The result was a slaughter, referred to by the American participants as the "Great Marianas' Turkey Shoot." More than 460 Japanese pilots perished. Japanese naval air power was a mere shadow of its former self and, with the exception of the kamikaze corps, had little more than nuisance value for the remainder of the war.

The Guamanians wondered what American intentions were. At first, life under the Japanese had not been brutal, but as the tide of war turned, the Japanese grew senselessly and arbitrarily cruel. Leading citizens were executed for no apparent reason. Life became a living hell, but reconquest of the island was delayed by the assignment to Saipan of the only reserve in the area, the Twenty-seventh Division. The Americans had not forgotten Guam, however, and just over one month after the invasion of Saipan, U.S. forces arrived.

The Americans enjoyed advantages on Guam they had not heretofore known. There were excellent maps of the area. Also, a small but very effective resistance movement provided last-minute intelligence data. After a sporadic seventeen-day bombardment by naval and air forces, the marines and the Seventy-seventh Army Division landed on Guam on July 20, 1944. Three weeks of fighting ensued, costing the lives of 1,290 Americans and 10,690

Japanese. Meanwhile, on July 24, Tinian was invaded; 5,700 Japanese and 390 Americans perished.

The Mariana campaign, including the carrier battle, demonstrated to the Japanese ruling elite that all hope of winning the war had disappeared. In Tokyo, the emperor exclaimed, "Hell is upon us," and, after an imperial expression of disapproval of the way he was prosecuting the war, Premier Tojo resigned on July 18, 1944. Some viewed it as high time for Tojo to step down. For many weeks his household had been receiving generic phone calls, all to the same effect: "Why hasn't Tojo committed suicide yet?"

This was the last instance in which the emperor appeared to believe that the conflict might still somehow be resolved in Japan's favor. He even briefly considered appointing a general and an admiral as co-premiers, but when the chosen navy candidate, Adm. Yonai Mitsumasa, declined, retired Gen. Koiso Kuniaka replaced Tojo, with Yonai as his navy minister and deputy premier. The emperor, speaking through Kido, urged an end to interservice rivalry and all due speed in reversing Japan's decline.

MacArthur Returns to the Philippines

At the time little was known in Washington of the vicissitudes of Japanese internal politics. The joint chiefs and the president had more pressing matters at hand. Should the next target be the Philippines, which MacArthur was now ready to approach, or should the islands be bypassed in favor of seizing Okinawa, and perhaps Formosa as well, as many in the navy, particularly Admiral King, desired? Never had interservice rivalry been more evident, or the Europe-first decision brought into more question—particularly by Admiral King. And it was an election year. Roosevelt was running for an unprecedented fourth term as president. Stressing his role as commander in chief, he chose to resolve the debate in person, or at least to give that impression. Sailing on the heavy cruiser *Baltimore*, via San Diego, Roosevelt reached Pearl Harbor on July 26, 1944, for a conference with MacArthur and Nimitz. The president brought with him only his White House chief of staff, Adm. William Leahy. They conferred at a former civilian residence on Waikiki beach, where they also spent the night.

Roosevelt must have been aware of his health as seldom before. He knew it was poor. Further, according to one of his sons, he had suffered an acute attack of chest pain just before he left the West Coast. Perhaps this made him more susceptible to MacArthur's arguments that he had a moral obligation to liberate the Philippine people from the Japanese yoke as soon as possible. Some writers have suggested that during the evening of the 26th, MacArthur secretly sought out the president and offered further arguments; a few have even claimed that the general might have promised to relinquish all presidential ambitions for 1944 if the president would approve immediate invasion of the Philippines. But there is no proof of any of this, and while speculation is interesting, such bargaining between the two remains improbable.

Nonetheless, MacArthur's largely political argument won the day, backed by the general's suggestion that the electorate might be disenchanted if Roosevelt seemed to desert the Philippine people. On July 27, in the course of an automobile drive, Nimitz sensed from conversation between MacArthur and Roosevelt that the general had indeed persuaded the president. "We've sold it," MacArthur told his staff aboard his own aircraft as they left the islands, referring to the proposed liberation of the Philippines in what must seem, in or out of context, a somewhat flippant manner. Still, Washington in general and King in particular were skeptical. It was several weeks before they agreed to the invasion of Luzon.

In late August and early September 1944, Nimitz sent Halsey on a series of preemptive strikes against the Bonin Islands, Yap and the Palaus, and Mindanao. Halsey's aviators found the southern Philippines and their approaches more lightly defended than they expected. As a result, the first of MacArthur's landings in Mindanao was canceled and MacArthur was authorized to bypass that island and strike directly at the island of Leyte, in the central part of the Philippine archipelago. MacArthur would begin liberating the Philippine people two months ahead of schedule.

Nimitz and MacArthur, however, wanted the Palaus group to be secured before any further advances were made on the Philippines. This would ensure that MacArthur's flank would be safe. The marines were very near the area already, so Washington gave its approval and the First Marine Division was slated to conquer the island of Peleliu. The decision to attack Peleliu was curious given the willingness to isolate other strongholds. MacArthur had argued vociferously for the conquest of Rabaul, but had eventually been convinced that the cost was simply too high and that base had been a major staging area for Japanese air and naval power. While Peleliu was a stronghold with an airfield, assaulting it represented a violation of a fundamental tenet of island hopping, avoiding and isolating enemy strong points whenever possible.

Intelligence had determined that there were as many as 10,000 Japanese on the island, but that only 6,000 were actually battle-ready. The pre-invasion reconnaissance of the island had failed to disclose the extensive bunker system that permeated the island, so when the marines hit the beaches on September 15, they were greeted with a most unwelcome surprise. The Japanese opted not to strongly contest the landing but rather husbanded their forces. They had dug in extraordinarily well and evidenced stiffer resistance than was normal even for them. By the end of the first day's fighting, the marines were forced to commit all of their reserves to the battle. This bloody struggle went on for nearly a month before the defenders had been rooted out. One in four of the marines who fought on Peleliu was buried there. The losses suffered by Americans were horrendous in comparison to the gains they made. All but 200 of the 11,000 defenders of the island were killed, and those captured were largely suffering from wounds or shelling that rendered them unconscious. A live documentary of the invasion of Peleliu was filmed, and nine combat photographers fell during the shooting. The film, entitled *Fury in the Pacific*, remains a graphic documentary of American and Japanese determination and combat operations.

The real tragedy of Peleliu is that the whole operation may well have been unnecessary. There was an airstrip on the island, but Mitscher's fast carrier force had reduced larger targets before. With American superiority in the air, what kind of problems could the Japanese have really caused from this tiny island garrison? After the war Nimitz admitted that the campaign in the Palaus area may have been a mistake. In any case, the stage was set for the glorious fulfillment of Douglas MacArthur's promise to return to the Philippines.

MacArthur was on the verge of committing a considerable military faux pas; he had been publicizing his return to the islands for quite some time, and the Japanese would surely be prepared to meet his arrival. MacArthur had been air-dropping items to the Filipinos with the motto "*I shall return*" printed or otherwise affixed to them. When he ordered a sudden and dramatic increase in the number of objects so dropped, he may not only have destroyed the chances of surprise but also, in the end, revealed the actual landing area. Some of MacArthur's staff had misgivings about his propaganda campaign but evidently kept their own counsel concerning the matter.

This propaganda campaign per se had its downside as well. Making such promises publicly, MacArthur had committed himself to location as well. Army strategy taught that a soldier should attack his enemy wherever he was found and that bypassing strongholds was logistical suicide. These reasons, along with the simple fact that MacArthur wished to make the Japanese in the Philippines pay for the humiliation he had suffered, had motivated MacArthur to propose an invasion of the southernmost island of Mindanao, followed by a stair-step campaign through the entire island chain.

But, as has already been recounted, during the pre-invasion strikes on the islands of Yap, Ulithi, and the Palaus, the navy had experienced less resistance than expected. Consequently the navy proposed moving the landings on Leyte up by two months from December 20 to October 20, 1944, and bypassing the Japanese garrison on Mindanao. MacArthur accepted this proposal, averring that it would return him to Philippine soil that much earlier.

The Japanese fully realized that American reconquest of the Philippines would enable the U.S. submarines to interdict what remained of their maritime supply lines to the southern resource regions. From the obscurity of retirement they called upon General Yamashita, the "Tiger of Malaya," to command the nearly 350,000 Japanese troops on the islands. Yamashita's task would not be an easy one. The Japanese had made the initial mistake of assuming that the Filipinos would greet them as liberators, not realizing that the inhabitants regarded themselves as an Hispanic American people. Long before MacArthur's approach, the Filipino underground had been nipping at the heels of the Japanese conqueror, especially in the Moro country, where the Japanese traveled in convoy or not at all. Further, most of Yamashita's air power had been used up in mid-October in a series of battles over and near Formosa. In Tokyo, a new strategy was formalized: the beaches were not to be contested. Japanese air power, including land-based aircraft, would strike at the American landing craft and/or support vessels on the beach.

None of this came soon enough to save the island of Leyte from American assault. After a very heavy naval bombardment, the first United States Army landings on Leyte began on October 20, 1944. The Japanese at once put the latest version of their "Go" (victory) plan into operation. Diesel oil had become so scarce in Japan proper that part of the Japanese fleet had to sail from ports in the southern conquered regions.

The Battle of Leyte Gulf

The Japanese naval strategy at Leyte was massive, intricate, and tardy. Ugaki, having survived the attack on Yamamoto, after much convalescence, had been assigned command of the First Battleship Division containing *Yamato* and *Musashi*. Among many laments recorded in his diary was the persistent complaint that the Combined Fleet was operating too slowly, and in the case of Leyte, the criticism appears justified. By the time the operation began to unfold, Allied forces had secured extensive beachheads on the island and begun construction and improvement of several airfields. Many of the supplies had been unloaded and the support vessels already departed. Certainly the big guns of the Combined Fleet could have caused some havoc among the soldiers ashore, but that plan had failed already at Guadalcanal.

The Leyte operations ultimately demonstrated that IJN planners were running on empty. Though the plan itself employed a large and varied number of ships, it might well have come from a Japanese naval academy textbook. Vice Admiral Ozawa commanded the northern force that served only one purpose—to lure Halsey and his fleet carriers away from the Leyte area. Ozawa commanded Japan's four remaining carriers, along with two battleships, three cruisers, and eight destroyers. But he reputedly had only 116 operational aircraft, flown by inexperienced pilots, and divided among his carriers, although Halsey did not know this. The plan called for Ozawa to expose his carriers and lure Halsey away from the invasion beaches, thus leaving the support vessels there vulnerable to the big guns of the Combined Fleet.

Rear Adm. Kurita Takeo commanded the center force, which had rendezvoused from several southern ports including Singapore and Lingga in Indonesia. The Combined Fleet had split and was staging out of bases in the south, where fuel was plentiful but ammunition scarce, and also the home islands, where ammunition abounded but it was difficult to keep the voracious battle fleet fueled. The southern force included the super-battleships *Yamato* and *Musashi* of the First Battleship Division, both of which when fully loaded displaced well over 70,000 tons. Kurita was to make for the San Bernadino Straits, where the behemoths would fire their eighteen-inch guns in action for the first time. Kurita ringed his giant ships with his three remaining battleships, twelve cruisers, and fifteen destroyers. The indestructible Ugaki sailed with Kurita, and his enthusiasm for the coming battle, regardless of his prior misgivings, was typical. Based on false attrition reports and overconfidence in land-based Japanese air power, Ugaki believed that the IJN might actually be capable of delivering the crippling blow to the Allied naval forces in the decisive battle for which it had planned so long.

To Kurita's south, Vice Adm. Nishimura Shoji commanded two battleships, one heavy cruiser, and four destroyers; he was to be aided by Vice Adm. Shima Kiyohide, whose force comprised three cruisers and four destroyers. Nishimura and Shima were to traverse the Surigao Strait. The northern and southern forces were to converge on Leyte Gulf, where, if American landing craft were no longer apparent, they would destroy the American supply train and, if possible, direct their fire on American troops ashore.

For the superstitious in the Japanese navy, plans began to go astray from the first. American submarines *Darter* and *Dace* sighted and torpedoed several of Kurita's cruisers (including his flagship) off of Palawan. Two days later Halsey's airmen attacked *Musashi*, and it took at least nineteen torpedoes; clearly lost, all Kurita could do was to order *Musashi* to engage flank speed, either forward or reverse, ground itself, and become a land battery! Since its steering capacity had been impaired, this proved impossible, and at sunset that day, October 24, 1944, it sank, taking over 1,000 of its crew with it. At dusk that evening, Kurita turned westward. It appeared to the Americans as if the central part of the battle had terminated. In fact, Kurita was pulling back to regroup and intended to force the straits the next day. This should have been evident to the American command structure, for Kurita had a reputation for tenacity. Further, signal fires and lighthouses, never before lit by the Japanese in the San Bernadino Straits, glowed that evening, betraying Kurita's intention to return.

Nonetheless, Halsey evidently remained convinced that the fighting in the area was over; he proceeded to execute a standing order to sink Japanese carriers whenever possible. Along with Mitscher's fast carrier task force, coded Task Force Thirty-eight, he turned northward on October 24 to pursue Ozawa's decoy force. He did not inform Rear Adm. Thomas Kinkaid of this decision, and Kinkaid was left alone to guard the Leyte area. The men of Leyte were left with only a light screen of cover provided by the Seventh Fleet's jeep carrier task groups. The Japanese now had the situation they had hoped for. American landing forces at Leyte were compromised and the battleships could proceed nearly unmolested to shell the American supply vessels and troops.

Early on the morning of October 25, Adm. J.B. Oldendorf's PT boat picket line detected Nishimura's force attempting to navigate through Surigao Strait. Oldendorf had laid a trap for the approaching Japanese and ordered his PT boats to attack first. This harassment did not result in any hits, but it did disrupt the Japanese formation. Next his destroyers engaged the enemy and succeeded in torpedoing several Japanese ships, after which they retired. Nishimura pressed on through the strait in a storm front, which greatly limited his visibility. When he broke out of the front on the morning of October 25, he did so in the face of Oldendorf's defensive line, essentially placing himself on the wrong end of a T formation. Oldendorf used a force of six battleships, five of which had been sunk at Pearl Harbor on the first day of the war, to establish a wall of sixteen-inch guns. Once again, the victims of Pearl Harbor were able to exact a terrible revenge. Oldendorf's force of battleships, cruisers, and destroyers decimated Nishimura's force, sinking all but one of his destroyers. Admiral Shima's force managed to escape, but was harassed by American PT-boats. In the ensuing confusion, Shima's flagship collided with one of Nishimura's mortally wounded vessels, and one of his cruisers was lost. At this point, Oldendorf broke off contact, fearful of another Japanese advance toward the strait. Shima's few remaining destroyers retired from the battle. The southern advance having been successfully blunted, Kurita was on his own in the north.

At dawn on the 25th, Kurita reentered the San Bernadino Straits. This time he found American carriers unprotected, unsuspecting, and just within range of *Yamato*'s big guns. Taffy Five, the designation for Rear Adm. Clifton Sprague's jeep carrier force, was protecting the northern approaches to the landing zone and thought that Halsey was still in the area. Sprague's force of six escort carriers, three destroyers, and four destroyer escorts was the only unit in position to stop Kurita's advance. But Kurita did not know that he faced only the light carriers, for he radioed that "by an opportunity sent by the gods," he was about to engage American fleet carriers off the coast of Samar.

Kurita's sailors had been at battle stations for the better part of three days. Exhaustion was beginning to take its toll. Since the spotters on Kurita's ships reported Sprague's force as being Mitscher's fleet carrier force, Kurita ordered his gunnery officer to fire armor-piercing rounds. The initial salvos caught the Americans off guard, but provided a literally colorful spectacle. *Yamato* carried dye markers in each shell so that its turret crews could distinguish from the color of the water spray which geyser corresponded with which salvo, thereby allowing the gunners to adjust their aim accordingly.

The two forces were about twenty miles apart and well within range of *Yamato*'s eighteen-inch guns. Sprague's destroyers bravely charged the far superior force, while the few aircraft he had harassed the enemy by dropping fragmentation bombs, meant for close support of ground troops, on the decks of the battleships. Reinforced by aircraft from the other picket forces, Sprague was putting up a spirited defense. The American carriers benefited from being unhampered by the necessity to retrieve, fuel, and rearm their aircraft, as the American fliers were able to take advantage of the recently captured shore bases. Thus the American ships were free to maneuver at will. Even Kurita's bombardment of the carriers seemed to be having little effect, largely because the armor-piercing shells penetrated the wooden decks of the escort carriers but failed to detonate, many continuing on through the thin hulls without exploding. This produced large holes in the American ships, but only one carrier was actually sunk. The Japanese force, on the other hand, was forced to engage in evasive tactics to avoid the concerted assault of bombs and torpedoes from U.S. aircraft and destroyers. Even so, with victory in his grasp, Kurita almost inexplicably decided to retire through the San Bernadino Straits, terminating the engagement.

At nearly the same time that the two forces in the south were being reduced, Halsey's carriers caught up with Ozawa and his force. Meant from the beginning to be live bait for the aggressive Halsey, Ozawa had sent most of his aircraft to operate from shore facilities, and was unable to defend his carriers against the determined American attack. In the engagement, Ozawa lost four carriers and five other support vessels. The last from the First Air Fleet, *Zuikaku*, joined its sister ships in a watery grave. The First Air Fleet in particular, and Japanese naval might in general, was destroyed in the battles of Leyte Gulf. Japanese naval power would never recover. The raw materials —even the iron necessary—were not available to rebuild the fleet.

Although none of the participants realized it until it was over, this was the greatest naval battle in history. No less than 282 ships were engaged, and nearly 190,000 sailors. The United States lost 1 light carrier, 2 escort carriers,

2 destroyers and 1 destroyer escort, and about 200 aircraft, with a total of 2,800 battle deaths. The Japanese lost 1 fleet carrier, 3 light carriers, 3 battleships (including *Musashi*), 6 heavy cruisers, 4 light cruisers and 11 destroyers, some 500 planes, and suffered over 10,000 battle deaths.

From the American standpoint, the battle is very controversial. Sometimes called the "Battle of Bull's Run," naval historians have long debated whether "Bull" Halsey was justified in dashing northward, since he did exactly as the enemy anticipated. True, he sank four enemy carriers, but if Kurita had not lost his nerve at the crucial moment, Kinkaid would have had no effective defense against *Yamato* and its escorting ships. It was a calculated risk, but one that Kinkaid did not appreciate. Halsey was his usual impetuous self. Establishing behavior patterns in battle is potentially the worst sin a commander can commit. Halsey's impulsive behavior led him to do exactly as the enemy had anticipated. But since the Japanese did not take effective tactical advantage of it, Halsey had the best of both worlds.

But obviously Kinkaid, and more importantly, Nimitz at Pearl Harbor, did not approve of his actions. Their opinions count for more than all of the later comments that could be, and have been, made. Nimitz's inquiry to Halsey, "Where is Task Force Thirty-eight?," sent as Halsey was engaging Ozawa, reflected more than mere curiosity by Halsey's superior at Pearl. Nimitz obviously did not appreciate Halsey doing exactly as the enemy desired, if indeed he had left Leyte unprotected. Nimitz had never before sent such a seemingly routine inquiry over his own signature to Halsey, and that fact alone betrays Nimitz's judgment, at least at that moment, on the matter.

From the Japanese standpoint, victory at Leyte Gulf would have meant little. At best, it would have lowered American morale and postponed the invasion of the remainder of the Philippines. All the Japanese would have purchased would have been time—time in which the American fleet would have brought up reinforcements, time in which Yamashita could have consolidated his plans. The Battle of Leyte Gulf dramatically reinforced a lesson learned during the first weeks of the Pacific War: No surface force, regardless of its size and power, could operate safely or effectively without adequate air cover.

The Kamikazes

In the wake of the Leyte disaster came a Japanese plan to snatch victory from the jaws of defeat. The air battle over Leyte, like the sea battle, had been one of the largest in history. Its outcome, however, had been remarkably similar to the Marianas "Turkey Shoot." The Japanese combination of inexperienced pilots, inferior quality aircraft and fuel, and dwindling replacement capacity resulted in a marked inability to compete successfully for control of the skies with the Allies. These realities, added to the virtual destruction of the IJN surface fleet, forced Japanese planners to a desperate decision. The idea was that a fleet of thousands of aircraft would deliberately crash land into Allied warships. Theoretically, the plan could have resulted in the sinking of the entire active battle navy. Known officially as the Special Attack Corps, the air fleet had been founded by Vice Adm. Onishi Takijiro just before the Battle of Leyte Gulf, and a very few units had participated in the last hours of the battle, sinking the escort carrier *St. Lo*. The unofficial name was Kamikaze ("Divine Wind") corps, the name deriving from a typhoon that had once saved the Japanese home islands from invasion from mainland Asia. (Another reading of the same Japanese characters is *shimpu*, the corps' usual name in Japan during the conflict.)

After the organization became nationwide in Japan, virtually every civilian young man within the requisite age brackets volunteered. The phrase "one plane, one ship" became their motto. Though largely a volunteer organization, the kamikazes needed experienced naval aviators to act as guides and as leavening for the green recruits, and on occasion aviators whose normal units were decimated were also ordered to join. Admiral Toyoda sometimes ordered ordinary naval aviators to imitate the kamikazes. But a volunteer, elite esprit de corps was their hallmark. Statistics vary, but it appears that well over 4,000 volunteers died, and it is believed that about 330 American ships were damaged or sunk by these missions.

The only branch of the kamikaze corps that saw substantial action was its aviation wing. The Japanese later began to put together a naval surface group. Husbanded largely for the expected Allied invasion of the main islands, these men were to be pilots of suicide boats, vessels of small construction that would ram Allied landing craft. A very few saw service in the Philippine campaign. In addition, the long-lance torpedo was equipped for guidance by a human (*kaiten*), and underwater suicide frogmen (*fukuryu*) were also recruited.

The United States Navy never could properly rationalize kamikaze behavior. It was widely rumored, particularly among navy enlisted personnel, that kamikaze pilots were riveted into their cockpits, hypnotized, drugged, chained, or promised immediate entry into heaven upon death. None of this, of course, was true. Young men were literally happy to offer their lives for their emperor. Ugaki, having survived the debacle of the First Battleship Division at Leyte, hailed the kamikaze's valor and confided in his diary that Japan would have no concern for the future if its population of 100 million [*sic*] showed the same spirit. In Japan today it would probably be impossible. But in wartime Japan, a generation not dedicated to materialism was willing to give up their lives. The mystique was not at all difficult to grasp for the average Japanese youth, although some parents naturally regretted their children's decision.

Upon joining, the volunteer wrote out a will and also a farewell letter to his family. Then he was given training on the ground and eventually posted to an airbase. He then waited for a target to appear. When a target came within range, volunteers were called for, although if a trainee did not feel at peace with himself it was not necessarily a disgrace, in effect, to refuse the call. If time allowed, he had a farewell toast with his commanding officer, after which he embarked on his first and, hopefully, only suicide flight. An experienced pilot would guide his group to the target, and then each pilot was on his own. If the target disappeared, he returned to the ground, although landing with a planeload of explosives set to detonate on contact was no easy matter.

If his target was a battleship, he crashed at the base of a turret; if a carrier, he aimed for one of the flight elevators. Some special pilots were actually instructed to land on American carriers and hurl grenades at the gasoline supply lines, and a few did so. The kamikaze corps never was an effective physical weapon, though they caused considerable damage at Okinawa, as will be seen. But psychologically, they made the enemy seem superhuman, ready to make sacrifices the average American warrior would not comprehend. The United States Navy and Marine Corps could never successfully appreciate Japanese motives, much less successfully represent them to enlisted men, and the subject is one both services avoid to this day. Americans are too secular and rational to comprehend fully the motives of the young men who willingly gave their lives in the service of their country.

Leyte and Luzon Islands

With the Japanese navy now essentially out of the picture, except as a ferry service for army personnel, the United States Army was free to press its attack on Leyte. Once again the Japanese had determined to make Leyte a decisive confrontation. Japanese troops on the island were minimal at the beginning of the campaign, but some 45,000 reinforcements were sent in an attempt to stem the advance of the American forces. The battle for the island lasted a full two months, with the Japanese surrendering ground only after inflicting heavy losses on the U.S. forces. By Christmas Day of 1944, the United States Army could declare the island secure. MacArthur was in the habit of declaring an island secure before the enemy was entirely eliminated, a habit that was not appreciated by officers who had to write the families of enlisted men killed after the general's proclamation had been published in stateside newspapers.

Wartime humor, the Philippines, spring 1945. *(United States Army)*

General Yamashita had taken a substantial risk in committing so many of his soldiers to the fight on Leyte. He seriously depleted the number of troops that would be available to him for the defense of Luzon. Concurrently, by capturing Leyte, the Americans had cut the Japanese garrison on Mindanao off from the force on Luzon and could deal with the separate forces at their leisure.

MacArthur now prepared to retake the northernmost island of Luzon, with its capital city of Manila. Although he denied the fact, he chose to follow almost the exact same invasion route taken by Homma late in 1941. He would land troops in the north at Lingayen Gulf and push the Japanese to the south and east. He was also determined to make the men who had been responsible for his humiliation early in the war pay for their insolence. With no danger of Japanese naval intervention, the landings on Luzon were scheduled for January 2, 1945.

The Japanese still had a force of a quarter of a million men under the command of General Yamashita. Yamashita did not advocate following MacArthur's strategy of 1941—retreating to Bataan—because of American naval strength, but instructed his field commanders to fall back and defend the airfields and then the mountains of the east coast. Yamashita himself withdrew to the Philippine summer capital, Baguio, situated on what amounted

147

to a small mountaintop. Here he was isolated in every sense of the word. Dispatch runners took an inordinately long time, or did not get through at all, because of guerilla activities. And his radios worked perhaps one-fourth of the time because of defective batteries, evidently weakened by the humidity. Yamashita was ill-informed concerning MacArthur's progress, and few of his ordered countermeasures were implemented. Instead, local commanders issued their own orders to oppose MacArthur's advance, or they were not issued at all. Portions of Luzon fell to MacArthur largely by default.

On January 9, 1945, Lt. Gen. Walter Krueger landed in Lingayen Gulf, almost without opposition. By January 23, he had reached the vicinity of Clark Field. In late January and early February elements of Gen. Robert Eichelberger's Eighth Army made landings to both the north and south of Manila.

Yamashita promptly declared Manila an open city—a city that would not be defended. Rear Adm. Iwafuchi Mitsuji decided nonetheless to contest the city, after a fashion. Using his 18,000 troops, largely Imperial Marines, he ravaged and pillaged the city for its last three days of Japanese occupation. The U.S. Thirty-seventh Division and other elements of the Sixth Army approaching from the north, together with elements of the Eighth Army approaching from the south, had the unenviable task of liberating the city, block by block, beginning on February 3, 1945.

The Japanese committed unspeakable atrocities. They entered hospitals, tied patients to their beds, and set the beds afire, using gasoline where available. They gouged out children's eyes, raped and then killed women. Years later, witnesses and survivors recounted those last terrible days of Japanese occupation, and almost exclusively they named Iwafuchi's Imperial Marines as the guilty parties.

On March 3, 1945, MacArthur declared Manila secure, but only after a month of bitter fighting, including the destruction of Intramuros, the old inner walled city, which was nearly impregnable in a pre-nuclear age. And Corregidor had been stubbornly defended as well, requiring a parachute drop on February 16 to help retake it. The fight was everywhere bitter, and civilian casualties were appalling in a city with so high a population density. At least 20,000 Japanese died defending the city and environs. MacArthur then wisely used Manila as a port from which to pour in supplies and reinforcements for the liberation of the remainder of Luzon.

Western Prisoners of War

The liberation of Luzon and especially Manila meant the end of two and a half years of Japanese oppression of the Filipinos and also the end of captivity for a large group of men who had been held in prison camps since very early in the war. There were several prominent POW camps near Manila; hence, General MacArthur had made a point of liberating Allied POWs as rapidly as possible. The men who were released from the camps rarely resembled the men who had entered them in 1942.

The code of *bushido* does not allow for a soldier's captivity. Since they themselves would willingly die rather than become POWs, the Japanese thought that Western soldiers shared similar beliefs. It came as something of a shock when entire garrisons chose to give themselves up rather then risk being killed in a hopeless pitched battle. The Japanese first experienced a crisis with excessive numbers of prisoners at Singapore, when Percival surrendered his garrison of nearly 100,000 men. They were unprepared to deal with that large a number of enemy personnel. The resulting movement of troops to prison camps, under the most brutal conditions, cost the lives of many Allied soldiers. Japanese programs to exploit the prisoner population later in the war would account for many more casualties.

The Americans who defended the Philippines in 1941 had suffered terribly at the hands of the Japanese. As with the case in Singapore, when Bataan fell in April of 1942, the Japanese had not anticipated having to deal with so large a prisoner population. Arrangements had been made for the transfer of troops from the front lines to camps prepared for them in the rear. The system collapsed when the materials necessary for the move were not available, and the imminent attack on Corregidor demanded full Japanese attention. The resulting trek from the tip of the peninsula to Camp O'Donnell became known as the Bataan Death March.

Adequate supplies of food and water were not available for the men, and their pre-march condition was never taken into account. Many were forced to make the entire sixty-two-mile trip without eating, and only received water, if at all, from the Filipinos who happened to populate the route. During the march, the Americans and Filipinos were subjected to various forms of abuse, ranging from searches and theft to physical violence and outright murder. Stragglers were not tolerated; the slightest infraction of a Japanese command could mean instant execution. Most of the men were weakened from the five-month struggle before the march began. Those who survived the tribulation found conditions at the various camps ultimately a worse ordeal than the march.

The diminished physical condition of the prisoners rendered them extremely susceptible to numerous diseases. Malaria, dysentary, beri beri, and other jungle infections, which ordinarily could be controlled with a healthy diet and proper medication, killed large numbers of men in all camps during the early stages of the Japanese occupation. The filthy living conditions and poor diets of the prisoners resulted in a death rate of nearly one in four men in Japanese captivity.

On May 30, 1942, Prime Minister Tojo ordered that in order to receive food rations, prisoners would have to complete certain amounts of work related to the area in which they were being held. For some men this meant an opportunity to escape from the death that pervaded the camps, if only for a short time. For others it was certain death. Already malnourished, the men were put to work on building projects intended to strengthen Japan's hold on its empire. The most famous of these, the Thailand to Burma railroad, provided the setting for *The Bridge on the River Kwai*, a movie based on POW life under the Japanese. (In truth, however, the POWs who built the bridge were French, not British.)

By the end of 1942, the number of Americans held in Japanese POW camps was estimated at 20,000. The main body of these was located in the Philippine Islands. As the war began to progress to Japan's disadvantage, an effort was made to transport POWs to the home islands to serve as a work force in war industries. This project was not particularly successful because of the effectiveness of America's submarine campaign. Most of the enlisted prisoners remained in the Philippines, while senior officers were transported to camps in Manchuria and China.

When American soldiers liberated the POW camps in 1944–45, the men they found were scarcely recognizable. Physically they were shells of the men they had once been. Psychologically they had been forced to reconcile themselves to the idea of being prisoners and had become conscious of the value of their own lives to their Japanese captors. Often, they had survived by coincidence or luck, and had only good fortune to thank for not having become a casualty of the Japanese brutality. These men were rapidly repatriated and were welcomed home as heroes, but were incapable of playing any further role in the downfall of the nation that had held them in captivity since 1942.

There was an active underground force in the Philippines and some prisoners did escape and join its forces. Mindanao was the location of the greatest concentration of such an underground because of the nature of the terrain, fierce hostility on the part of the Filipinos, and the fact that the Japanese had a smaller force to patrol it than Luzon. Here the Filipino resistance forces operated in the hill country with little interference from the Japanese. However, men captured while serving with these groups or men caught attempting escape to serve in them were executed almost without exception. For the men in the POW camps of Luzon, the primary concern was simply living to see the next sunrise; ultimately, the hope of liberation was all that sustained them.

A combination of factors determined life in captivity: the attitude of the commanding officer, a prisoner's physical condition, mental attitude, and above all, whether or not a buddy system was established in the camp. Here, in the few instances when Americans were quartered with captured Britons, they learned from their allies. Otherwise, in an every-man-for-himself climate, few but the hardiest or most stoic of individuals survived. Those few men who remained together as cohesive units survived far better. One group of marines who was allowed to remain together during the Bataan Death March emerged alive, almost to a man, at the end of the conflict. The average internee liberated by MacArthur had been through a nightmare he could not even begin to recount unless he had somehow managed to keep a diary. MacArthur could only apologize to the survivors. Many perished even after repatriation, for captivity had rendered the prisoners sensitive to disease, both mental and physical, long after the end of the war.

The Liberation of the Philippines

The campaign for the Philippines must have seemed as long-lived to MacArthur as the captivity had seemed to the men he liberated. The Philippine archipelago contains some 7,000 islands, 5,000 of which are inhabited. Luzon itself is covered by much rugged terrain; indeed, Yamashita surrendered on his mountaintop headquarters only upon hearing the emperor's surrender broadcast on August 15, 1945. The actions on Luzon cost the United States nearly 8,000 dead, while Japanese battle deaths have recently been placed as high as 192,000. The Philippine underground had done a good deal to aid the liberation of the islands, as virtually any participating Filipino still alive today can recount. Everywhere the Filipino people rallied to MacArthur and rose up against the Japanese. No reliable estimate of Filipinos killed during the liberation has ever been made, but it was doubtless high.

MacArthur now violated the cardinal principle of island hopping. He went southward to attack Mindanao. His desire to do so is perhaps understandable. The island held POW camps and two full Japanese divisions. The American Eighth Army made over fifty landings before even reaching Mindanao. Here, landing on April 17, 1945, they were greatly aided by the inhabitants, who in some instances rose up and literally hacked the local Japanese garrisons to pieces with bolo knives. About 50,000 Japanese perished, as well as perhaps 2,500 Americans. But MacArthur now went further. He instigated a basically Australian reconquest of portions of Borneo, using the Seventh Fleet and portions of the Army Air Corps under his command as well. Since he had recrossed the equator, he could also command Australian forces. Allegedly, he wanted to procure oil-rich regions, but he conquered real estate long since bypassed, and as far as Tokyo was concerned, isolated and useless. Again MacArthur, who would claim, inaccurately, to have originated the island-hopping strategy, violated its basic tenets.

The Japanese greatly regretted the loss of the Philippines. For Tokyo it was a staggering blow. Japan's critical supply routes to the southern resource regions ran astride the Philippines, and these were now completely severed by the American submarine effort against the Japanese merchant marine. The populace in general was told that the Americans were being lured toward the home islands, where they would be destroyed in a decisive battle, one in which the entire populace would be expected to participate. The decisive battle was now an army dream as the navy no longer existed to meaningfully challenge the Allies. But for the elite that ran the country, the Philippines held both physical and symbolic value. It was the logistical touchstone of the Japanese empire, and the Americans had conquered it. Life at home had in fact become a nightmare, thanks to the American submarine effort against Japan. That campaign must now be examined.

Suggestions for Further Reading

Philip Crowl, *Campaign in the Marianas* (Washington, DC: Army Historical Office, 1960) is the U.S. Army's semi-official account. Stanley Karnow, *In Our Image: America's Empire in the Philippines* (New York: Ballantine, 1990) gives a novel insight into that area's wartime years, but must be used with caution. Edwin Hoyt's *To the Marianas* (New York: Van Nostrand, 1980) and *The Battle of Leyte Gulf* (New York: Weybright and Talley, 1972) are acceptable, if superficial and undocumented. Probably the best account of the Leyte Gulf operation, although brief, remains James A. Field Jr., *The Japanese at Leyte Gulf: The Sho Operation* (Princeton, NJ: Princeton University Press, 1947); but see also C. Vann Woodward, *The Battle for Leyte Gulf* (New York: Macmillan, 1947)—the author, renowned for his writings in another field of American history, was in naval intelligence during the conflict; Donald McIntyre, *Leyte Gulf: Armada in the Pacific* (New York: Ballantine, 1970); Adrian Stewart, *The Battle of Leyte Gulf* (New York: Charles Scribner's Sons, 1979); and Stanley Falk, *Decision at Leyte* (New York: Norton, 1966). Timothy Maga, *Defending Paradise* (New York: Garland, 1987) contains interesting information on life in wartime Guam. Samuel Eliot Morison's volumes in his history of U.S. naval operations during the conflict are still quite worthwhile, especially *New Guinea and the Marianas, March 1944–August 1944* (Boston: Little, Brown, 1958). For a fascinating view of the progress of the war from a Japanese perspective, see Donald M. Goldstein and Katherine V. Dillon, eds., *Fading Victory: The Diary of Admiral Matome Ugaki* (Pittsburgh, PA: University of Pitsburgh Press, 1991). The kamikaze corps is best chronicled in Rikihei Inoguchi, Tadashi Nakajima, and Roger Pineau, *Divine Wind: Japan's Kamikaze Force in World War II* (Annapolis, MD: Naval

Institute Press, 1959). For the POW experience, see Donald Knox, *Death March: The Survivors of Bataan* (New York: Harcourt Brace Jovanovich, 1981); E. Bartlett Kerr, *Surrender and Survival: The Experience of American POWs in the Pacific, 1941–1945* (New York: William Morrow, 1985); Captain Edwin Dyess, *The Dyess Story* (New York: Putnam, 1944); William E. Brougher, *South to Bataan, North to Mukden* (Athens: University of Georgia Press, 1971); and finally, Hank Nelson, "The Nips Are Going for the Parker [pen]: The Prisoners Face Freedom," *War and Society* 3 (September 1985): 127–43.

8

Submarines, Firebombs, and Survival

This chapter deals with several of the most controversial elements of the Pacific War. Submarine warfare, mass-scale aerial bombing, and home front scarcity and deprivation make up the bulk of the following discussion. Viewed with the luxury of hindsight, these may well be some of the most inglorious elements of this conflict and are testimony to the price paid by all participant populations.

Almost universally condemned during World War I, the submarine came to be an integral part of all the fleets of the world during the interwar period. Their use in World War II as commerce raiders and forward strike vehicles dwarfed that of the period 1914–18 and provides one of the most dramatic and important stories of the war. Submarines, the men who sailed them, and the purposes to which they were turned will be examined closely in this chapter.

Also decried as immoral and contrary to the acceptable articles of war, aerial bombing of largely civilian targets was practiced by nearly every belligerent, and came to be a core element of the Allied campaign to bring Japan to its knees in 1945. Precision bombing of specifically military targets gave way to the wholesale devastation of hundreds of square miles of Japanese urban areas by incendiary bombing, as the latter was found to be far more destructive, if not more effective in bringing the empire to heel. The progression and effect of the Allied bombing campaign will be discussed in this chapter and further pursued in Chapter 10 as well.

Finally, elements of life on the home fronts in Japan and the United States will be examined as they relate to the progress of the war. The price of war must often be measured in more than battle casualties and territory lost and won. The manner in which a population deals with the inherent fear and sacrifice associated with war often says a great deal about the character of the population and the prospect for rebuilding after the end of hostilities.

Submarine Warfare

World War I proved the value of the submarine as a naval weapon, but on a relatively small scale. In World War II all of the major belligerents planned and executed submarine campaigns against their enemies, with varying results. The German effort in the Atlantic is popularly believed to be the most successful example of undersea conflict. This is not so; the Pacific theater provided a far larger arena of operations for the submariners. While slow to achieve effectiveness, the American effort in the Pacific eventually, when taken within context, dwarfed that of Nazi Germany in the Atlantic in terms of the result it achieved against its intended target.

The Japanese and American submarine campaigns could scarcely show greater diversity. The Japanese possessed advantages at the outset. Specifically, their navy possessed the long-lance torpedo for submarine use. Because it was oxygen driven, it did not leave a tell-tale stream of bubbles in the water. These torpedoes were among the deadliest of the war from the standpoint of low malfunction and nonexplosion rates. Equipped with a reliable contact detonator when fired from a submarine, they would usually run true.

The Japanese delivery vehicle, the *I*-class submarine, was potentially just as fearsome. Displacing 2,200 tons, it was slightly larger than American submarines, had higher surface speeds, and, almost identical with them, had a safe diving depth of about 300 feet. Its usual complement was eighty officers and enlisted men. The average *I*-class submarine carried seventeen or eighteen torpedoes, but it could not be effectively rigged for silent running. And the *I*-class had a cruising range of 10,000 to 17,000 miles, which was slightly greater than that of its American counterpart. Unfortunately for the Japanese, the Imperial Navy did not equip submarines with radar, whereas radar was routinely installed aboard American subs after late 1942.

Worse, Yamamoto evidently agreed with the naval general staff in Tokyo, which decreed that American warships were the submarines' targets of choice. More often than not, Japanese submarines served as support vehicles to surface operations. Submarine captains were given little incentive to pursue aggressive individual action. Ugaki often berated submariners during the Solomons campaign for what he described, sometimes unfairly, as a decidedly passive attitude on the part of submarine skippers and an unwillingness to closely engage the enemy Relegation of the submarine to a second-tier role proved to be a major error because it failed to take into account America's far longer supply lines in the Pacific. The American merchant marine would have been a vulnerable, tempting target indeed had the Japanese directed a major, sustained effort against it. The obvious choke points existed: from the Panama Canal, to San Diego, to the Hawaiian Islands, Australia, and New Zealand. But the Japanese simply did not use them to attempt to disrupt Allied supply lines.

In the opening days of the war the Japanese effort was dogged by bad luck. During the attack on Pearl the midget subs had nearly given away the attack prematurely, while the fifteen *I*-class subs that ringed Hawaii had sunk nothing of consequence, if only because the air raid itself was so successful. At Midway, the submarines assigned to screening duties between Pearl and Midway arrived too late to warn Nagumo that American carriers were indeed headed toward his carrier force. The midgets further failed at Port Darwin during the Midway operation. They did manage, in a contemporary attack (May 30, 1942) at the harbor of Diego Suarez on Madagascar, to damage a British battleship and sink a tanker. The British did not realize that the midgets operated from a mother craft. Fearing that the Japanese had a secret base somewhere in the vicinity, they seized the entire island, to no avail.

Yamamoto placed little faith in the midget subs, however. This was probably justified, as they automatically rose to the surface after discharging their torpedoes, which he regarded as too great a risk for the two-man crews. He also displayed little knowledge of wartime conditions in the United States. For the first year of the war he maintained a screen of at least three *I*-class subs off the West Coast, where they did indeed sink a few merchantmen. Some were equipped to carry not a midget sub, as they had at Pearl, but a small pontoon-equipped floatplane, which was used on several occasions to drop incendiary devices on the forests of the Pacific Northwest. This was their designated target, on the assumption that a forest fire would do the greatest material damage to the American war effort. Perhaps it did. But the effect of dropping the odd explosive device on, say, San Francisco, was evidently never even considered. What the effect would have been on the most populous of West Coast cities will, of course, forever remain a matter for speculation.

The Japanese did score a few glittering prizes with their torpedoes. The carriers *Yorktown* (June 1942), *Wasp* (September 1942), *Hornet* (October 1942), and later the cruiser *Indianapolis* (July 1945) were the greatest kills achieved by Japanese submariners, and indeed some American merchantmen were sunk also. No really accurate count is available, but the totals were miniscule compared to the losses the U.S. merchant marine suffered in the

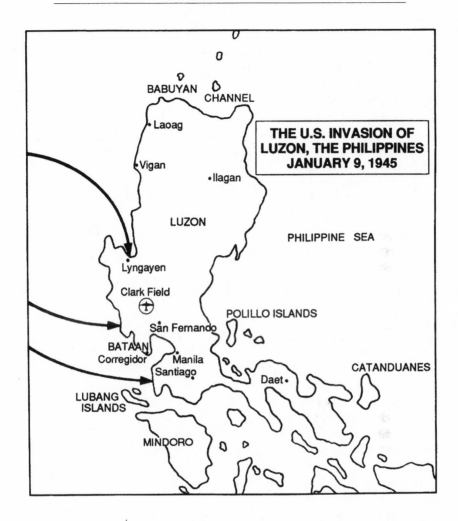

BABUYAN CHANNEL

• Laoag

• Vigan

• Ilagan

LUZON

**THE U.S. INVASION OF
LUZON, THE PHILIPPINES
JANUARY 9, 1945**

PHILIPPINE SEA

• Lyngayen

Clark Field ⊕

San Fernando

POLILLO ISLANDS

BATAAN
Corregidor • Manila
Santiago

Daet •

CATANDUANES

LUBANG
ISLANDS

MINDORO

Atlantic. As the Americans began their advance across the Pacific, the submarines were all too often asked to run supplies to garrisons bypassed and
now isolated behind American lines. Indeed, the Imperial Army actually developed a small fleet arm in the guise of special garrison duty submarines.
There can be no duty more fatal to morale than that of playing blockade
runner for a beleaguered garrison. By 1945 the Japanese submarine service
was a shadow of its former self, with roughly 130 of the Imperial Navy's
subs having been lost at sea, out of a basic number of 170 that engaged in
one or more wartime patrols.

The American submarine effort was far different. Roosevelt had asked
Congress that a state of war be declared against Japan as of the beginning of

the attack against Pearl, on the chance that an American submarine might have torpedoed a Japanese vessel, though none had. The first days of the American submarine effort were not glorious: Adm. Thomas Hart, in charge of the small Asiatic Fleet, discovered that many of his skippers were a bit too cautious, although the gold bullion of the Philippine government was successfully evacuated by submarine.

When Nimitz took command at Pearl, the submarine service underwent swift and positive changes. Although in many ways a submariner by temperament, Nimitz quickly gave the submarine command at Pearl to Vice Adm. Charles Lockwood. Lockwood soon split his submarines between Pearl Harbor and the base at Fremantle, near Perth, on the western coast of Australia. Rear Adm. Ralph Christie commanded Fremantle, though he remained subordinate to Lockwood. Neither man hesitated to cut deadwood out of the command structure. This was especially true after the battle of Midway. Lockwood, though brand new to the job, swiftly retired those he found to be overly cautious. Nimitz had hoped the submarines would play a significant role at Midway, but they did not.

Perhaps the most basic trouble was American torpedoes. On Pearl Harbor day, the United States Navy had seventy-three submarines in the Pacific and the Japanese had sixty. The standard American sub was *Gato* class. In the course of the conflict, the United States operated a total of 250 submarines, of which 52 were lost, accounting for a total of 3,505 men killed. A *Gato*-class sub displaced about 1,500 tons, had a surface speed of slightly over 20 knots, and carried a crew of 77 men. Torpedo inventory, at exactly two dozen "tin fish," was greater than that of the *I*-class sub, although the *Gato*'s effective cruising range was less, at about 10,000–12,000 miles. But from the first, American submariners complained that their torpedoes were defective.

Nonetheless, from the opening day of the war unescorted Japanese merchantmen fell prey to American submarines. Unknown at the time, however, American steam-driven torpedoes ran at a greater than set depth, often as much as eight to ten feet deeper. Their magnetic detonators, which could theoretically break a ship's spine by exploding beneath the vessel's keel plates, usually failed to function at all. Further, their contact detonators were defective: torpedoes seemed to explode when transecting with the target at anything but a ninety-degree angle, which was supposedly the perfect, "textbook" shot. Given the number of torpedoes fired and ships sunk, it took over seven torpedoes to sink the average Japanese ship. This was obviously a high average.

In mid-1943 the turning point came for the submariners. They had already taken a significant toll, having sunk about 142 Japanese merchantmen by the end of 1942. The basic Japanese naval cipher for merchantmen—

Crowded quarters aboard an American submarine; the *Gato*-class sub was approximately twenty-seven feet in diameter. (*United States Navy*)

tankers included—was not broken by the Americans until early 1943, when its secrets fell victim to an American cipher team attached to the command structure at Pearl. The suffix *maru* is attached to all Japanese merchantmen, and the *maru* cipher was cracked at precisely the moment when the Japanese had begun convoying in an attempt to stem their merchantmen losses. Now the location of each convoy was laid bare to prying eyes at Pearl, and in a very precise manner: the exact coordinates for each convoy were given nearly every day, as well as names of individual ships, cargo carried, and what specific escort each convoy had for protection. Seldom has cryptography yielded such useful fruits.

American submarine captains subsequently found hunting very worthwhile indeed. The matter of the *maru* cipher was a very closely guarded secret during the conflict. Each submarine captain was required to sign an oath to the effect that he would not reveal its existence to anyone, including his officers or crew. Some captains did tell their second in command, and the ships' radio personnel knew as well, but the Japanese never suspected that the Americans had penetrated the code.

The only problem lay with the naval Bureau of Ordnance, which issued torpedoes. Its officers continued to insist with a stubbornness that must have been maddening that American torpedoes were *not* defective. Then on July 24, 1943, came the submarine *Tinosa* and her encounter with the 19,000-ton whaling factory *Tonan Maru III*. Targets this large were rare. *Tinosa's* skipper fired a total of fifteen torpedoes at his target, of which eleven were duds and none were fatal. Saving his final torpedo for the Bureau of Ordnance, he turned his prow back to Pearl. The Bureau, however tacitly, admitted that something was wrong. Tests in the water and then on land—the torpedoes were dropped from a cherry picker—disclosed that a ninety-degree hit would crush the exploding pin before detonation could take place. By this time, the magnetic detonators had been deactivated and the problem of running deep was also solved. A new torpedo, electrically driven, was introduced and dubbed the Mark XVI. It was slower than the former steam driven torpedoes, but otherwise an almost quantum-leap improvement. The result would be disaster for the Japanese merchant marine.

Tankers were always priority targets since Japan had almost no oil resources of its own. By November 1943 the number of Japanese cargo vessels was smaller than on December 7, 1941. New Japanese ship construction was concentrated almost exclusively on oilers. The combined fleet, in order to lessen the load, moved its basic anchorage to Tawi Tawi, south of Mindanao, and then to Singapore itself by mid-1944. Of all the steel allocated in Japan for shipbuilding in 1944, only one-sixth went for new warships; the remainder was allocated for the merchant marine, and almost all of that for tankers. Some commentators have contended that the United States Navy should have concentrated exclusively on sinking tankers. This argument ignores the fact that each convoy in turn was attacked; concentration exclusively on tankers would have revealed American's penetration of the *maru* cipher.

When warships were encountered, Lockwood naturally ordered that carriers be regarded as the primary targets. Ten Japanese carriers ultimately slid beneath the waves as submarine victims. The most important of these was probably *Shinano*. Begun as a slightly larger version of *Yamato*, *Shinano* was the largest warship ever constructed to that date. Since time had proven the now deceased Yamamoto correct concerning the value of naval air power, the naval general staff decreed that *Shinano* be finished as a carrier. The Japanese had already been experimenting with a battleship/carrier hybrid. Battleships *Ise* and *Hyuga* had their fan tails modified to include a landing deck. Though never able to operate as fully functional carriers because of lack of planes and pilots, the battleship/carriers had been part of the "bait" used to lure Halsey away from Leyte in 1944. Had it ever been completed and battle ready, *Shinano* would have dwarfed all other true carriers, displacing close to 72,000 tons when fully loaded. However, with a flight deck of steel and concrete, it left Yokohama scarcely seaworthy. It sailed with an untrained crew and had no aircraft aboard.

It was bound for Hiroshima on the Inland Sea, but the submarine *Archer Fish* found it well before that. In the early morning hours of November 29, 1944, *Archer Fish*'s skipper fired four torpedoes into *Shinano*. *Shinano*'s captain, Abe Toshio, was at first not overly concerned. *Musashi*, after all, had taken no less than nineteen torpedoes at Leyte Gulf before sinking. But *Musashi* had been manned by a full complement of highly trained and experienced crewmen. *Shinano*, it turned out, had not been properly tested for watertight integrity, and the electric pumps for evacuating seawater did not operate properly. By mid-morning it sank, taking over 1,000 men with it.

One of the most prodigious submarine skippers of the war was Richard O'Kane, captain of the *Tang*. Until his ship was sunk and O'Kane became a prisoner of war, he sank twenty-four Japanese merchantmen for a total of 93,824 tons. In October 1944, during the Leyte Gulf action, O'Kane encountered several Japanese merchant convoys. He fell victim, ironically, to one of his own torpedoes, which, in a not-unknown malfunction. described a full circle and detonated against the hull of his own ship twenty seconds after firing. Manning his own conning tower, O'Kane was thrown into the water. Captured by Japanese who had been aboard a ship he had just sent under, O'Kane was probably glad to be transported to an actual prisoner of war camp. In addition to the Congressional Medal of Honor, O'Kane received three Navy Crosses and an equal number of Silver Stars.

By the end of 1944, with the reconquest of the Philippines, American submarines began to venture into the Sea of Japan. This was no mere propaganda stunt. Something of a "sub scare" eventually ensued, as many fishermen refused to venture out of sight of shore—if even that far—in their sampans. By early 1945, American aircraft began attacking not only merchantmen but also Japan's larger, seagoing sampans; the results for the diet of the civilian population were catastrophic. Japan has always had a basic diet of fish and rice; its fish catch was now reduced nearly 40 percent, while the rice crop for the last years of the war was poor (the worst since the famine year 1931), largely because of climatic conditions. Despite an offensive in China that provided a direct land link to Indochina (except that ultimately the rice had to be shipped by sea from Korea to one of the home islands), little rice from Southeast Asia reached Japan. Some farmers in Indochina had been forced to plant jute instead, while Chinese bandits plundered Japanese land supply lines with Indochina. As a result, malnutrition became widespread in the home islands while resultant diseases, especially tuberculosis, were increasingly endemic.

Not long after Yamamoto's death in 1943, the Japanese began to organize convoys, although never to the extent that the American navy did in the Atlantic. American submarine forces responded by wolfpacking, or concentrating, their submarines, with catastrophic results for the Japanese. By the spring of 1945, thirty-five out of forty-seven regular Japanese convoy routes between Japan and its possessions south of the Philippines had been completely abandoned. By the end of the war, U.S. submarines would send no less than 1,113 Japanese merchantmen to the bottom. A somewhat smaller but significant number of freighters was also eliminated by airpower, and 201 Japanese warships of all types were sunk by submarine action as well.

While losses in the American submarine service were within acceptable limits, they were far from insignificant. Although only 2 percent of the navy's total manpower served in submarines, a staggering 22 percent of those 16,000 men perished. The sailors received combat pay, but little else, except the occasional decoration, in return.

Life in an American submarine service was not the glamorous life Hollywood has projected. Nature, human nature, and the enemy always posed obstacles for any submarine skipper. Even more than carrier aviators, submariners required onshore recreational facilities beyond the ordinary and these were not always to be had, especially in Fremantle and its environs. Worse still, the navy developed Midway Atoll as a submarine base as the war progressed, and Midway possessed virtually no first-class shore facilities.

Life was cramped, noisy, difficult, and dangerous under the best of circumstances. Of the fifty-two U.S. submarines lost during the war, all but two perished in the Pacific. The submarines operated out of Pearl (Midway was sometimes substituted as a home port for subs based out of Pearl) or Fremantle, or later, just at the end of the conflict as the Japanese empire contracted, Guam or Luzon. The later bases afforded fewer opportunities for recreation, but yielded in the long run fewer hours at sea and probably higher kill ratios. And, of course, in the tradition of the silent service, there was little in the way of public recognition. Life was not always pleasant, and the sacrifices probably seemed unheralded.

Life in Japan

By 1943 life in Japan had become truly squalid, largely because the U.S. submarine campaign severed contact with the overseas empire. The Japanese may have conquered the El Dorado of the South, but they never enjoyed its fruits since the American submarine effort isolated them from their newly acquired territories before they could begin proper exploitation of the areas. Serious, official rationing had begun as early as April 1941, six months before Pearl Harbor, when rice purchasing was restricted in many cities. Other commodities were added to the restricted list on an as-needed basis, and the system spread from Japan's cities to embrace the entire nation. This in turn led to the inevitable black market operations, which became so blatant that in some provinces the authorities actually encouraged them, since the profiteers sometimes seemed to have access to commodities that the authorities had believed exhausted.

Dealing with the black market required finesse. Usually, payment was demanded not only in cash, but also in the form of family heirlooms, art objects, and the like. The Japanese who ran the black market were true professionals as such things go. They had their own law in the guise of territories controlled, standardized methods, even specific hours and places of operation. Dealing with them was not pleasant, but it became a necessity for the majority of urban Japanese by the late summer of 1945.

The most serious military shortages were fuel oil and aluminum. The oil shortage was compensated for in part by whaling, which harvested a combustible fuel, and by pressing the roots of pine trees, which also yielded a serviceable fuel. But the results in both cases were meager. In fact, some gasoline destined for civilian use was reportedly diluted with sake. The very few Japanese who still operated automobiles found it necessary to push them to the tops of hills and then drift the vehicles downhill in first gear in order for the gasoline to spark. Some Japanese attempted to convert their cars to burn solid fuels, but this was not officially encouraged and met with little success in the long run. There was, however, no substitute for bauxite ore, and by early 1945 there was almost no aluminum left in Japan. In desperation, the Japanese manufactured planes out of magnesium, whose low combustion temperature made this practice counterproductive from the pilot's point of view. In a desperate search for all metals, Japanese housewives were called on to turn in unneeded objects. The Japanese also ransacked their conquered empire, even commandeering coins to be smelted down for their brass content.

The most restricted civilian commodities were rice, coal, iron ore, salt, and virtually any edible commodity one can think of. By the spring of 1945 only the army's secret police, the dreaded *kempetai*, very high ranking civilians, and flag- or star-grade military officers were officially given gasoline for private or official automobiles, and then only in small quantities. The Americans' restrictions of two-and-a-half gallons per week would have seemed an incredible luxury to the Japanese.

Homes went without coal for heating, pneumonia became commonplace, pipes froze, and sanitation was difficult, particularly for city dwellers. Long lines at markets became common. Any neighbor with a close relative who owned a farm suddenly became the most popular person on the block—he or she was, in effect, a potential source of food. Even the silk industry was curtailed. Kimonos became scarce, and a national standard of dress was introduced, reducing life to the truly shabby. Metal objects for civilian use were no longer manufactured. While the government still encouraged early marriage with many children, young couples had to wait and literally inherit a frying pan, much less a hibachi.

As early as March 1943 the government had tacitly admitted that all was not well when it proclaimed a national "smile week" to raise public morale. Worse, in February 1944 the press announced a fifteen-point program for the "simplification" of the standard of living. These measures included the conversion of consumer items factories to war goods production, the closing of geisha houses, the conservation of energy, fewer holidays, and increased employment of women in the civilian work force. School grounds were to be planted with vegetable gardens. Even afternoon newspapers were discouraged, a measure of desperation in what was surely the most well-read population of all the belligerents. Few complained, but Tojo, chief of the army general staff as well as premier and minister of the army, obviously did not endear himself to the working population, especially when the seven-day workweek became common.

Women for the first time played an acknowledged role in the economy, if only because so many men of draft age had been called to the colors. The munitions industry in particular began employing them. Premier Tojo's wife shattered all precedent when she made public appearances in factories and urged women to increase worker productivity. She also made radio broadcasts to the same effect. The Japanese used their secret weapon—long hours and hard work—to produce what they could of the modern military necessities. Travel became a luxury. Pullman cars were discontinued on almost all train runs, or else they were restricted to military officers. Police permits were necessary for civilian train travel beyond routine commuting. Foreign nationals of neutral nations were increasingly harrassed by frequent nocturnal visits from *tokko*, the special police that usually monitored the activity of foreigners.

Amphetamines were distributed to civilian workers. Until their use was restricted to prescription distribution (this occurred only in 1950), misuse was common, probably in part because of their appetite-reducing effect. The entire nation was on a nationalistic binge. Teaching of foreign languages was curtailed. In one sense wealth, property, and even social rank no longer mattered, for neighbors were now all equal: all of urban Japan joined or participated more intensively in required neighborhood societies, groups that became in effect a firewatch/bucket brigade for each block. Air raid practice became common, blackouts frequent. Entire rural districts were put on electric power rationing, with electricity generated only during the hours immediately after dark. Chemical fertilizer became rare, and Koreans living in Japan, who had long been regarded as second-class citizens, were pressed into farm labor forces.

In short, life was no fun. Many stage and film theaters were closed, and virtually the only movies shown were leftovers from the 1930s, which depicted the Chinese and Westerners in general as vicious beasts. Even book printing was curtailed. The only available literature was the current propaganda, which demonstrated how Japan was winning the conflict with the clever strategy of drawing the Americans close to the home islands before defeating them. Though not all truly believed the official line, most probably wanted to believe it and therefore accepted the deception and its correspondent calls for greater endurance and effort.

Tokyo Rose and Japanese Wartime Propaganda

Just before the conflict broke out, a young lady from California arrived in Japan to visit a sick aunt. A graduate of UCLA with a degree in zoology, on

Pearl Harbor Day she became an enemy alien. Iva Ikuko Toguri avoided being sent to a detention camp by volunteering to do English-language broadcasts for the Japanese. At first she was identified simply as "Tokyo Ann," as in *ann*ouncer, and she frequently simply identified herself as "Orphan Annie, your favorite enemy," but her eventual favorite nickname became simply Tokyo Rose. She had a silky, bedroom-like voice and for a salary of $6.60 a month, she broadcast nightly.

The propaganda she disseminated was obvious. Indeed, she even panned her own material on occasion. The remainder of Tokyo's radio broadcasting personnel was not as effective, but did include captured United States Navy and Army officers who broadcast rather obnoxious propaganda to their colleagues still in the service of their country. Tokyo Rose alone, however, was widely listened to by United States Navy and Marine personnel, in part because she always seemed to have an adequate supply of Glenn Miller recordings, probably obtained via one of the neutral embassies in Tokyo. Every evening a Japanese colonel, whose name is lost to history, spoke after her program was over. To the last day of the conflict he sought to disabuse his unseen American audience of the notion that the United States was winning the war.

To oversee the nation's radio grid, the *kempeitei* set up a special monitoring facility in Tokyo. Every station in the country was monitored day and night, with the police ready to arrest any announcer who even hinted that all was not well. In truth, an arrest was never made, and the entire effort proved unnecessary in the end. A great majority of the Japanese unquestioningly and dutifully believed the official government line. Though the sentiment was not universal, by war's end many Japanese were questioning the policy of national self-sacrifice. Some were even criticizing the military and political leaders, though in a muted fashion. Most Japanese, however, were shocked when the emperor spoke over the radio in August 1945 and revealed the truth to his subjects.

Hard though it was, life in the home islands remained tolerable until the night of March 9–10, 1945. On that evening a flight of over 300 American B-29 bombers began the first and probably most successful fire bombing in the Asiatic theater of the conflict. (See Chapter 10 for a discussion of American bombing strategy.) Maj. Gen. Curtis LeMay's B-29 bombers, employing incendiary bombs and aided by gale-force winds at ground level, reduced the sixteen-square-mile Shitamachi district of Tokyo to ashes in a conflagration that burned for four days.

Life for the emperor's conquered subjects in the empire outside of the home islands was another matter. The Greater East Asia Co-Prosperity Sphere was quickly and quietly dubbed the "Co-Poverty Sphere" by the emperor's newly conquered subjects. Certainly, it quickly became just that. The Bank of Japan did not hesitate to print money on an "as needed" basis, and the result of this was chronic inflation. China in particular was never treated with even an outward semblance of decency. On the basis of Tojo's radio pronouncements in particular, it remains unclear if Tokyo ever considered China part of the Prosperity Sphere. Korea fared very poorly, receiving treatment unequaled among the conquered nations in its inhumanity. Korean men were drafted into the Imperial Army and Navy to perform menial labor. Korean women were recruited to serve as the nucleus of Comfort Battalions, which "serviced" troops in the field in the sexual sense. After taking them prisoners, the Americans set these "comfort women" to work as practical nurses, a task at which they proved excellent.

Tokyo's Asian puppets felt increasingly ridiculous as the war progressed. Henry Pu-Yi, once the child emperor of China, ruled Manchuko for the Japanese. He became increasingly subservient to the Japanese Kwantung Army, which administered his domains with an absolute hand, engaging in hideous atrocities against the Chinese populace openly and on an unbelievably wide scale. Soldiers raped thousands of Chinese women publicly, sometimes literally in the street. Young Chinese were occasionally used for live bayonet practice. Wang Ching-wei, a Koumintang turncoat who became ruler of a portion of the remainder of China in 1940, also found his authority greatly eroded by the army. He remained but a puppet, while the army brutalized his supposed subjects.

Even in Burma, the most cooperative of Japanese possessions, the originally tiny Burmese Independence Army, which resisted the domination of the Japanese just as they had resisted the British before, swelled in size as Japanese oppression increased. The Japanese, who had promised almost immediate independence to the Burmese, increasingly treated Premier Ba Maw, a fervent collaborationist, as an inferior. While the northern portion of the country initially had been relatively free of Japanese occupation troops, before long the Japanese had to extend their occupation to the entire country.

Indonesia, which had also at first welcomed the Japanese, was oppressed by the army as early as March 1942, when the right of political protest was severely curtailed through a series of crudely worded military proclamations. Nationalists like Achmed Sukarno were put under police surveillance. The Japanese army divided Indonesia into three occupation zones, and study of the Japanese language, even the singing of the Japanese national anthem, became mandatory. None of this endeared the Japanese to the Indonesians. As in all the other Japanese possessions, there was a relatively small but highly effective civilian resistance movement in operation long before 1945.

Japan Prepares for Invasion

By the summer of 1945 the Japanese braced themselves for the first invasion wave of Americans, which they expected momentarily. All prepared
for what would be the supreme test of Japanese morale: resistance to the
Allies. The Japanese organized a national guard-like force of 27 million
civilians, most of whom were armed with the basic weapons for members
of this force—sharpened bamboo spears. Men and women alike were issued rifles when possible, and children were shown diagrams of American
tanks and instructed where to place (and hold) a grenade in order to destroy one. Trenches were dug around each maritime or coastal village. The
ministries of War and Navy were partially evacuated from Tokyo to rural
areas. The many caves that are spread throughout Japan's four home islands were stockpiled with provisions and made into improvised fortresses.
It was in two such cave complexes that the sections of the two ministries
removed from Tokyo were relocated.

Civilians were prepared for the worst. One extremist even proposed that
elderly people, women, and children be eliminated in advance to conserve
the remaining food supplies, but the army rejected this suggestion as overly
zealous. When one civilian reportedly asked the military what they would
do if the Americans did not invade the country but simply left the Japanese
to starve and burn, he drew the interesting reply, "We'll really be in a fix
then." The slogan "One hundred million die together," abbreviated *ichioku*,
became the new national wartime slogan by midsummer 1945. (This betrayed the Japanese official belief that 100 million people now inhabited
the home islands: this was, however, only a target figure. As far as we
know, the home islands comprised 79 million inhabitants.) Military circles
called for the "Yamato Spirit" from the population and swore to die as one
rather than submit.

The kamikaze corps (see the previous chapter) prepared for its most he-
roic effort. Virtually every young man of eligible age in the nation had his
name inscribed on a basic recruitment roster. The Japanese had prepared
kamikaze planes with portions of their fuselages manufactured of silk, to
conserve metal. Planes and fields, with supplies of gasoline secured nearby,
were later found during the American occupation that had been completely
unknown to the Allies earlier. The kamikaze boat squadrons also prepared
for their first substantial action. The same was true for the suicide torpedoes
(*kaiten*): long-lance torpedoes were adapted to be driven into their targets by
a human operator. And underwater frogmen (*fukuryu*) were recruited for suicide missions against American vessels, especially landing craft.

Finally, the Japanese attempted to intensify an effort already under way to bring the war to the North America mainland. Operation Flying Elephant had begun on November 3, 1944 (the emperor Meiji's birthday), reportedly from the slopes of Mount Fuji. Flying Elephant was meant to avenge Doolittle's unexpected bombing of Tokyo in April 1942. Large hydrogen-filled balloons, thirty-two feet in diameter, were put into the air with the hope that they would drift eastward in the jet stream. They carried both incendiary and antipersonnel charges. They were, for their day, sophisticated weapons. There was some talk in Japan of using them to carry pathogenic bacteria to the North American continent, but this was never done. Conversely, the worst fear in the United States seems to have been that they would be used to carry a saboteur to this country, particularly if the Japanese developed large prototypes. The balloons were released, roughly along the fortieth degree of northern latitude, and were meant for the American Pacific Northwest, where it was reasoned that they would come to earth before encountering the Rocky Mountains. They would take two days to reach North America. Some 9,300 balloons were so released, the last in early August 1945. Civilians were pressed into service to construct the paper balloons in theaters no longer open to the public because of the war.

No one was sure of the results achieved. The facilities that had manufactured the balloons had been largely burned down by late spring 1945, but many were in storage and had survived. The results in the United States were mixed. Some brush fires were undoubtedly started. A total of 285 balloons were found in the United States, or otherwise known to have arrived. The actual number that arrived will never be known. Balloons were found as far north as Alaska, as far south as Mexico, and as far east as Michigan. Six people were killed by one explosion in Oregon. The American atomic bomb project was briefly interrupted when one of the balloons caused a power outage at the atomic energy plant at Hanford, Washington. As late as the 1960s an unexploded balloon was found in Alaska. A 1973 U.S. government pamphlet warns that hundreds are probably still to be discovered and remain dangerous.

Operation Sunset was the essential American response. A series of special radar stations were established to detect incoming balloons. In addition, the Army Air Corps from the Aleutians to Los Angeles was kept busy searching for and destroying the devices. The results achieved by the balloons were obviously poor, but the Japanese did not know until the 1970s, when a U.S. government pamphlet described their effort, that they had been moderately successful in some respects.

In the far reaches of what remained of the empire, Japanese subjects were safe from the Allies concentrated attacks on the home islands, but local populations fell under increasing exploitation and outright brutality as the end of the conflict obviously approached. What was in effect slave labor began, and the army everywhere enrolled so-called volunteers to build emplacements and fortifications. Japanese promises of independence now seemed ridiculous. (A general grant of independence had been given to almost the entire empire in mid-1943.) The closer the Allies came to a particular conquered area, the more brutal the Japanese army, the almost exclusive occupation authority, became. One of the most egregious examples of this occurred in the Philippines, where hundreds of thousands of Filipinos were killed in the name of guerilla suppression. Rarely were these mass murders confined to the male population of fighting age. Women, children, and the elderly were often killed alongside soldiers and other suspected Allied sympathizers.

Even by its own standards, the army practiced brutality on its enlisted personnel. Corporal punishment was common. Striking of enlisted men was actually encouraged in the course of maintaining discipline. The number of deaths in basic training, usually held in Manchuria, grew, and as the army found itself frustrated by defeat, it literally devoured its own. In the Philippines, garrisons on bypassed islands, reduced to starvation, sometimes resorted to cannibalism of the least fit garrison soldiers. The worst examples of Japanese brutality, however, probably occurred in China.

The Japanese Kwantung Army became a replica of the local Chinese warlords whom it had never quite managed to exterminate. Chinese laborers were maltreated to such an extent that they survived only a very few days. One notorious facility, Camp 731, located north of Mukden at Pingfan, engaged in large-scale medical experiments, sometimes on American personnel. Tests were performed to establish human endurance to such extremes as cold, frostbite, and blood loss. Surgical experiments were conducted to study human resistance to severe trauma and resultant infection. And inevitably, since American POWs were involved, there were tests made to compare Caucasian and Asiatic reactions to extremes of disease and climate.

Worse, the camp authorities, under Lt. Gen. Ishii Shiro for most of the conflict, engaged in chemical and bacteriological warfare against the Chinese, spreading bubonic plague behind Chiang Kai-shek's lines. Ishii and his colleagues also experimented with anthrax, typhoid, typhus, and other diseases as methods of warfare. The Chungking regime complained of Japanese biological warfare to both Washington and London, but Chiang's claims went unbelieved at the time. After the conflict, however, American authorities carefully debriefed some of Camp 731's personnel and verified the nature of their experiments and work. Small wonder that the

A Japanese *maru*, or freighter, heels to starboard on her way to the bottom after being attacked by the American submarine *Guardship* on September 4, 1942. This photo was taken through a periscope. (*United States Navy*)

Japanese made efforts at the end of the war to eradicate Camp 731 physically. These attempts were unsuccessful. Like the Germans, the Japanese discovered that death camps could not readily be made to disappear without a trace.

When the Soviets entered the war in August 1945 and promptly invaded Manchuria, the Japanese officers of the Kwantung Army fled in cowardice and terror. Ranking officers commandeered trains, which left enlisted men to the unenviable fate of becoming Soviet prisoners of war. Everywhere the army left behind hordes of executed civilians as defeat approached. The Imperial Army betrayed its own honor. After the surrender, the only factor preventing local war crime trials from enacting a greater number of indictments was the fact that Japanese troops were needed to preserve order until legitimate governments could be reestablished.

In the end, survival became the solitary goal of the inhabitants of Japan's empire, both on the home islands and elsewhere. From the euphoria of the first six months of the conflict, Japan was now on the verge of an Allied invasion. Fittingly, had the Japanese known it, the Pentagon plan for the invasion was code-named Downfall. It envisioned a conflict that would last at least until the fall of 1946, and might entail as many as 1 million Allied (not solely American) combat deaths. This does not seem an unreasonable estimate. Invasion of the home islands would have brought about a slaughter unprecedented in all of human history. The civilian population as well as the military would have resisted to the last, using the caves that honeycomb the home islands. Little of Japanese society would have survived, and the Japanese battle deaths and civilian casualties would have been enormous. The army's slogan, "One Hundred Million Die Together," suggests the Japanese mind-set in the late summer of 1945. It seemed that only a miracle could prevent the invasion from taking place. Washington named Douglas MacArthur to command it. Had he done so, his reputation in postwar Japan would certainly not have been as positive as it turned out to be.

Early in the conflict the American military and civilian establishment had been eager to gain Russian participation in the eventual invasion of the home islands. The Americans expected a costly invasion and the Soviets apparent lack of concern about casualties made them an attractive ally. President Roosevelt obtained a definite pledge in February 1945 at Yalta that the Soviet Union would enter the war several months after Germany surrendered, in return for which he promised the Kremlin numerous Japanese possessions, from the northern portion of Korea, to the Kurile Islands, to the Japanese portion of Sakhalin. Critics have contended that this was unnecessary largesse, in part because the atomic bomb would soon render

An Oakland, California, newsstand, February 27, 1942. (*American History Slide Collection, Instructional Resources Corporation*)

the Japanese defenseless, and in part because the Soviets would probably have desired to participate in the war against the Japanese in any event, once Germany was defeated.

There is a degree of truth in these arguments, but it is the logic of twenty-twenty hindsight that motivates Roosevelt's critics. No one could have been sure that the atomic bomb would function, since it had not yet been tested when Roosevelt made the promise. Further, a test date had not yet been projected. And, as will be seen, when the atomic devices were used, they did not compel Japanese surrender. Doubtless, the Soviets would have participated in the conflict, but one may argue that Roosevelt simply wished to codify or formalize their gains. The Soviets were not promised any portion of the home islands, and finally, their participation in the conflict did compel the prompt surrender of the Japanese, which saved many American lives.

Invasion would have meant an incalculable number of Japanese deaths. It would have entailed house-to-house fighting, with tremendous civilian casualties. The effect on the American personnel participating in such a conquest would have been severe. There were even those in Washington who urged that chemical weapons be used against the population of the home islands, but there is no evidence that such suggestions were seriously considered.

Japanese Americans in the United States

Americans of Japanese ancestry living in the United States fared far better than the Japanese in Japan, but life was not what it might have been for many of them. Though long accustomed to being treated as second-class citizens, and though they endured nothing compared with the Japanese in Japan as the war neared its end, life quickly turned unpleasant after Pearl Harbor. There had been much talk on the West Coast, and even in Hawaii, the most tolerant of American possessions, of a Japanese "fifth column" that was waiting to betray the United States and open the country—particularly the coastal portions of the West—to a supposed Japanese invasion.

On Pearl Harbor Day, 127,000 Americans of Japanese ancestry lived in mainland America, with over 112,000 in the Pacific seaboard states of California, Washington, and Oregon. Soon after Pearl Harbor, rumor had it that many Issei (first-genereation Japanese) had purposely settled near vital defense installations, especially in California. Feelings ran so high that many Chinese Americans literally put makeshift cardboard signs around their necks proclaiming their nationality in order to protect themselves against open racial discrimination and even beatings. And in Hawaii, Buddhist temples and Shinto shrines were closed for the duration of the conflict. Canada, together with Mexico and many other U.S. friends south of the border promptly gave in to pressure from the U.S. State Department to relocate their Japanese populations. It is hard to imagine what danger the two Japanese living in Paraguay posed to that nation's vital interests, but they were nonetheless promptly interned. The one nation that might have had something of a case against the Japanese, Chile, where the Japanese ambassador bullied the government during the first six months of the war, intimating that a Japanese fleet was just over the horizon—did nothing against its miniscule Japanese population.

Several Latin American countries literally sent their entire Japanese populations to the United States: Peru was especially craven in this respect. In the United States itself, and particularly in California, pressure was intense to intern Japanese. Some of the concern was doubtless sincere, such as that of Earl Warren, then California's attorney general, who evidently believed that some Americans of Japanese ancestry posed a danger to the national interest. Warren later recanted his statements in his memoirs and regretted them and their consequences for the rest of his life. Others, including local commerce groups, made their case so vehemently and with such unction that their greed for the land owned by Americans of Japanese ancestry was glaringly evident.

In this case, culpability must be apportioned throughout the American government to its highest levels. Indeed, even Franklin D. Roosevelt must share some of the blame as he was complicit in ordering the evacuation to what he referred to as "concentration camps." Roosevelt's issuance of Executive Order 9066 in the spring and summer of 1942 authorized the roundup and internment of all persons of Japanese descent, regardless of status or citizenship. A War Relocation Authority (WRA) was established, headed for its first three months by Milton Eisenhower, brother of the future president. The WRA relocated approximately 110,000 Americans of Japanese ancestry, 70,000 of who were American citizens by virtue of birth in this country (naturalization of Japanese had not been permitted since 1790). In general, the victims of the authority had two weeks to sell their belongings, since they were allowed to take with them only what they could carry. Selling of land and possessions was not compulsory (one could simply "abandon" them), but many did sell land to speculators. Those who did not usually had friends who promised to look after their property. Nonetheless, many of those who did not sell returned home after the war to discover that their property had been vandalized.

The people to be relocated were tagged like cattle, due to a common stereotype that claimed all "orientals" looked alike. Initially, the internees were moved to mass staging areas, like the Santa Anita racetrack, where they were housed in temporary facilities, including horse stalls. They were

Americans of Japanese ancestry on their way to relocation camp. (*American History Slide Collection, Instructional Resources Corporation*)

later moved into tar-paper barracks at permanent sites, most without individual sanitary facilities. There were ten official relocation centers, the furthest east was in Arkansas, in addition to numerous temporary staging centers. The smallest relocation or internment center housed 7,000, the largest 20,000. A few internees became so embittered that they asked to be repatriated to Japan, going so far as to renounce their American citizenship. Some, including numerous college students, were able to leave the centers on "indefinite leave" status. Many others would be temporarily released to harvest farm crops. All were held in overcrowded conditions, however, that were several times worse than was permitted by law in federal penitentiaries. Compared to the treatment meted out to American POWs and civilians in Japan, the Japanese Americans made out fairly well. But the United States was a democracy, with the majority of those affected being U.S. citizens, and U.S. law should have prevented the internment in the first place. There was talk as well of interning aliens of German and Italian ancestry, but this never took place with the exception of a few "enemy aliens." Such an operation would have entailed the internment of quite a large number of citizens indeed.

In Japan, the general population was well aware of America's interment policy. The Japanese people were then and are now probably the most voracious newspaper readers in the world, and their press frequently reprinted excerpts from neutral papers that told of the interment. The Japanese government protested via neutral governments—particularly those of Spain and Switzerland—to no avail. It was particularly incensed when the entire Japanese population of Panama was arrested on Pearl Harbor Day and treated in a very inhumane manner.

Worst was the Tule Lake episode. In Tule Lake, in northernmost California, a camp was established for what became the most recalcitrant internees. Among them were those who had stated they would like to be repatriated to Japan as well as those who failed a federally ordered loyalty test for persons of Japanese descent. The camp was a 2,900-acre truck farming operation that provided produce for the U.S. military. The local population learned only by rumor of what was happening within the camp. They were quite naturally disturbed about having such a facility in the area. After some serious rioting in November 1943, the army moved in, doubtless an overreaction. For a week or two newspapers on the West Coast wrote of Tule Lake more than of the war in either theater of conflict.

News quickly reached Tokyo. The State Department had been in communication with the Japanese government, largely via the Spanish government, concerning the exchange of 6,000 sick or disabled American POWs in Japan for Japanese who wished to return to their homeland. There had been two prior successful exchanges involving several thousand civilians. Negotiations for a third, to consist largely of POWs, stalled after the army arrived at Tule Lake, and were never successfully resumed. Perhaps they would never have succeeded. (After the war, lawyers in California successfully argued that many of those requesting transport to Japan had done so under duress and therefore should have their citizenship reinstated.) But the Japanese, who scarcely needed any incitement to mistreat POWs, reacted to the United States Army's arrival at Tule Lake by further abusing American prisoners, sometimes telling their victims that their torture was in response to the doings at the internment camp.

The last of the interment camps was not closed until the end of 1946. Remarkably, a few elderly Japanese did not want to leave the camps and actually had to be removed by force! Having disposed of their property and possessions, and fearing further discrimination, older persons requested to stay in the internment facilities and be maintained at federal government expense. This was refused. Japanese internees had also been held at other facilities, nationwide, including Ellis Island in New York harbor. So far as is known, all were released by the end of 1946.

Civil liberties are frequently curtailed in wartime, but not until 1988 did Congress and the White House apologize for this breach of civil liberties and make payment of $20,000 to each surviving internee. And, again, however cold the comfort, it was likely better than the treatment Americans of Japanese ancestry would have received had they been returned to Japan. Still, the entire internment procedure was part of an interracial war, and as such, comprises one of the most regrettable episodes on the entire conflict.

The average Japanese knew nothing of the mistreatment of American POWs during the war, nor the atrocities committed in China, until the late 1970s, when the Japanese press aired such subjects for the first time. During the conflict the Japanese faithfully accepted whatever the official propaganda line was. But no words could allay the fear that gripped the population of the home islands by the summer of 1945. An American invasion was expected imminently. Indeed, a fear gripped the Japanese such as was felt probably only by the Carthaginians at the approach of the Roman army. All Japan prepared for the worst as the summer of 1945 waned.

Suggestions for Further Reading

Clay Blair, *Silent Victory* (New York: Lippincott, 1975) is the best account so far of the American effort against Japan, but it must be supplemented by Ronald Lewin, *The American Magic: Codes, Ciphers, and the Defeat of Japan* (New York: Farrar Straus Giroux, 1982); and John Prados, *Combined Fleet Decoded: The Secret History of American Intelligence and the*

Japanese Navy in World War II (Annapolis, MD: Naval Institute Press, 1995). Richard O' Kane's story is the best told in his own book, *Clear the Bridge! The War Patrols of the U.S.S. Tang* (Novato, CA: Presidio Press, 1989). The most useful account of the Japanese submarine effort, outdated but not supplanted, is Mochitsura Hashimoto, *Sunk! The Story of the Japanese Submarine Fleet, 1941–1945* (New York: Holt, 1954); an individual Japanese account is provided by Zenji Orita, *I-Boat Captain* (Canoga Park, CA: Major Books, 1976). A first-rate reference book for both American and Japanese submarines is Erminio Bagnasco, *Submarines of World War Two* (Annapolis, MD: Naval Institute Press, 1977). Joseph Enright, *Shinanao!* (New York: St. Martin's Press, 1987) recounts well the sinking of that ship. Information pertaining to life in wartime Japan may be found in Thomas Havens, *Valley of Darkness: The Japanese People and World War Two* (New York: Pantheon Books, 1978); Haruko Taya Cook and Theodore Cook, *Japan at War: An Oral History* (New York: The New Press, 1993); Hoito Edoin, *The Night Tokyo Burned: The Incendiary Campaign Against Japan, March–August 1945* (New York: St. Martin's Press, 1987); and Tessa Morris Suzuki, *Showa: An Inside History of Hirohito's Japan* (New York: Schocken Books, 1985). By far the best study dealing with the interracial nature of the conflict is John Dower's seminal work, *War Without Mercy: Race and Power in the Pacific War* (New York: Pantheon Books, 1986). *Japan's Greater East Asia Co-Prosperity Sphere in World War Two: Selected Readings and Documents*, ed. Joyce V. Lebra (New York: Oxford University Press, 1975); and Grant K. Goodman, ed., *Japanese Cultural Policies in Southeast Asia During World War Two* (New York: St Martin's Press, 1991) provide some positive information on the topic. The plight of the comfort women has been brought to light in the past decade in studies like Yoshimi Yoshiaki, *Comfort Women: Sexual Slavery in the Japanese Military During World War II* (New York: Columbia University Press, 1995); George Hicks, *The Comfort Women: Japan's Brutal Regime of Enforced Prostitution in the Second World War* (New York: W.W. Norton, 1997); and Nora Okja Keller, *Comfort Woman* (New York: Penguin, 1998). The only biographical study of Tokyo Rose in English is Masayo Duus, *Tokyo Rose: Orphan of the Pacific* (New York: Kodansha, 1978). Ryuji Nagatsuka, *I Was a Kamakaze* (London: Schuman, 1972) has some interesting comments on the subject. The materials on Operation Flying Elephant are drawn primarily from Robert C. Mikesh, *Japan's World War II Balloon Bomb Attacks on North America* (Washington, DC: Smithsonian Institution Press, 1973), but see also Bert Webber, *Retaliation: Japanese Attacks and Allied Countermeasures on the Pacific Coast in World War II* (Corvallis: Oregon State University Press, 1975). The latest work on Japanese chemical and biological warfare is Sheldon H. Harris, *Factories of Death: Japanese Biological Warfare, 1932–1945, and the American Cover-up* (New York: Routledge, 2002), though it should be used with caution and should be supplemented with Peter Williams and David Wallace, *Unit 731: Japan's Secret Biological Warfare in World War Two* (New York: Macmillan, 1989). The most informative studies of Japanese internment in this country during the war include U.S. Commission on Wartime Relocation and Internment of Civilians, *Personal Justice Denied* (Washington, DC: Government Printing Office, 1982); Dillon S. Meyer, *Uprooted Americans* (Tucson: University of Arizona Press, 1971); Morton Grodzins, *Americans Betrayed* (Chicago: University of Chicago Press, 1949); and Michi Weglyn, *Years of Infamy* (New York: William Morrow, 1976), although the last must be used with some caution. A great number of studies have come out on this topic in the past decade as well, including Donna Nagata, *Legacy of Injustice: Exploring the Cross Generational Impact of the Japanese American Internment* (New York: Plenum Press, 1993); Sandra Taylor, *Jewel of the Desert: Japanese American Internment at Topaz* (Los Angeles: University of California Press, 1993); Page Smith, *Democracy on Trial: The Japanese American Evacuation and Internment of Civilians* (New York: Simon & Schuster, 1995); *Personal Justice Denied: Report of the Commission on Wartime Relocation and Internment of Civilians* (Seattle: University of Washington Press, 1997); Greg Robinson, *By Order of the President: FDR and the Internment of Japanese Americans* (Cambridge, MA: Harvard University Press, 2001). Scott P. Corbett, *Quiet Passages: The Exchanges of Civilians Between the United States and Japan During the Second World War* (Kent, OH: Kent State University Press, 1987) details a little known facet of the conflict.

9

The China–Burma–India Theater

China, Burma, and India constituted what was known as the CBI theater of the conflict. It was under a unified Allied command for most of the war. Allied veterans who participated in campaigns there consider that they have long been ignored. In truth, their real complaint may be that fighting in the CBI theater was not decisive in defeating the Japanese. The theater was at the end of the longest supply line in the world. It was constantly undersupplied in comparison with every other theater of the conflict. And it never received its fair share of publicity or attention in either the American or British press. The CBI theater was the backwater area of Allied operations and was to the main area of the Pacific what the Italian campaign was to the Allied effort against Germany—an interesting but ultimately indecisive sideshow.

But secondary though the CBI theater may have been, it possessed its own intrinsic importance. The areas involved were vast. Many were very densely populated. And, as will be seen, the political makeup of the region today largely derives from the Japanese conquest and its political consequences.

China

President Roosevelt took a special interest in the China theater, as did the Luce publications, *Time* and *Life*. Henry Luce, editor in chief of these two magazines, had been born in China of missionary parents. He therefore displayed a natural interest in things Chinese. In Roosevelt's case, the interest stemmed from familial connections with that nation. His mother's family, the Delanos, had made their fortune during the nineteenth century in the China trade, including, so it appears, opium. Roosevelt in particular hoped that China would be a great democratic power, or at least presence, in the postwar world. In this he would encounter considerable opposition from the British. In fact, Prime Minister Winston Churchill had an opposite view, believing that China would not be a power for many decades to come; indeed, Churchill held a decidedly nineteenth-century Victorian view of the matter and thought the Chinese would not be capable of effective self-government without, at the very least, substantial advice from the occidental powers until after the conflict.

China had been ruled by the Manchu dynasty until 1911, when a republican revolution forced the abdication of the last emperor, the boy Henry Pu-yi. Sun Yat-sen, widely regarded as the father of the revolution, was not in China when the revolution toppled Pu-yi from his throne. Traveling in the United States to raise money for the revolutionary cause in the various Chinatown areas on the West Coast, Sun was caught by surprise in Denver when the revolution occurred. After hurrying home, he was soon elected president of the Chinese republic, but there were always those who contested his claim to power. Indeed, he never headed a regime in Peking, which would almost certainly have brought him diplomatic recognition as head of government by the Western powers. And Sun himself seemed to oscillate between periods of dreamy idealism and ones of hard-headed political realism. His party was the *Kuomintang*, the Nationalist party, which aimed at modernizing China.

Sun died suddenly of cancer in 1925. His heir apparent was Chiang Kai-shek, who had been working with the Soviets to reform the Chinese military, although Chiang himself never embraced Marxist ideology. He had founded the Whampoa Military Academy, China's first substantial attempt to emulate West Point. A man of humble origins, Chiang was adept at accumulating personal power. He did not hesitate to employ his cadets and academy graduates to strengthen his political position. Everywhere he consolidated his power, even marrying to further his ambitions. In 1927 he wed the wealthy Soong Mei-ling, who belonged to a Shanghai family that had converted to Christianity. Chiang's own conversion to that religion, which was basically sincere, increased his standing as a reputable head of state in the eyes of the Western powers.

Mei-ling, one of three quite ambitious sisters, had gone to both high school and college in the United States. Some Westerners in Shanghai, within the international settlement in that city, referred to her contemptuously as a "banana," a Chinese who was Westernized—still yellow in skin tone but white on the inside. This was unfair. Mei-ling was a patriotic Chinese, although on occasion she did not hesitate to put her own fortunes first and those of China a distant second. She was perfectly fluent in English, was widely idealized in the American press, and appeared on the cover of *Time* magazine several times in the 1930s and 1940s.

Chiang married Mei-ling for her wealth as well as her Christianity. He had been married twice before and his two sons were products of these prior unions. Mei-ling could not bear her husband another child, a fact that, she claimed, ultimately led to an all-but-open dissolution of their marriage by late 1944.

Chiang never had a proper chance to implement his plans for reform. In 1937, after the Marco Polo Bridge incident, Chiang was even more openly at war with the Japanese as they invaded additional portions of his country. Chiang was forced to borrow money abroad, although he did not hesitate to manipulate the exchange rate of the Chinese currency to enrich his family's coffers.

Chiang's second greatest problem, after the Japanese, was the Chinese Communist party, under Mao Tse-tung. At first the Communists' power base had been in the south. But in the famous "Long March," Mao set out in November 1934 for north China. He began with 85,000 followers. His own brother died during the march, and Mao had abandoned two of his own infants before it began. In the course of 235 days he moved his men 6,600 miles. Averaging seventeen miles per day, crossing eighteen mountain ranges and twenty-four major rivers, the Communists marched across eleven Chinese provinces, almost every inch of the way contested, all on foot! Mao established himself near the relatively (by Chinese standards) prosperous northern town of Yennan, within Shensi province, although only about 8,000 men survived the march. Mao then began a vigorous campaign effort for recruits to the Communist cause, spreading his own brand of rural Communist ideology.

Chiang was ever Mao's bitterest enemy, although Mao and his guerillas proved a burden to the Japanese as well. On very rare occasions Chinese troops actually cooperated with the Japanese when Mao was their common enemy. As Mao's power increased and the area of Japanese rule expanded, rural China fell more and more into the hands of bandit chiefs, who formed a local second government. Even within the international settlement in Shanghai, gangs terrorized Chinese merchants at night, forcing them to pay tribute or protection money. Chiang himself even took to collecting taxes years in advance, evidently to help finance his campaigns against the bandits, Communists, and Japanese. Thus, by 1941 Chiang had his hands full. He was understandably relieved when he learned of the Japanese attack on Pearl Harbor.

On Pearl Harbor Day Chiang realized that the United States would indeed eventually defeat the Japanese. He determined to make no further substantial effort to oust the Japanese from his country. The various local Chinese military commanders were ordered to cease all but the most minimal resistance

Chiang Kai-shek, Madame Chiang, and General Stilwell, April 1942. *(United States Army)*

to the Japanese. In effect, something of an unofficial truce with the Japanese was cemented in some areas. The Japanese in particular did not hesitate to violate these truces around harvest time, when they would engage in "rice raids" to pillage the local rice crops. They were thus able to gain foodstuffs for their own army, while denying them to the Chinese. Nonetheless, for two years there was almost no formal fighting between Chinese and Japanese troops in China.

This obviously disturbed the United States. China received Lend Lease supplies after Pearl Harbor, as well as numerous loans. Roosevelt was determined to see that the material and money sent to China were not squandered, although he enjoyed almost no knowledge of conditions in China, either political or military. Consequently, in March 1942 Gen. Joseph Stilwell arrived in Chiang's capital, Chungking, to serve as chief of staff to the Chinese army. In effect he was second in command, second only to Generalissimo Chiang himself. Stilwell was fluent in Chinese, having had prior military service in China.

Not only did Stilwell know China well, he was on very good terms with Chief of Staff George Marshall in Washington, and reputedly the only officer who regularly addressed Marshall by his first name. So far, so good. But Stilwell had a sarcastic nature, which was evident well before his advent in China. Indeed, he had long been known by the nickname "Vinegar Joe," and he evidently relished his reputation as a cynic. An energetic worker, he was intolerant of lassitude, corruption, or simple complacency in high places, which meant that he was inevitably bound to become a fervent critic of Chiang. After several weeks at his new assignment, Stilwell had already undertaken some very basic, sorely needed reforms of the Chinese army, which were to win him the almost universal respect of its officers and enlisted men alike. But Stilwell soon engaged in his penchant for sarcasm: he code-named Chiang "peanut," and Chiang almost surely knew about this. On one or two occasions of extreme impatience, in a tasteless parody of Roosevelt's infirmity (the president was confined to a wheelchair), Stilwell referred to his commander in chief as "Rubberlegs." Stilwell had scarcely arrived in China when Chiang began a campaign to have him relieved, working partially through his ambassador to Washington. But largely because of the support of General Marshall, Stilwell remained, for the moment, at his post.

Chiang had an ally in his attempts to relieve Stilwell in the person of Maj. Gen. Claire Chennault, a rather maverick Army Air Corps general who had arrived long before Pearl Harbor to command the Chinese air force. Even then, Chennault had mainly American flyers under his command. He was a tactical genius. The first American general to see the Japanese Zero fighter plane in action during the year 1940, he wrote Washington of its potential and enclosed something like blueprints for construction of an aircraft to combat it effectively, but was unfortunately ignored. General Marshall in particular had little use for Chennault, and not without some justification. Marshall frequently, and quite correctly, referred to Chennault as nothing but a "paid agent" of Chiang. Chennault accepted very large sums either as pay or as outright gifts from Chiang. Further, when Chennault's Americans actually entered into combat against the Japanese after Pearl, they required very large pay incentives, sometimes even to take to the air. Money seemed to be the cement that held Chennault's group of flyers together.

To be sure, there was precious little else to attract American flyers to China, except the promise of adventure itself. In the mid-1930s, the Italians had been in charge of the Chinese air force. Chennault had taken over after they left and inherited many problems they had created. First, the Italians had graduated as pilots almost every candidate who applied for flight school, regardless of vision, aptitude, and the like. Second, when the Italians left, they took all the aerial maps of China with them. Thus, Chennault had to begin at square one by establishing a basic cartography operation, which, given China's vastness, was not always as successful as he and his flyers would have liked.

Chennault's flyers adopted the name "Flying Tigers," and they were greatly romanticized in the American press. Chennault was naturally a firm believer in air power. Although virtually blind in one eye, he became an ace; eventually he accounted for no small number of downed Japanese aircraft. His importance became all the greater after February 1942, when the Burma Road from Lashio in Burma to Kunming in China, the only support route left into China, was permanently closed because of the Japanese conquest of Burma. Supplies now had to be flown from northwestern India into China. Because of a Japanese air base at Myitkyina in northern Burma, this air route went over the eastern Himilayan Mountains, from India to Kunming in southern China, at an altitude of 21,000 feet. Known as "flying the hump," it was dangerous work indeed: anyone lost over the mountains could not be rescued.

Chennault's American airmen, who were allowed to down Japanese aircraft only after the attack on Pearl, suffered a major setback early in 1942 when they officially became part of the Army Air Corps as the Fourteenth Air Force. Put on normal combat pay and evidently denied further incentive pay, almost all of the original pilots quit as of July 4, 1942. (One who left for future adventures in the Solomon theater was Gregory Boyington, hero of a future television series.) Chennault had the unenviable task of having to train replacements rapidly. But Stilwell now demanded that greater emphasis be given the Tenth Air Force, under Brig. Gen. Clayton Bissell, which had charge of bringing in supplies flown over the hump as well as materials for the Chinese army, while Chennault, perhaps understandably, wished to transport, almost exclusively, supplies for his own aviation effort against the Japanese.

In response, Chennault, with Chiang's blessing and encouragement, began deluging Washington with position papers and, when possible, personal letters stating that air power alone could defeat the Japanese, at least in the Chinese theater of the conflict. This led to bitter disagreement between Chennault and Stilwell, the latter maintaining that Chennault's argument was put forward in part to ingratiate himself with Chiang. Stilwell also contended that Chennault carried not only supplies but also contraband in his aircraft, a charge that doubtless carried substantial truth, since bribery was then the mainstay of bureaucratic existence in China. Anyone who wished to work effectively with Chiang's government often found it useful, if not absolutely necessary. Stilwell was one of the few Westerners in China who probably did not resort to it.

Stilwell and Chennault spent their time in China locked in internecine conflict. Stilwell undoubtedly had by far the better grasp of the military realities of the situation, and he alone was fluent in Chinese. But Chiang sided automatically with Chennault, and from the first, Chennault did everything humanly possible to have Stilwell relieved. To say the very least, their situation was not American military cooperation at its best, but it was probably inherent in the circumstances in China, with its blatant, rampant corruption.

Chiang closeted himself in his chosen capital of Chungking and in effect began husbanding supplies for the civil war with the Communists, which he correctly predicted would begin the day the Japanese surrendered to the Americans. Washington, understandably, took a dim view of his attitude. American leadership also never accepted Chennault's contention that air power alone could defeat the Japanese. But every morning that Madame Chiang was in China, she sent a lengthy epistle to General Stilwell, filled with her husband's supposedly sage advice, espousing the virtues of "deep column tactics" as opposed to the "adventures" in which Stilwell hoped to engage against the Japanese. Stilwell did what he could with the 300-division Chinese army and organized the first effective medical service in that army's history.

The Japanese put a price on Stilwell's head. This Stilwell actually found advantageous. Whenever he ordered a front-line general in the Chinese army to advance and the order was disobeyed, Stilwell would simply appear at the recalcitrant general's headquarters. This would attract much Japanese sniper and patrol attention, evidently in the hope that they could literally cash in on the reward posted for his head. In turn, the Chinese general would usually be moved to some minimal military action, if only to get Stilwell out of his command area. It was a negative command method, but it did ensure some resistance to the Japanese, who otherwise moved more or less at will throughout the Chinese countryside.

Eighty-five percent of China's people lived in rural areas. The average amount of land farmed by each family was only one and one-seventh acres, and in some areas less. These peasants probably did not care who governed the nation, except that they opposed the Japanese occupation when their areas were effected. Stilwell perhaps understood their sentiments better than any of the leaders in Chungking. Whenever possible, he took care not to allow his military operations, maneuvers, and inspections to interfere with the peasants' crops, and there is some evidence that he knew how susceptible many of the peasants would be to Mao's particular brand of peasant communism.

Stilwell managed to piece together several divisions that could operate with artillery support (usually referred to as *Y* force, although this designation was not consistently used in Washington). But he never managed to engage the Japanese seriously, which was always Washington's advice.

Chiang remained aloof in Chungking, ignorant of the state of his armies. Stilwell routinely sent him reports on military matters, but these evidently went unread. On one occasion, when informed of the incompetence of one of his generals, Chiang turned his cane on the offending officer, apparently believing that a good public thrashing would restore competence. Chiang evidently had a shortsighted view of his ultimate command responsibilities and was not infrequently unaware of conditions *inside* his own capital.

Madame Chiang, as the American press usually dubbed her, visited the United States from November 1942 through May 1943, in part for medical treatment. She was greeted by an astonishing outpouring of public approbation and addressed capacity crowds in the Hollywood Bowl and Madison Square Garden. Behind the scenes, ensconced on the second floor of the White House, she behaved like spoiled, petulant royalty. As might have been expected, she sang Chennault's praises and castigated Stilwell. The joint chiefs were particularly alarmed by her visit, for she made it no secret that she thought America's "Europe first" decision an error that she intended to correct. Probably the highlight of the visit was her address to a joint session of Congress, but she made no headway in reversing the Europe first decision. Almost everyone in Washington breathed a sigh of relief when she departed.

Roosevelt kept an open attitude toward Chiang himself until the First Cairo Conference, held in November 1943. For the first time, Chiang was questioned personally about the state of his army, his plans concerning the Japanese, and his possible aid in ousting the Japanese from Burma, which had once been a Chinese tributary province. Chiang had been sent in advance numerous position papers, studies, and war plans by his allies, but if he actually received them, he did not read them. To Chiang, future military planning consisted, perhaps understandably, of ways and means to contain and defeat the Communist menace within his own country.

At Cairo, much to Churchill's annoyance, Roosevelt insisted that China be the first topic discussed by the participants. It was Chiang's curtain call, although he did not know this. When quizzed by the commander in chief for the Far East, British admiral Louis Mountbatten, about the state of his own armed forces, Chiang could not answer the most basic questions, much less give a detailed summary of his planned operations against the Japanese, since in fact he had none. Stilwell fielded most of Mountbatten's questions while Chiang watched with growing anger. Then Chiang revealed the depth of his own ignorance. The Allied leaders began a discussion of Buccaneer, a planned amphibious operation against Burma, later canceled partly for lack of landing craft. Someone made mention of the monsoon season. Madame Chiang, who had insisted on acting as her husband's interpreter, suddenly began a heated discussion with him in Chinese. After a decent interval, Mountbatten interrupted to ask what the discussion concerned. Madame Chiang informed Mountbatten that Chiang had never heard of the monsoon season and evidently refused to believe it really existed. There could have been no greater demonstration of Chiang's military ineptitude. He could not describe military conditions in his own army, much less anticipate what those conditions might be elsewhere.

Everyone left Cairo disillusioned with Chiang, who alone thought he had given a passable performance. Roosevelt reputedly wondered aloud if his government might not find a substitute for Chiang, although if he did have such thoughts, no action was taken, even though it was known in Washington that Madame Chiang's ambitious and very wealthy brother, T. V. Soong, wanted to replace Chiang. Thereafter Roosevelt was more susceptible to the views of his secretary of the treasury, Henry Morgenthau, who had previously warned the president that every loan in cash made to China ended up in Chiang's own foreign bank accounts or in those of his wife's family.

The Chinese continued to press for financial aid, arguing in what amounted to financial, diplomatic, and military blackmail that if China dropped out of the war, a million more Japanese troops would be free to fight the American troops engaged in the Pacific. Roosevelt and Morgenthau were evidently moved by this logic. They continued to pour money into the coffers of Chinese officialdom. The Luce publications in this country continued to extol Chiang and his wife as the saviors of China, but behind the scenes the federal government in Washington now had only contempt for a man who practiced blackmail on them. All told, Chiang received over $1.5 billion in American aid. If recently revealed FBI files are correct, over $1 billion of that amount was routed into personal bank accounts. Further, while China, including Manchuko (as Manchuria had been renamed), contained a million Japanese troops, many were raw recruits in training or were otherwise surprisingly inept. Witness that when the Soviets invaded Manchuko in 1945, they experienced only the most token opposition. Had Washington known the true quality of the Japanese military on the Asian mainland after Pearl Harbor, the United States might have been less inclined to tolerate Chiang's blackmail.

In October 1944, Roosevelt caved in to pressure applied by Chiang and announced General Stilwell's recall. As a sop to Stilwell, Roosevelt pointedly remarked to the press that a personality clash was involved and that basic military competence was not in question. Stilwell's successor, Maj. Gen. Albert Wedemeyer, did not have Stilwell's China background, but he was able to concentrate exclusively on China itself, without having to devote undue attention to the Burma problem that had long plagued Stilwell. But the Chinese army had been at its peak under Stilwell. His loss was a blow from which it did not recover.

At almost the same moment as Stilwell's recall, a new American ambassador arrived in Chungking: Gen. Patrick Hurley blundered into the post without prior knowledge of the Orient. Soon code-named "albatross" by the Office of Strategic Services (OSS), Hurley addressed Chiang as "Mr. Shek." On occasion he let out Oklahoma Indian war whoops, which in one instance evidently temporarily convinced the generalissimo that Hurley was unbalanced. Hurley visited Mao Tse-tung and his lieutenant Chou En-lai at Yennan, and promptly urged Chiang to allow Communists to participate in his government. Chiang's reaction to this proposal can well be imagined. Chiang had little use for the ambassador; on one occasion, as Hurley was leaving his residence, Chiang loudly ordered that the windows be opened right away to let the smell of the foreigner dissipate.

In Washington Roosevelt was now preoccupied with the Soviets and the fate of postwar Europe. He paid the Chinese problem less attention as each month passed. In May 1944 the Japanese exploded the myth that they could not move at will in China when they launched an offensive in southern China to gain a land route for transporting the Indo-Chinese rice crop to Japan and also to seize some of Chennault's key airfields. It was their largest offensive in China since 1938. It cost them few casualties, at least from Chinese fire. Since an all-land route to Indochina was ultimately impossible for Japan, the offensive gained them little, except for the airfields, which were of marginal value.

When Harry Truman became president in April 1945 after Roosevelt's death, he encouraged Chiang to consider the wisdom of a coalition government that would include Communist party members, on the grounds that this was the only realistic solution to the China problem. Such an agreement was eventually reached, but it was never executed.

For the Americans who were part of Stilwell's or Chennault's command, serving in China was doubtless the experience of a lifetime, despite the poverty-stricken, wartime conditions. Stilwell's prediction concerning the Chinese leadership held true. Chiang's government would fall of its own weight, and he and his clique became exiles in 1949. He lost power because of his lack of knowledge of his own people, in whose fate he had often seemed so disinterested.

Burma and India

In the CBI theater the only real Allied military successes were in Burma. There, the British were desperate to regain the initiative against the Japanese. They had lost Burma in early 1942, thereby giving the Japanese empire a border on India, the brightest jewel in Britain's own imperial crown.

The Japanese victory in Burma had been so rapid and well executed that it appeared that the Japanese would be capable of driving on to India with little delay. British political power in Burma was completely displaced by mid-May of 1942. The Japanese chose to consolidate their power in a receptive Burma, waiting for the rainy season to pass before even considering launching any further advances in south central Asia. With the demise of British military in Burma and the failure of any Allied naval units to challenge Japanese control of the seas, this delay did not seem unreasonable. The victories that had already been achieved had placed the Japanese forces well ahead of schedule, and for the army there seemed time enough to conquer India later, if they so desired. Domestic unrest in that country had already begun to work in favor of the Japanese. Still, the Indian subcontinent remained surprisingly calm, despite the evident threat of Japanese invasion. Indeed, about 2 million Indians volunteered for service with the Indian armed forces, which came to constitute one of the greatest volunteer forces in the history of warfare.

To give at least the illusion of being on the offensive and lend credence to its claim that Burma would again be under British rule after the conflict, the British high command initiated a series of limited offensives against occupied Burma. Thus came into being the "Chindits," the Seventy-seventh Indian Brigade, under Brig. Gen. Orde Wingate. Wingate conceived of the nuisance raid. He proposed to penetrate Japanese lines, relying on air drops for supplies. The Chindits first entered service in February 1943, when they set out to sever two railways in Burma. One was cut, but the damage was quickly repaired. Wingate's forces were scattered and returned to India in small groups, some taking months to make the journey. The raid was a military failure, but this was not the view taken by the English-language press in India, which hailed it as a military coup.

The next move came from Stilwell. Frustrated by his growing inability to command troops in China, since Chiang almost always managed to countermand his orders, Stilwell decided to lead a Chinese army into Burma. His ultimate goal was to reopen the Burma Road. In this he would not succeed, although he did liberate a portion of northern Burma. Stilwell's Thirty-eighth and Twenty-second Chinese divisions kicked off in October 1943, pushing southward into Burma from India through the Hukawng Valley. He was sup-

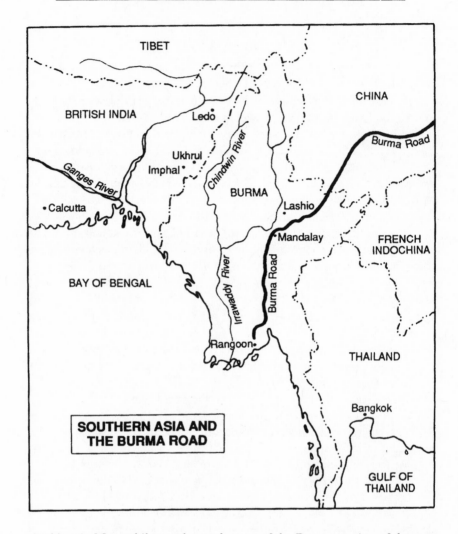

TIBET

CHINA

BRITISH INDIA

Ledo

Chindwin River

Ukhrul

Imphal

Ganges River

Burma Road

BURMA

Lashio

Calcutta

Mandalay

FRENCH
INDOCHINA

Irrawaddy River

Burma Road

BAY OF BENGAL

Rangoon

THAILAND

Bangkok

SOUTHERN ASIA AND
THE BURMA ROAD

GULF OF
THAILAND

plied by air. Meanwhile, work on a bypass of the Burma portion of the supply route had begun, pushing east from Ledo.

Also in October, Vice Adm. Louis Mountbatten became Supreme Allied Commander of the Southeast Asia Command. At first he operated out of Delhi, but he later moved his headquarters to the cooler city of Kandy in central Ceylon (now Sri Lanka). Mountbatten had as his area commander in Burma Lt. Gen. William Slim, who proved excellent in training men for jungle duty.

In 1944 the American provisional infantry regiment known to history as "Merrill's Marauders," under the command of Maj. Gen. Frank Merrill, arrived in Burma. Their efforts inflicted serious losses on the Japanese, but were not as successful as had been anticipated.

The Burma Road, early in the war. (*United States Army*)

A second Chindit expedition was prepared, again under Wingate. In early March 1944, employing gliders, it landed behind Japanese lines but could not disrupt the Japanese offensive against India, which had just begun. Wingate was killed on March 25, 1944, when his aircraft crashed into a mountain in the jungle. He was replaced by Maj. Gen. W.D. Letaigne.

The Japanese meanwhile had reorganized their forces in Burma. As with all of the Japanese forces holding conquered lands in 1944, the army in Burma was forced to deal with new realities. The empire was no longer capable of properly sustaining all of its far-flung forces. Area commanders were increasingly instructed to stand and fight with the resources they had, enjoying little hope of future assistance. The Japanese army in Burma now found itself facing this situation. Any offensive measure had to be successful because every loss was irreplaceable. The British had recovered well enough to make a substantial commitment to the defense of India and the reconquest of Burma on land; the Japanese navy could no longer sortie into the Indian Ocean. In all, it appeared that the time of Japanese imperial expansion had passed.

The senior command of the Japanese Burma army was now under Lt. Gen. Kawabe Shozo. His immediate superior was Field Marshall Count Terauchi, headquartered in Saigon. The Burma army contained six divisions. Two were in southwest Burma, under Kawabe's command; the other four, in the north, were under Lt. Gen. Mutaguchi Renya. Kawabe had asked General Mutaguchi to prepare for an offensive against eastern India. Mutaguchi's force would consist of three divisions that had been reinforced to almost 100,000 men, all veteran combat troops accustomed to jungle life. Mutaguchi had a dual objective; first, to seize the fortress town of Imphal, just across the border and key to domination of the Imphal–Kohima plain of Manipur, which would be the base of any British attempt to reconquer central Burma; second, to sever the railway line into Assam, which passed through Manipur and carried supplies to the southern terminus of the Hump. Strategically significant, however, was that in order to accomplish these goals, Mutaguchi would have to cross the vast mountain ranges in eastern India.

On March 6, 1944, Mutaguchi began his invasion of India from central Burma when he crossed the Chindwin River. One division was dispatched toward Kohima, two toward Imphal. The British had been expecting the offensive, possibly aided in advance by cryptography (the materials are still classified). But they had no idea of its size. The British managed only at the last moment to reinforce Imphal. On April 4, the Japanese invested Imphal and began its siege. Three British divisions defended it. General Slim organized an airlift for Imphal and Kohima as well and began a relief campaign from India, which reached Kohima on April 20.

The Japanese besieged Imphal with a stubbornness unusual even for the

Imperial Army. Slim continued to aid the besieged garrison via airlift. But the Japanese, who had counted on capturing British supplies, did not take equal measures to sustain their troops and began to suffer from attrition. They encountered stiff resistance, and the revolt in India they had hoped for did not materialize. Then the monsoon rains began, making further resupply efforts by the Japanese almost impossible. They had delayed too long—they should have begun the offensive several weeks earlier. After eighty-eight days, the siege of Imphal was broken on June 22, 1944. But the Japanese retreated relatively intact and slowly. They had lost 65,000 men, the majority to disease, malnutrition, and drowning. Slim pursued them, inflicting further losses.

The Japanese brought in Gen. Kimura Hoyotaro to replace Kawabe. During the summer monsoon rains, when the temperatures can remain high and the humidity can make one yearn for the return of the dry summer heat, Kimura reorganized his army. He received reinforcements, reaching a battle strength of 250,000 men. His strategy was realistic. He would slowly yield ground to the enemy, allowing them to conquer portions of central Burma. Gradually his supply lines would contract, while the Allies' lines would lengthen.

What Kimura did not appreciate was Allied air power—not so much combat air power as logistical strength, which allowed all manner of supplies to be dropped to the British, something the Japanese never imagined. Parachutes were used for supplies that might break; otherwise, supplies were "free dropped," without chutes.

By early 1945 four major Allied armies were busy reconquering Burma: the British XV Corps were pushing toward Akyab on the Bay of Bengal; Slim was advancing on a broad front; a Chinese force was moving toward Burma from the north; and Lt. Gen. Daniel Sultan was approaching the old Burma Road from the west. The Japanese resisted, but General Kimura deliberately let the enemy penetrate central Burma.

Merrill's Marauders were attempting an end-run maneuver of the Japanese army, hoping to cut them off and crush them against the mass of Allied soldiers approaching from the north. Kimura realized what was happening, since this was a favorite tactic of the Japanese themselves. He turned his full attention to Merrill, leaving only enough soldiers in the north to prevent the Allies from pouring through on his flank. He then attacked Merrill's comparatively smaller force in strength and nearly crushed it, managing to escape the trap planned for his troops. Kimura was then forced to withdraw the main body of his surviving forces into Thailand. There he had little respite, for that nation, like the other Japanese conquests, had mounted a resistance movement against the Japanese conqueror.

Slim conducted a brilliant campaign in the north and his training methods paid off. Aided by some native tribesmen, who revolted behind enemy lines, he was able to make rapid gains against the weakened Japanese force. Following these campaigns, the Japanese force in Burma was reduced to little more than a nuisance.

In early spring of 1945 the British extension to replace the Burmese portion of the Burma Road was completed. If it had been operative when originally planned, six to twelve months earlier, it might have enabled the Chinese army to mount at least a limited offensive against the Japanese. Opened as the Ledo Road, after its new Indian terminus, it was soon renamed the Stilwell Road. It had a pipeline running its entire length, which allowed a greater amount of supplies than ever to reach China.

By mid-spring, the British realized they could seize Rangoon, the capital city and a major port, before the May monsoon rains began. Thus, the interservice race for the city began on April 1, 1945. On May 1, an amphibious landing was made at the mouth of the Rangoon River, in a display of an "I will get there first" attitude, which in the long run was not helpful. The British, too, suffered from interservice rivalry.

On May 1, 1945, the Japanese evacuated Rangoon, but the British did not know this. The next day, however, a British plane overflying the city reported that there were no Japanese in the city, at least none in uniform. The pilot landed, helped the local population release prisoners of war, and then paddled down the river to tell the army that the Royal Air Force had liberated the capital!

At this point the British had succeeded in routing a Japanese army that was hardly its equal. The Japanese in Burma were suffering from all of the effects of the successful Allied submarine effort and were incapable of retaining the fighting capacity they had once possessed. As soon as the siege of Imphal was broken, the Japanese commanders were forced to commit the remainder of their reserves to a doomed withdrawal effort. The focus shifted from increasing the empire to merely sustaining the existing forces. The campaign became only a sideshow to the main attraction that was taking place in the waters surrounding the home islands of Japan.

There was no further substantial action in Burma after May, since the monsoon rains began and the Japanese forces began a slow withdrawal to Thailand. Mountbatten began planning for a major amphibious operation against Singapore in 1946. Had this come about, he would probably have had considerable success, for the Japanese army in Malaya had its hands full with a growing indigenous resistance movement.

The remaining theater under Mountbatten's command, India itself, witnessed conflict, but not of the overt military nature seen in Burma. Instead, India was on the very brink of civil revolt, which would undoubtedly have

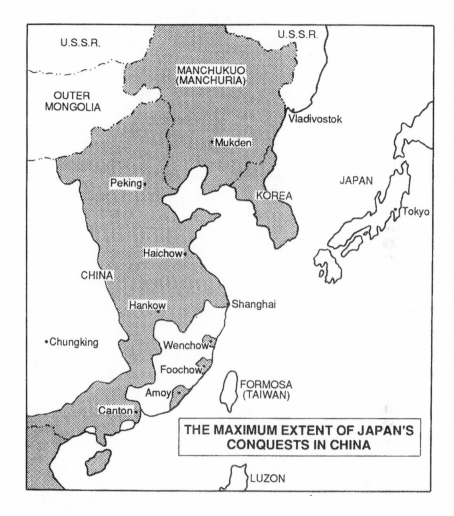

THE MAXIMUM EXTENT OF JAPAN'S
CONQUESTS IN CHINA

been followed by a religious civil war between Hindus and Muslims. This civil war smoldered just below the surface throughout the greater portion of World War II.

Roosevelt had hoped at first that the British might make substantial concessions toward Indian self-rule. He raised the matter with Churchill only once, at least in person. Churchill's reaction was frosty, and Roosevelt let it drop, although for more than a year after Pearl Harbor the American liberal press continued to raise the subject from time to time.

The Indians themselves did not neglect the matter, however. The two greatest Indian political figures were Mohandas Gandhi, the leader of the Congress party, and Muhammed Ali Jinnah, the Muslim leader. Gandhi had organized a campaign of "individual civil disobedience" to British rule and on occasion stated that he would prefer Japanese rule to that of Britain, if it were India's immediate two choices. By May 1941 some 15,000 Indians had been jailed for civil disobedience. Britain eventually promised independence but only after the conflict ended, which satisfied no one. Gandhi thereupon asked that the British "Quit India" at once, in which case he promised to resist the Japanese. When the British authorities tacitly refused, Gandhi's followers engaged in more active resistance to British rule. Several thousand were arrested. Gandhi himself was put under a form of house arrest, during which his wife died. India was fortunate to have a new viceroy in the person of Archibald Wavell. He handled a terrible growing food crisis (more than 1.5 million people died of starvation in the Bengal) quite adeptly and calmed some of the anti-British sentiment in the nation as well. The Congress party grew less restive. Jinnah, however, remained free throughout the crisis and frequently stated that Japanese rule would be preferable to British, although he may have made these statements out of simple political expedience.

Churchill refused to consider independence during the world war. He argued that even after the war, independence would mean a religious war, which in fact later occurred. Probably the key to retaining India, even for a few years, had been the successful British campaign in Burma, which impressed many Indians with British determination, while demonstrating that the Japanese could be defeated even in an area that had initially welcomed them as liberators.

In Indochina the Japanese had been in control longer than in any other of the Southern Resource Areas. Here, a rebel known as Ho Chi Minh opposed the Japanese occupation. He and his guerilla forces, a combination of nationalists and Communists known as the Viet Minh, had received aid and supplies from the United States, and some also from Chiang Kai-shek, who supported them because they were anti-colonialist. By the time Japan surrendered, almost all of northern Indochina had been liberated. When on September 2, 1945, Ho Chi Minh proclaimed Indochina independent, an American adviser was standing on the platform with him.

The Significance of the CBI War

The CBI theater was obviously of life-and-death importance to the men who fought there, and the individual acts of bravery by soldiers on both sides of the conflict are too numerous to recount. The war, however, was neither won by the Allies nor lost by the Japanese in this theater of the conflict.

But despite its peripheral importance to the outcome of the conflict as a whole, the CBI struggle was of vast importance to the millions who inhabited those nations. It helped lead to a civil war in China, which eventuated in the establishment of a Communist regime. It led in India, soon after the war, to a British promise of Indian independence and Commonwealth status. It also gave the Burmese something of a taste of independence and paved the way for the British loss of Burma as well. Similarly, the resistance movement in Malaya would eventually turn on the returning British overlords. As a few Americans (including Pearl Buck) had warned the White House from the first, the average Asian, at least in theory, would prefer Japanese domination rather than domination by the white man, and, at least in the first instance, this was true. Britain and the other colonial powers might try to reestablish their empires, but in the long run they would not succeed. The fact that in many areas the surrendering Japanese forces had to be given back their weapons to keep order until the European colonial powers' forces could arrive in strength did not help white prestige in Asian eyes. Everywhere, Japanese conquest paved the way for the independent nations in southeast Asia that exist today.

Suggestions for Further Reading

The best English-language studies dealing with wartime China are biographies of the major figures involved: see especially Barbara Tuchman, *Stilwell and the American Experience in China, 1911–1945* (New York: Macmillan, 1970); Martha Byrd, *Chennault: Giving Wings to the Tiger* (Tuscaloosa: University of Alabam Press, 1987); Sterling Seagrave, *The Soong Dynasty* (New York: Harper and Row, 1985); and William Slim, *Defeat into Victory* (London: Weidenfield & Nicholson, 1960). The best military studies on China during its civil war period are Peter W. Kozumplik, "The Chinese Civil War," in the West Point Military History Series, *The Arab-Israeli Wars, the Chinese Civil War and the Korean War* (Wayne, NJ: Avery Publishing, 1987); F.F. Liu, *A Military History of Modern China, 1924–1949* (Princeton, NJ: Princeton University Press, 1956); and the more general but quite valuable work by James Sheridan, *China in Disintegration: The Republican Era in Chinese History, 1912–1949* (New York: The Free Press, 1975). Unfortunately, much of the available material on the campaigns in southern Asia is often romanticized and tends to lack objectivity. One exception to this is Louis Allen, *Burma: The Longest War, 1941–1945* (London: Phoenix Press, 2000). Until the mainland Chinese can devote attention to this turbulent period in their history, the best basic source for the era remains The Asia Society, *Encyclopedia of Asian History*, 4 vols. (New York: Charles Scribner's Sons, 1988), which contains a wide range of articles on many political and military topics, all of considerable perceptiveness.

10

The Final Campaigns

As 1945 opened, the Americans found themselves approaching the very home islands of Japan. Victory was almost inevitable, but the timing and cost were still unclear. The final rungs on the ladder leading to the home islands, a small volcanic island and the heavily populated keystone of the Ryukus, remained to be conquered. Both the British and the Soviets promised to become fully engaged in the Pacific conflict as the year progressed, further ensuring future success. Similarly, a new weapon, the B-29, held tremendous, though unproven, potential for use over the vast expanses of the Pacific. For Japan, escape from total devastation rested on the familiar gamble for a decisive battle. Military planners in Tokyo placed their last hopes on exacting such a heavy cost in Allied lives in the approaching campaigns that negotiated peace would substitute for unconditional surrender and Japan could somehow salvage a portion of its once vast empire. Both sides were committed to their chosen course of action, and the result was the most fierce and costly fighting of the Pacific War.

Iwo Jima

Iwo Jima is part of a small island group very aptly named the Volcano Islands. A geologist's paradise, Iwo is eight miles square, experiences frequent earth tremors, and lacks any vegetation. It has steaming sulfur pits, an abundance of volcanic rock formations, and, on rare occasions, hot lava flows. The air reeks of sulfur since ocean breezes are rare. Almost exactly 750 miles south of the Japanese capital, the island was ruled as part of Tokyo Prefecture itself. It was regarded as an integral part of the Japanese home islands, at least for administrative purposes.

The Allies would almost certainly have overlooked this island but for its strategic function: the Japanese had transformed it into a sophisticated observation platform, which included more than one radar installation. It functioned as their forward air raid warning station, advising of approaching American bombers from the Mariana Islands long before they reached Japan. In addition, the Japanese obviously intended to use the island as a forward fighter base to interdict American air strikes against the home islands. If the island were conquered, the Americans could reverse this role and use Iwo Jima for fighters to cover raids against Japan. More importantly, an airstrip on the island, if sufficient in length, could be used to land crippled B-29 bombers returning from raids on the home islands.

As early as July 1944, after the loss of Saipan, the Japanese garrison on Iwo, under Lt. Gen. Kuribayashi Tadamichi, began preparing to meet the Americans on the assumption that the Allies might bypass the Philippines and head directly for Iwo. The Japanese decided to defend the high ground at either end of the island. Iwo Jima was topographically dominated by Mount Suribachi, nicknamed "Hot Rocks" by Americans even before the invasion. The island's volcanic ash combined with concrete to form a substance far harder than even the Japanese had at first hoped. They honeycombed the island with bunkers, emplacements, and machine gun nests, all well camouflaged. Many of the Japanese emplacements were impenetrable even to direct naval gunfire. Iwo's defenders had no less than three airfields from which the island might be contested, with a garrison of about 22,000 men to defend it.

The United States Navy did what it could for the marines scheduled to seize the island. It unleashed an intense three-day naval bombardment, including fire by no less than six battleships. But Iwo's fortifications remained largely intact. At dawn on February 19, 1945, Maj. Gen. Harry Schmidt's Fifth Amphibious Corps, comprised of elements of the Third, Fourth, and Fifth Marine Divisions—well over 30,000 men—landed on its beaches. They were surprised, just past the water line, to find themselves ankle deep in ash. The first day's casualties were more than 2,000 marines killed.

It took a full forty days to conquer the island, although on February 23 five marines raised the American flag on Mount Suribachi, a scene immortalized in what became the most reproduced photograph of the war. American battle deaths were 6,800; the Japanese lost their entire garrison, with the exception of 212 who were taken prisoner. To this day, geological expeditions to the island uncover caves with Japanese bodies sealed in them. The marines wondered aloud whether it had been worth it. The Air Corps had no doubt. On the day the island was declared secure, March 16, 1945, sixteen B-29s returning from bombing the Japanese home islands made emergency landings there. By war's end, 2,251 other B-29 pilots did the same, saving the lives of 24,761 Allied flyers. Iwo Jima became a small but vital cog in the American war effort against Japan.

A P-51 fighter takes off from Iwo Jima. *(American History Slide Collection, Instructional Resources Corporation)*

Okinawa

This left one last island before Japan itself: Okinawa, the key island in the Ryukyu chain, which was needed as a staging area for the invasion of the home islands. Here was a direct preview of what the conquest of Japan itself would be like. Okinawa was considered by many Japanese to constitute a fifth, if unofficial, home island, even though its inhabitants were culturally perhaps as much Chinese as they were Japanese. Japan had officially annexed Okinawa in 1879. Although the Okinawans considered themselves to be loyal Japanese, the Japanese did not arm civilians on the island (in contrast to what they would attempt on the actual home islands to prepare for an Allied invasion). Okinawa is sixty-seven miles long and from three to twenty miles wide; the average width is eight miles.

The Okinawa campaign was the first substantial British participation in the Pacific since the fall of Singapore and the ill-fated ABDA force the Japanese had decimated at the Battle of the Java Sea in February 1942. For the first time, British warships participated in an island-hopping campaign. On the direct orders of Prime Minister Winston Churchill, the admiralty had begun transferring capital ships from the Atlantic to the Pacific as of late November 1944 to fulfill Churchill's pledge that the moment the German navy was essentially defeated, he would begin shifting British naval might to the Pacific.

The American navy, proud of its rapid expansion since Pearl Harbor, did not relish British aid, even though the British carrier *Victorious* had previously served in the Pacific from March to August 1943, when it was sorely needed (after the loss of the *Wasp* and the *Hornet*). The specter of a species of international naval rivalry raised its head and might have taken a serious form had the Allies invaded the home islands. In Washington, Admiral King, who had never approved of the Europe-first decision, was especially reluctant to accept British aid. Indeed, the further one was from the actual battle scene, the more opposition to British participation one seemed to find in the American naval establishment.

But practical considerations slowly overcame all objections. First, Churchill had made the promise of British aid at American insistence early in the conflict. Indeed, at one point the Prime Minister had offered to incorporate the promise into a formal treaty, but Roosevelt said that he accepted Churchill's word on the matter. The only real drawback to actual British participation turned out to be the lesser fuel capacities of the Royal Navy's ships, which gave them a shorter operating range; they were also somewhat slower than their American counterparts. British carrier decks were constructed of steel, whereas American flattop decks were made of

American teakwood, which allowed for a softer landing if a crippled aircraft came in. But the British decks were soon to prove as kamikaze-proof as anything yet devised by the Allies.

No fewer than five British flattops, each about 25,500 tons, would help in the operation. These included HMS *Formidable*, *Illustrious*, *Indefatigable*, *Indomitable*, and *Victorious*. All but the second of these suffered direct kamikaze hits during operation, and all sustained, relatively speaking, less damage than the American carriers in the area similarly afflicted. British battleships and cruisers aided, as well.

The United States Navy code-named the Okinawan conquest Operation Iceberg, which seems inappropriate for an island devoid of snowfall but that is often literally muddied by an annual rainfall of over 120 inches. Ashore, the Japanese Thirty-second Army, commander Lt. Gen. Ushijima Mitsuru, prepared his 130,000 men, mostly Manchurian veterans, to meet the Americans. He also conducted extensive propaganda among the island's nearly half-million civilian inhabitants. He assured them that they would die if they fell into American hands. His officers actually informed the Okinawans that American soldiers, and marines in particular, brought gorillas with them to tear apart civilians as part of the American marines' idea of a sporting event. As farfetched as the claim was, no small number of Okinawans believed it. If questioned, the Japanese army solemnly gave assurances that in order to join the Marine Corps in the first place, a recruit was required to shoot one of his parents in the presence of a recruiter. Though it seems implausible, cultural misunderstandings and misinformation like these were at least partially responsible for the mass civilian suicides earlier at Saipan, a gruesome scenario that would be repeated on an even larger scale on Okinawa.

On March 14 American carriers under Mitscher and British flattops under Vice Adm. Sir Bernard Rawlings began the isolation of Okinawa by bombing nearby islands, especially those that had airstrips or operational military harbors. Here, for the first time, kamikazes began their intended role on a large scale. One dramatic photograph shows the carrier *Franklin* receiving a hit, its deck crew gazing in both wonderment and fear and just beginning to react physically, as a Japanese pilot crashes his plane high above into its masts. The *Franklin* was so badly mauled that, while officially "saved," it was never operational again. The new carriers *Yorktown* and *Wasp*, namesakes of the prior carriers of the same name, were also hit. Special fire-fighting apparatus designed by the New York Fire Department extinguished the fire aboard all three flattops, but 825 crew members perished. And in between jazz recordings, Japanese radio propaganda broadcasters gave nightly assurances that this was a mere prelude to future horrors.

The U.S. Tenth Army under Lt. Gen. Simon Bolivar Buckner led the con-

The American carrier *Franklin* receiving a kamikaze hit in her masts, March 1945. *(United States Navy)*

quest for the island. He initially commanded four army and two marine divisions. This was the first time an army general commanded a major assault on a Pacific island. The marines were hesitant to accept his leadership but had no choice after Nimitz agreed to the arrangement. Later, some marines and naval officers lodged bitter complaints against Buckner's leadership, but a certain amount of negative commentary may have been inevitable given the formidable task the Americans faced on Okinawa. And, of course, interservice rivalry, which had been a problem ever since the days immediately following Pearl Harbor, when each service had unofficially tried to place principle blame on the other for the attack, played a role in motivating the complaints. That rivalry now reached its wartime zenith, with each side expressing reservations about the arrangement. No one knew then that Okinawa would be the last conquest of the war, or that it would also be the bloodiest.

On March 23, 1945, the Allied naval force began both the bombardment and aerial strafing of the island. The Japanese were fully aware of the approaching Allies and declared the forthcoming battle for Okinawa a *tennozan*, or decisive battle. Like the navy before them, the Japanese army was staking its hopes on a single decisive battle with the Allies to turn the tide of the war. They would find success no less elusive than had the navy. However, General Staff members received some brief encouragement when radio stations at home broadcast several erroneous reports of successful repulsions of Allied forces. For their part, the Allies were attempting to reduce Japanese resistance as much as possible before embarking on the conquest of Okinawa. On a nearby island, about 350 suicide boats were captured before they could receive their crews. Each was to have been operated by two or three men and carry something like an underwater bomb attached to a pole for ramming purposes, as well as hand grenades, to pitch into American landing craft.

On the morning of April 1, 1945—Easter Sunday—the Allied task force, employing the relatively new amphtrac or tractor-like landing craft, reached the beaches of Okinawa. The Japanese had decided not to contest the island at the waterline, in part because it had served as a prewar artillery school, and the Japanese garrison therefore knew every topographical feature and contour of most inland areas, meter by meter. Japanese artillery fire would be coordinated, accurate, and deadly as never before. This fact was evidently unknown to the Allied high command structure beforehand.

The marines and army troops literally walked ashore in some areas, as initially only a very few snipers fired at them. General Buckner ordered some of his forces to turn both north and south. The northern portion of the island fell with relatively little resistance compared to what was to ensue elsewhere. When the American troops turned south, they promptly encountered the Machinato Line, part of an interlocking system of fortifications that extended south almost to the very end of the island. Artillery was skillfully hidden in cave mouths, which made even sighting it almost impossible for the Americans. Buckner's forces, well over 100,000 men strong, promptly engaged the Japanese in intense fighting, sometimes hand to hand. It was to be their worst trial of the war. Soldiers and marines frequently took temporary refuge in lyre-shaped burial vaults (Okinawans bury their dead above ground in concrete and stone tombs), especially during Japanese artillery barrages. Flamethrowers were used on an unprecedented scale, and Okinawa witnessed the first military use of the helicopter, albeit in a very limited and experimental fashion (it was used primarily to evacuate wounded).

In Tokyo, the Army Ministry described the struggle for Okinawa as a fight to the death and a decisive campaign. The emperor's seemingly innocent query as to the role of the IJN in the struggle for Okinawa produced immediate and disastrous results. In order to salvage some dignity, rather than admit that it could in no substantial way support the soldiers on Okinawa, the Naval General Staff decided to order super battleship *Yamato* to undertake an almost hopeless mission. On April 6, *Yamato*, escorted by one light cruiser

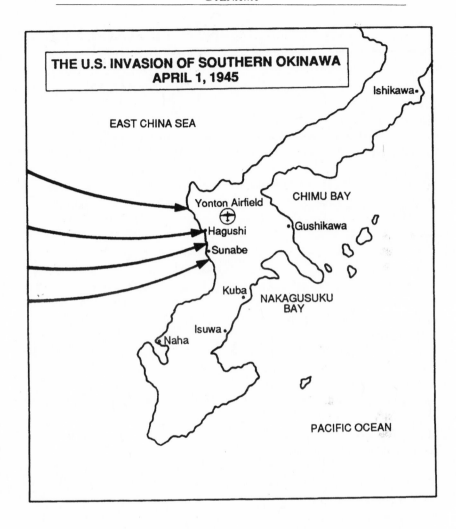

THE U.S. INVASION OF SOUTHERN OKINAWA
APRIL 1, 1945

Ishikawa•

EAST CHINA SEA

Yonton Airfield

CHIMU BAY

•Hagushi

•Gushikawa

•Sunabe

Kuba

NAKAGUSUKU
BAY

Isuwa•

•Naha

PACIFIC OCEAN

and eight destroyers, left for Okinawa, with its fuel tanks only 63 percent
full. This was by any definition an obvious suicide mission. Its training cadets were compelled to leave the ship before it sailed. It also sailed without
the benefit of air cover. *Yamato*'s supposed task was to destroy American
landing craft and engage the Allied fleet. Finally, if possible, *Yamato* was to
be beached and employed as an unsinkable fortress. Admiral Spruance, warned
by U.S. submarines of its mission, sent Mitscher's carriers after *Yamato*. The
next day Mitscher's aviators located the task force, and successfully placed
at least seven torpedoes into *Yamato*'s hull, along with numerous contact
bombs. At 4:23 P.M. *Yamato* went under, as did its accompanying cruiser and

four destroyers. It was the last sortie of the IJN. Following this vainglorious gesture, there was no conventional naval strength of any consequence left in Japanese home waters.

Yamato's demise did bring about favorable circumstances for one group of defenders of Okinawa, however. With the departure of Mitscher's fast carriers and their accompanying air cover to pursue *Yamato*, the transports supporting the invasion were left vulnerable to assault. The kamikazes utilized this opportunity to launch what was to be their greatest effort of the war. Their campaign at Okinawa was named Ten-Go operation, the Heavenly Air Offensive. It was divided, roughly, into ten separate series or waves of attacks against the Allied fleet. Over 3,000 sorties were flown, and twenty-one American ships were sunk. Naval casualties included the fleet carrier *Hancock*, damaged with seventy-two deaths, and the battleship *Maryland*, a Pearl Harbor survivor, damaged with sixteen killed.

The greatest toll, however, was taken on the light support vessels. Numerous destroyers and transport vessels were sunk or damaged so severely that they were removed from active service. Hundreds of American sailors were killed and thousands more injured during the devastating attacks. It was a terrifying experience. Hospital bays were soon filled to capacity, mainly with burn victims. On some vessels navy corpsmen literally exhausted their supply of morphine attempting to quell the cries of the injured. More than one officer wondered what sort of effort the Japanese might make to defend the "sacred soil" of their four home islands. They may have been motivated to ponder so by Tokyo Rose, who assured anyone listening that the kamikaze effort at Okinawa was just a pale preview of efforts to come. In all, 330 Allied naval vessels required repairs, or were permanently out of action, in addition to those that had been sunk outright. Marines who returned to ships at the end of the campaign, and saw sailors writhing under bandages from the burns inflicted by the kamikazes, resolved never to criticize shipboard personnel ("blue jackets") again.

Buckner continued to experience trouble in pushing south, but the problem was evidently now isolated and was most evident on his right flank. There the Twenty-seventh Army Division, whose performance had been weak at Saipan, gave a poor showing once again and was soon relieved by marines. The Machinato Line was pierced on April 24, although the Americans promptly encountered a second line, the Shuri, two days later.

Buckner was now faced with an obvious choice: He had absolute control of the sea, with the exception of the kamikazes. He could attempt a landing on southernmost Okinawa, thereby bypassing the fortifications, or he could use direct frontal assaults to reduce the Japanese positions. Many of the marines under his command, veterans of prior campaigns, fervently hoped he would choose a second landing. Instead Buckner decided to implement something of a compromise: a direct frontal assault but with a double envelopment, which would push forward on both his right and left flanks at the same time. Given the casualties engendered, it would probably have been wiser to attempt a landing on southern Okinawa. Only on May 11 was the double envelopment offensive launched, and on May 31 both the Japanese right and left flanks were pierced but with appalling losses to the attackers.

On June 1 the final offensive to penetrate the last Japanese fortification line on southern Okinawa began. Buckner did not live to see his task concluded. A bursting Japanese artillery shell claimed his life on June 18, 1945. Four days later General Ushijima, having been promoted by Tokyo to full general in recognition of the price he had made the Americans pay for the island, took his own life as enemy troops approached the cave in which he had his headquarters. A few days later the island was essentially secure, except that many Japanese survived in caves. Some soldiers emerged days, weeks, and even months later to engage in their own one-man *banzai* charges.

The casualties were the heaviest that any single island had cost the American forces. About 7,400 American were killed outright on the island, but the navy had lost perhaps 5,000 more men killed while offshore, mostly by kamikazes. Japanese losses can only be estimated. About 107,000 were killed outright, while an additional 20,000 were sealed in caves to die of starvation, suffocation, or cremation when gasoline had been poured in after them and ignited. About 4,000 Japanese planes were lost, while the United States Navy lost 763 aircraft, with no fewer than 458 falling in combat. The Japanese had well-camouflaged airfields on the islands adjoining Okinawa, and numerous planes had gotten in the air to engage Allied aircraft in dogfights. The air battle was a greater contest than the Marianas Turkey Shoot, but it has received little attention from historians, and American authorities suppressed news of it at the time. It seemed at the time a spectral view of the air battles to come once the United States attempted to invade Japan's home islands.

Conditions on Okinawa had been extraordinarily grim. Civilians had frequently been caught up in the fighting. Here, at least, they had not to any appreciable extent openly aided the Japanese army, although no small number took their own lives rather than be captured by the Americans. About 75,000 civilians perished during the campaign. Many, however, were prevented from suicide by Americans of Japanese ancestry who, for the first time, were employed on Okinawa as translators and were equipped with bullhorns to advise the local population that death would not be their fate if they peaceably surrendered.

Civilians were not the only ones who experienced brutal conditions on Okinawa. Even for experienced soldiers, the savagery of the combat brought about unusual results. Not least among these was the first substantial number of Japanese soldiers willing to surrender, over 7,000. Even the environment seemed to conspire to make Okinawa as deadly as possible. The frequent rains—on occasion so heavy that men literally could not see their hands in front of their faces—had sometimes made hand-to-hand fighting almost like mud wrestling. In some cases Americans and Japanese had literally strangled each other to death. Excavations on the island to this day occasionally disclose skeletons with their hands locked around each other's throats. American physicians logged 14,077 cases of battle fatigue or neuropsychiatric casualties among the troops who participated in conquering the island. Thus, the equivalent of a full division had to be relieved, some of course only temporarily, for reasons other than wounds or physical illness. The heavy artillery bombardments accounted for no small number of these cases, as did the very extensive use of flamethrowers, which were sometimes accidentally used on civilians. It was hard to tell, in combat conditions, whether Japanese soldiers or Okinawan civilians occupied a particular cave. While the costs of an invasion of the four home islands can only be conjectured, of course, many of the American soldiers and marines who had participated in the Okinawa campaign later wept unashamedly out of relief when they learned of Japan's surrender.

The B-29

As early as January 1944, Maj. Gen. Henry "Hap" Arnold, head of the Army Air Corps, had informed the White House that an invasion of the home islands might not be necessary. He cited the new B-29 bomber as a promising alternative. Arnold was immensely proud of the American nation's new air weapon and seriously concerned that it would be misused. Indeed, he always reserved decisions concerning its strategic use for himself. He was probably motivated in part by the disappointing record of the B-17 in sinking ships.

Although described earlier, the B-29 Superfortress merits further discussion for the unique role it was to play in the bombardment of the Japanese home islands. The B-29 was capable of carrying up to 20,000 pounds of bombs, including the first nuclear weapons, while the earlier B-17 Flying Fortress would usually carry only 6,000 pounds of bombs on a mission and lacked the ability to carry the new weapon. The Superfortress cruising speed of 290 miles per hour was much greater than the 182 miles per hour of the Flying Fortress. Also of great advantage over the vast expances of the Pacific was the B-29's 3,250–statute-mile range, over three times that of the B-17. In addition, the B-29 came equipped with pressurized crew stations for comfort at high altitudes, ground mapping radar, and remote-controlled gun turrets.

The number of aircrew on board fluctuated between ten and fourteen, depending upon the mission requirements.

Ordered into production in January 1942, the B-29s flew their first operational mission on June 5, 1944. The B-29 had the heaviest airframe constructed by any nation to that date. Fully loaded, it could carry over 100 percent of its own weight in the air, gasoline included.

Small wonder, then, that Arnold did not want his B-29s under the command of General MacArthur. He was also leery of a navy commander, especially Nimitz, giving his airmen orders. The B-29 had first been used in the China–Burma–India theater of the conflict but with mediocre results. Beginning in early June 1944, flying from airfields in the vicinity of Cheng-tu in China, the B-29s were used in attempted air raids against the Japanese home islands. But aviation gasoline was scarce in China and the bombers had bugs that were still to be worked out. Still, these obstacles would not have proven insurmountable save for the fact that all fuel, parts, personnel, replacement craft, and ordnance for the bombers had to be ferried over "the hump." Also, their production had not yet been standardized. Further, bomber command in China did not seem to grasp fully the new bomber's potential. And their bases were technically vulnerable to Japanese attack as well as to raids by local war lords, who were always in search of booty. With all that, though, the short time the B-29s spent in China did serve to bolster wavering indigenous support for the Chiang regime and quieted American critics who claimed that the United States had abandoned China to its own fate.

As a result, after the Marianas were secured in July 1944, the B-29s were husbanded there. In December 1944 the B-29s in China were withdrawn and stationed there as well. Arnold's B-29 commander in the Marianas was Maj. Gen. Heywood Hansell, who headed the Twenty-first Bomber command. Hansell basically decided to emulate the European theater of the conflict, ordering daylight strategic bombardment from high altitudes of aircraft factories in Japan.

Thus on November 24 more than one hundred B-29s attempted a raid against an aircraft factory in the greater Tokyo area. This inaugurated a series of over one hundred bomber raids, at about five-day intervals. The aircraft loss rate became about 6 percent, as opposed to the 5 percent that had been considered the greatest acceptable loss figure. True, most of these losses were due to operational problems rather than enemy action. The early B-29s proved very temperamental and broke down rather readily under the strenuous conditions, resulting in a high abort rate for their bombing missions. Contributing to mechanical difficulties and reducing overall effectiveness of the B-29s was their operating from altitudes of 30,000 feet or greater, frequently placing the bombers in or near the jet stream, which greatly affected their accuracy, fuel consumption, and navigation, as well as often interposing heavy cloud cover between the aircraft and their target.

Aircraft factories remained the priority targets. Results on the ground, however, were disappointing, as reconnaissance photographs clearly disclosed. Frequently the factories that were hit were only slightly damaged, or on occasion the bombers missed altogether, releasing their payloads into the countryside. Nonetheless, as the year 1944 ended, Hirohito specifically warned his service chiefs that weather and altitude alone could not protect Japan against American bombers. His warning evidently made little impression on the Japanese military.

On January 19, 1945, the first truly successful raid was conducted. Some sixty bombers smashed an aircraft plant near the town of Akashi on the Inland Sea, reducing its production by about 90 percent. Meanwhile, Hansell also began experimentation with incendiary bombs against Japanese targets, evidently on Washington's suggestion. But Arnold was now clearly impatient. Hansell's days in command of the B-29 bomber force were clearly numbered.

LeMay and Firebombing

Thus the stage was set for Maj. Gen. Curtis LeMay, who was to become the patron saint of those who wished to see Japan bombed into oblivion. LeMay had won his spurs as an airman in Europe, where he was an advocate of daylight precision bombardment. He had then briefly taken a bomber command in India. Finally, on January 20, 1945, he assumed command of the Twenty-first bomber force. At first he did little differently from his predecessor, with the same disappointing results. Then, on February 19, Arnold suggested that LeMay try incendiary strikes. On February 25 LeMay launched a 231-plane raid on aircraft plants in the Tokyo area. While the raid failed to produce the spectacular results of later efforts, it did prove the value of firebombing against virtually any Japanese target. This fact was scarcely lost on LeMay.

LeMay now carefully studied his options. He believed, evidently, that Japanese anti-aircraft shells could not be fused to explode below 10,000 feet; doubtless he was also aware of the lack of fuel remaining for the remnants of Japanese air forces. Reportedly after learning of the results obtained against a mock Japanese city constructed in Utah and subject to firebombing, he chose his strategy. Not specifically informing Washington in advance, he decided to risk all on a gigantic fire raid on Tokyo. He deliberately selected a flimsy, low-income district of the Japanese capital for extinction. LeMay ordered the bombers almost completely disarmed (only their tail guns remained in most instances), for he would send them in at night when Japanese fighter opposition, which had no radar direction, would be at a minimum. This partial disarmament would allow an even heavier bomb load than usual. LeMay ordered his planes to

This "moonscape" is Osaka, Japan, after an American firebomb attack in late spring, 1945. The craters are from high-explosive contact bombs that were used to make firefighting efforts more difficult. *(United States Army)*

approach the target at several altitudes, varying from 5,000 to 8,000 feet, safely below the jet stream, thereby greatly increasing the accuracy of the planes' bombsights. He also ordered his airmen to bomb in an X pattern, allowing fires to start that would burn toward their center.

The majority of the 334 B-29s that left the Marianas on March 9, 1945, dropped their bomb loads over Tokyo. Their payload was napalm, which spread fire on the roofs of many dwellings in the target area. While the raid progressed, LeMay paced the floor of his headquarters, fully aware that his reputation was almost certainly at stake, since General Arnold had become visibly impatient with him. The attack lasted three hours. Gale-force winds were blowing on the ground, guaranteeing the spread of any fires that were started. Supposedly executed to support the Allied operation against Okinawa, the raid was instead a test of LeMay's hope that he could kill Japanese civilians in so great a number and so rapidly that the conflict would be brought to a swift conclusion.

At least 150,000 civilians perished in the course of the raid. Indeed, the resulting fires burned for four days. Japan's records reveal that 267,161 buildings were destroyed. The actual number was probably higher, although that total alone represents almost one-quarter of the buildings in the Tokyo city area itself (as opposed to the greater Tokyo–Yokohama area, for which no records are available). Indeed, some of LeMay's pilots became physically sick from the stench of burning flesh, which rose to greet those who participated in the later phase of the raid. LeMay instituted systematic firebombing of other cities as well as of the remaining portions of the greater Tokyo–Yokohama area, until he literally expended the American arsenal of incendiary weapons. Victims of the bombing raids were, in LeMay's words, "scorched and boiled and baked to death."

Japanese cities were unfortunately built to burn, and were far better incendiary targets than European urban centers. In the series of fire raids that ensued, the death rate was very high, and the social dislocation engendered was also disastrous. The Japanese attempted to implement a system in some cities to identify the dead and the missing, but the records centers themselves were urban and burned to the ground together with their contents.

On Roosevelt's orders, the imperial palace was left untouched. But one night in May 1945, during a firestorm resulting from the bombs, flaming debris leapt the moat and razed a portion of the imperial residence within the 500 acres that comprise its grounds. Thereafter the royal family, at the insistence of the court officials, slept in special underground shelters. Legions of children were orphaned in Japan's cities, more rapidly than anyone could count them. By the late summer of 1945 they roamed the streets of what remained of the cities of Japan at will, preying upon the unwary by practicing cannibalism. Cities became depopulated. Police restrictions notwithstanding, the populace sought refuge when possible with relatives in the country.

The authorities evacuated children from the cities in some instances. They were sent to farms or small country villages, but the rural population often failed to nourish them adequately, and many perished from tuberculosis. A fair number discovered that they were orphans only at the end of the war, when they returned home and discovered their families were dead.

Initially, Japan offered substantial and spirited, if largely ineffectual, aerial resistance. Hundreds of fighters rose to meet the B-29s in the first months of the campaign, but they faired badly against the fast, well-armored, and armed heavy bombers. As the summer of 1945 progressed, lack of planes, fuel, and personnel led to fewer and fewer imperial aircraft in the skies over Japan. By July, American aircraft flying from the northern Mariana Islands and from carriers roamed at will over Japanese cities. Life for the Japanese had become another species of living hell. Entire square miles of Japanese cities ceased to exist. Perhaps worst of all, anyone could die without suffering a visible burn. The firestorms left oxygen deprivation in their wake, and the elderly especially, whose vital capacity to absorb oxygen was diminished, would be found dead in the morning, sometimes many miles from the area of combustion. Yet, the Japanese showed little sign of capitulation.

If the sirens sounded and American bombers appeared, Japanese left their homes at once and headed for the nearest stream or river, in which they immersed themselves. But if the fire was too close or too intense, the stream would probably boil, and anyone in it would die. The total number killed in the fire bombings is unknown, but it is certainly far greater than the official 330,000 figure released by Japanese military authorities at the time. The most recent estimates put the number closer to 2 million. This was in addition to millions more who were left homeless as a result of the fires. The Imperial Army dismissed the raids as "routine" while they encouraged the neighborhood firewatch associations to greater efforts against American incendiary bombs. But since American incendiary devices contained napalm or, at the end, generated their own oxygen, normal fire-fighting procedures with water alone were unavailing—a fact the Japanese army would never publicly admit. The B-29s—nicknamed *B-sans* by most Japanese—became so dreaded that surviving crew members of the few that were downed were frequently killed by the normally law-abiding civilians.

The firebombing raids that followed were a great success from a military standpoint. The fire torch was applied not only to Tokyo again but also to Nagoya, Osaka, Kobe, Kawasaki, and Yawata. LeMay showed great interest in the raids, sometimes personally debriefing pilots and crews. He was particularly impressed when a thermite magnesium bomb became available, for such a bomb could, under the proper conditions, burn through steel.

On June 16 LeMay began rotating targets, switching temporarily to medium-sized urban centers. The few reconnaissance photographs released to the press were on rare occasions published in the United States. LeMay had obviously adopted the technique the British used in Europe—simple terror bombing, the exact opposite of precision daylight bombardment. Earlier, Washington had vehemently opposed the use of terror bombing against Germany. Now, however, few seemed to notice or care. The clerical and liberal press in America raised occasional questions about the morality of mass civilian bombing and frequently cited President Roosevelt's request, made in 1939 at the outbreak of the war in Europe, that all belligerents refrain from bombing purely civilian targets.

But after Pearl Harbor and Bataan most Americans came to accept that slaughter of the enemy, whether in uniform or civilian dress, was the quickest way to end the conflict. Further, LeMay genuinely believed that Japanese military industry was in part handicraft industry and that Japanese workers took home part of their work to be completed after their hours in the factory were done.

There was undoubtedly some truth in this assertion, although not so much as LeMay thought. Workers in the silk industry, especially women, had traditionally engaged in such work. It also held true for a few other segments of production as well. But it was the exception, not the rule, a fact LeMay should have certainly realized. Instead LeMay justified the wanton destruction of residential areas as part of the campaign to destroy Japanese industrial strength.

Time magazine in particular supported LeMay, which was understandable since its owner, Henry Luce, was a devoted Sinophile. *Time* frequently told its readers that LeMay would bring a speedy end to the conflict, thereby saving American lives, and gave its readers the impression that LeMay had embarked on nothing less that a holy crusade against the barbarous Japanese. Other American magazines duplicated *Time*'s copy, although debate about the efficacy and ethics of such bombings continued, even occasionally in the *New York Times*. Some went even further, advocating the use of poison gas against the Japanese for good measure. One scheme bruited about in Washington was to spray the Japanese rice crop with the pesticide DDT; nothing came of it.

As the summer of 1945 progressed, the Japanese had no way to deal with the rain of death from the skies, except superstition. One prominent religious couple survived a fire raid but found their goldfish dead. Believing that their fish had somehow died for them, they put them in their shrine, and the practice caught on. Possession of goldfish became the goal of the more religious, superstitious, or frightened. When the supply of live goldfish was exhausted, porcelain ones were manufactured as substitutes. The social dislocation caused by the bombings, as described in Chapter 8, was great. LeMay almost certainly believed he was shortening the conflict: In actual fact he did not do so, as will be seen, but many in Washington, as well as London, believed otherwise at the time.

From July 10, 1945, onward, as the Japanese prepared for invasion, they also suffered from carrier raids against their home islands. Mitscher's task force, under Admiral Halsey, roamed the seas around Japan more or less at will. It was accompanied by British carriers, which used Ulithi as their staging area. More than 3,000 Japanese aircraft, the majority of them kamikaze, were destroyed on the ground. Japanese who lived in coastal villages on the Pacific were now subject to direct Allied attack. Allied aircraft strafed whole towns, as well as bombing strategic targets. The total number of planes involved included more than 1,000 American and nearly 250 British.

Operation Downfall and the Atomic Bomb

The Allies considered several alternatives for concluding the war, mostly service specific. The navy favored a strangling blockade aimed at starving out the Japanese. Though this option seemed very capable of success, it

Marines raising the American flag on Mt. Suribachi. (*National Archives*)

would not be so in the short term and all leaders agreed that a speedier end was desirable. The air force commanders suggested a sustained bombing campaign that would continually reduce the Japanese capacity for resistance and eventually force submission. Again, this scenario seemed acceptable as few ground troops would be lost, but appeared to be a long-term proposal. Douglas MacArthur and the army championed a full-blown invasion of the Japanese home islands. Barring any substantial change in the war situation, this proposal was most favored by the Allied leaders. Not only did it promise a quicker conclusion to the war, but it also included the participation of the most recent belligerent in the Pacific theater, the Soviet Union. Roosevelt had secured a promise from Josef Stalin at the Yalta meeting in early 1945 that the Soviets would declare war on Japan three months after the fall of Germany. The German surrender in May 1945 meant that a fall invasion would include Soviet troops and both a China and a home island front for the defending Japanese. Operation Downfall, the invasion plan, placed MacArthur in charge of the land forces with Nimitz in charge of landing all troops. The first of MacArthur's forces was scheduled to land on the home island of Kyushu on November 1, 1945. Honshu was scheduled for invasion on March 1, 1946, the objective being nothing less that the seizure of the greater Tokyo–Yokohama area itself.

Projected Allied casualty totals have been a topic of much debate in recent years, mostly by way of justifying the atomic bomb attacks by theorizing some gruesome casualty tally board. Indeed, Truman was desperately concerned with casualty projections for the forthcoming invasions and became increasingly frustrated at his chief advisers' unwillingness to commit to any consensus estimates. MacArthur's staff projected almost ridiculously low figures based on misinformation about the total and level of troops available for the defense of Kyushu and Honshu. Naval estimates were much higher (perhaps to justify the blockade option). Other government agencies projected numbers according to their own interests. Unfortunately most of the numbers bruited about were based as much on the particular agenda of the agency involved as on solid military information. Some numbers did range as high as 1 million casualties (including those incurred by Soviet forces participating in the attack) before all resistance in Japan ceased, though most envisioned tens of thousands of Americans killed with potentially hundreds of thousands injured. The truth is that no one knew or could know the death toll an invasion would incur. These numbers did not begin to take into account the tremendous numbers of Japanese killed and wounded, both military and civilian, if that is the proper designation for the nearly 27 million Japanese enlisted in the home defense forces. Consequently, most soldiers and marines were understandably lacking in enthusiasm for the forthcoming campaign.

For a few privileged insiders there seemed to be an alternative: a newly developed weapon, which, if it functioned as planned, promised to end the war quickly. The atomic bomb, America's most secret project during the war, was in large part made possible by Hitler's racial bigotry.

Individual American physicists had undertaken nuclear research in the 1930s, but their efforts were uncoordinated and sometimes overlapped, and work progressed slowly. Many of the scientists who would eventually spark the bomb project had been residents of Nazi Germany. A fair number left in the late 1930s when it became evident that Hitler would indeed implement the racial policies he had outlined earlier in his autobiography, *Mein Kampf.* Most at first settled in Great Britain.

The refugees in question may have been scientists of international repute, but Britain's most urgent scientific project at the time was radar. Hence, German scientists found university teaching positions, although they continued their nuclear research, concentrating on the theoretical aspects of atomic fission. Then Professor Frederick Lindemann (knighted as Lord Cherwell), Churchill's only scientific adviser during the war, organized the scientists into the world's first truly workable atomic bomb project. But Britain was bankrupt and work did not progress beyond the theoretical stage. Further, there was no place in the United Kingdom that could not be bombed by the German air force. Lindemann had given the project the code-name Tube Alloys.

The British offered the project to the American government. Roosevelt readily accepted. The American Manhattan Project was born in the early fall of 1942, when the refugee scientists arrived and joined forces with their American colleagues.

Maj. Gen. Leslie Groves, a West Point graduate with an interest in higher mathematics, headed the program. His qualifications proved limited, however. Groves proved adept at organizing the expensive, geographically disjointed, and highly secret operations of the Manhattan Project. In other ways, though, he was less gifted. Groves's idea of security was simplistic. On one occasion, he had the Selective Service draft illiterates to serve as janitorial help. At another juncture he wanted to draft the entire scientific staff into the army so that he could enjoy the luxury of giving them orders. Groves did eventually succeed in coordinating the efforts of his highly talented team to produce a prototype device that promised great destructive power, or at least a big flash. In fact, no one privy to the matter doubted that nuclear fission would release an incredible amount of heat and light; but some held that it would be a relatively slow process, which would mean in effect that the new weapon would have no explosive power per se.

The base project was established in a former boys' school in the town of Los Alamos, New Mexico. Work progressed simultaneously in Hanford, Washington, and Oak Ridge, Tennessee, but Los Alamos remained home base for the undertaking. Progress was uneven, although this was probably inevitable given the complexity of the task and the large number of researchers involved. The necessary uranium, fortunately, proved relatively easy to obtain, which was a decided plus for the scientists.

Many of the scientists working on the project were virtually professional pacifists; they labored to construct the world's first atomic weapon, at least in part, because Nazi Germany was known to have a similar project under way. Evidently no one knew that the Japanese also had such a project, although it was foiled by a lack of uranium. In late 1944 the U.S. government learned that Nazi Germany had more or less abandoned its atomic bomb project, but this did not deter work, since it was now widely assumed among those in the know that an atomic device would force Japan to surrender.

On the evening of July 16, 1945, the desert floor trembled as the first atomic device was successfully detonated in New Mexico. The decision was then made by President Harry S. Truman to use such a device on the Japanese, although not before considerable thought and reflection, something he would later downplay. (A recently discovered letter to his daughter Margaret reveals that the president did indeed agonize over the decision.) There were several compelling reasons to use the bomb. Development of the bomb cost over $2 billion, and failure to use it would have been difficult to justify to most Americans in the postwar world. Also, the family of any American killed or wounded in the invasion would have thought little of Truman's indecision about the rightness of using the weapon. Finally, given the lack of knowledge about the effects of radiation on humans, the atomic bomb appeared only slightly less inhumane than the massive firebombings already taking place. In the end, Truman decided that dropping the bomb would compel early Japanese surrender and thus, basically, save Japanese as well as American lives. LeMay was ordered to remove certain Japanese cities from his target list so they could serve as testing grounds for the new weapon.

Some critics have contended that the Japanese should have been invited to a demonstration of the new weapon. This is, at best, an idea of questionable merit. A nation with a kamikaze corps, a civilian defense force of 27 million, and professional samurai warriors would be unlikely to send a representative. To do so would have meant, in a sense, fraternization with the enemy, which is not encouraged by the Japanese military ethic. Others have suggested that an atomic device should have been detonated at high altitude over a Japanese city. But if this had occurred, the Japanese army would probably have written it off as "routine," which was in fact their precise response to the Hiroshima bomb. And such a high-altitude detonation would have released radiation, which later precipitation would have conveyed to earth, possibly inflicting in the long run far more damage over a wider area than explosion of the device at a conventional altitude.

The more interesting question is why the bomb was employed. Doubtless Truman thought he was shortening the war, although, as will be seen, the bomb alone did not do this. Then too, he probably wished to impress the Russians with its might and possibly repay the Japanese for the atrocities visited on American service personnel. Finally, the scientists themselves confessed a certain curiosity—albeit, at least in retrospect, perhaps a morbid curiosity—as to the effect the bomb would have on human beings. Thus, on August 6, 1945, the world's first atomic device was exploded over Hiroshima, and three days later the world entered the nuclear age when a plutonium device was detonated over Nagasaki. Japan would soon surrender, but not because of the devices exploded over those two cities. And so now it is to the surrender saga that we must turn.

Suggestions for Further Reading

For Iwo Jima, Whitman Bartley, *Iwo Jima* (Washington, DC: Government Printing Office, 1948) is a semi-official Marine Corps narrative of the island campaign; the United States Navy has provided a similar, brief narrative in its *Analysis of Air Operations: Iwo Jima, February–March 1945 and SOWESPAC Activity* (San Francisco: Pacific Fleet, 1945); Richard Newcomb, *Iwo Jima* (New York: Holt, Rhinehart, and Winston, 1965) is an early oral history study of the conquest of that island; there are three eyewitness accounts: Richard Wheeler, *Iwo* (New York: Lippincott and Crowell, 1980); Gallant T. Grady, *The Friendly Dead* (Garden City, NY: Doubleday, 1964); and Robert Leckie, *The Battle for Iwo Jima* (New York: Random House, 1967); and Donald McKinnon, M.D., "Battalion Surgeon on Iwo Jima," *Marine Corps Gazette 66* (February 1982): 28–37, gives a rare but very professional glimpse of the medical problems corpsmen and doctors faced on that island, and by inference on many other islands as well. The semi-official account of the Okinawa conquest is Roy Appleman, James MacGregor Burns, Russel Gugler, and John Stevens, *Okinawa: The Last Battle* (Washington, DC: Department of the Army, 1948); James H. Belote and William M. Belote, *Typhoon of Steel: The Battle for Okinawa* (New York: Harper and Row, 1969) is a workable account of the war's final campaign, but see also Ian Gow, *Okinawa 1945: Gateway to Japan* (New York: Barnes & Noble, 1988); George Feifer, *Tennozan: The Battle of Okinawa and the Atomic Bomb* (New York: Ticknor & Fields, 1992); Robert Leckie, *Okinawa: The Last Battle of World War II* (New York: Viking, 1995); Gerald Astor, *Operation Iceberg: The Invasion and Conquest of Okinawa in World War II* (New York: Donald I. Fine, 1995); and for a Japanese perspective on the campaign, see Hiromichi Yohara, *The Battle for Okinawa* (New York: John Wiley & Sons, 1995). A memoir account of the Okinawa campaign and Marine Corps Pacific island warfare in general is

William Manchester, *Goodbye Darkness: A Memoir of the Pacific War* (Boston: Little, Brown, 1979). John H. Bradley's *The Second World War: Asia and the Pacific* (Wayne, NJ: Avery, 1984) is a well-done overall survey that forms part of the West Point series of textbooks on American warfare; although sometimes more factual than interpretive, its sections dealing with Iwo Jima and Okinawa are particularly useful. A seminal history of Anglo–American relations during the conflict is provided by Christopher Thorne in *Allies of a Kind: The U.S., Britain and the War Against Japan, 1941–1945* (New York: Oxford University Press, 1978). An account including several interesting photos of the Japanese air and sea suicide efforts has been written by A.J. Barker under the title *Suicide Weapon* (New York: Ballantine, 1971); the latest title on the subject is Richard O'Neill, *Suicide Squads: The Men and Machines of World War II Special Operations* (Guilford, CT: The Lyons Press, 1999); but see also Nahuso Naito, *Thunder Gods* (New York, Kodansha, 1989). The best work on the firebombing campaign is Kenneth P. Werrell, *Blankets of Fire: U.S. Bombers over Japan During World War II* (Washington, DC: Smithsonian Institution Press, 1996); see also Martin Caidin, *A Torch to the Enemy: The Fire Raid on Tokyo* (New York: Ballantine, 1960); the United States Strategic Bombing Survey, *The Effects of Strategic Bombing on Japanese Morale* (Washington, DC: Government Printing Office, 1947); Ronald Schaffer, *Wings of Judgment* (New York: Oxford University Press, 1985); and Robert Guillain, *I Saw Tokyo Burning* (New York: Doubleday, 1981). The standard work on the Manhattan Project is Richard Rhodes, *The Making of the Atomic Bomb* (New York: Simon & Schuster, 1986), which is better on the physics and personalities than on the politics involved. Any student of nuclear politics during and after the conflict should consult Martin Sherwin's *A World Destroyed: The Atomic Bomb and the Grand Alliance* (New York: Knopf, 1975). Lauri Fermi, in *Illustrious Immigrants: The Intellectual Migration from Europe, 1930–1940* (Chicago: University of Chicago Press, 1968), gives an idea of the debt Americans owe the British and the European community in general for the Manhattan Project; see also Margaret Gowing, *Britain and Atomic Energy* (London: St. Martin's, 1964), and Leslie Groves's published memoirs, under the title *Now It Can Be Told* (New York: Harper & Row, 1962). Another work on the effects of the bomb is edited by Kyoko Selden and Mark Selden under the title *The Atomic Bomb: Voices from Hiroshima and Nagasaki* (Armonk, NY: M.E. Sharpe, 1989); but see also Ronald W. Clark, *The Birth of the Bomb* (New York: Horizon Press, 1961), and Ferenc M. Szasz, *The Day the Sun Rose Twice* (Albuquerque: University of New Mexico Press, 1984). Finally, Robert K. Wilcox, *Japan's Secret War: Japan's Race Against Time to Build Its Own Atomic Bomb* (New York: William Morrow, 1985) is innovative and helpful but should be used with great caution.

11

Allied Endgame

For Allied foreign policy makers the atomic bomb was one possible means to an end, the final defeat of Japan and the transition into the postwar world. For many Allied soldiers the atomic bomb meant deliverance if not from death, at least from a miserable and brutal invasion. For the Americans the bomb was the successful culmination of a massive program that combined the efforts of a large scientific community, the armed forces, and the central government. For England the bomb relieved the burden of fulfilling massive and expensive obligations to its ally in the Pacific after an enormous and nearly ruinous conflict in Europe. For the Soviet Union the bomb meant liberation from the commitment of an invasion of the Japanese home islands and was a message from the United States. The twin mushroom clouds over Hiroshima and Nagasaki demonstrated the totality of the Allied victory in the war. But the bombs did not provide ready answers to questions that had become increasingly pressing as the end of the conflict approached: When and how would final Japanese capitulation be accomplished? What would the relationship of the Allies be in the immediate postwar period? Who would emerge from the war as the real winners and losers?

Allied and American Postwar Planning

The task of planning for peace in the Allied capitals of Washington, London, and Moscow began almost with the first shots of the war. One of the great lessons of World War I had been not to allow postwar planning to wait until the end of hostilities. In this effort the Americans had helped take the lead. President Roosevelt had authorized the State Department to begin informal inquiries into postwar reordering during the first months of 1942. Those efforts were paying clear dividends by 1943 and resulted in commitments by nearly all of the Allied nations to continue a cooperative relationship after successful termination of the war.

American postwar planning efforts retained a good deal of New Deal ideology as the members of State who crafted the documents were heavily influenced by Roosevelt's depression-era policies. Postwar plans included calls for advanced economic planning and cooperative trade arrangements and international security. American plans also embodied many of the most popular points of Woodrow Wilson's plans for peace in 1919. The American plan called for national self-determination, international economic equality and opportunity, and collective security. These general desires proved easy enough for the Allies to agree upon during the early, dark days of the war when Allied victory did not seem as certain or as complete. As the war wore on, though, and Allied victory appeared more sure and total, the postwar planners attempted to turn these generalities into specifics. However, as the threat of Axis domination receded, the natural differences between republic, empire, and communist state began to emerge. Still, the Big Three of Roosevelt, Churchill, and Stalin were able to keep negotiations amicable, and hopes remained high for a smooth transition from wartime allies to peacetime partners.

One of the greatest areas of contention among the Allies was the framework for postwar security. Roosevelt and Churchill favored a policy known loosely as the "Four Policemen." The United States, Great Britain, the Soviet Union and, somewhat controversially, China would share the duties of "patrolling" the globe and settling regional problems before they became global conflicts. Differences arose over the regions to be "patrolled" and the nature of the relationship between the policeman and his territory, or sphere of interest. Roosevelt favored including China as the fourth member of the postwar collective security arrangement. Churchill and Stalin humored Roosevelt on this point early in the war, but privately harbored serious doubts about Chiang Kai-shek's abilities and control of the nation, as well as the Kuomintang's potential as a force for stability even within its own borders, let alone all of East Asia.

The Big Three addressed many of these issues at the summit meetings held during the course of the war. The last two of these meetings at Yalta and Potsdam were nearly completely dominated by discussions of postwar arrangements. By the time of Yalta in February 1945, Roosevelt's health was failing, China's value as a postwar policeman had all but disappeared, and Germany was clearly beaten. Roosevelt hoped to convince the Russians, who still had a nonaggression treaty with Japan, to enter the Pacific War after the final collapse of Nazi Germany. In return for agreeing to enter the war with Japan three months after the surrender of Germany, Stalin, whose interpretation of spheres of influence included direct Soviet control of strategic border territories, secured promises from a reluctant Roosevelt that included regaining control of those territories lost to Japan in 1905 as a result of the

Russo–Japanese War: Sakhalin Island, Port Arthur, and influence in Manchuria and Korea. Roosevelt then turned the tables on Stalin, calling for a second front in the Pacific, as the Soviets had so often done in Europe. Roosevelt was willing to make the concessions because he feared that the probable invasion of the Japanese home islands would cost hundreds of thousands of Allied casualties and that Soviet assistance would be beneficial. Many of Roosevelt's advisers also informed him that Stalin would most likely enter the Pacific War anyway and this might be a way to secure commitments from Stalin regarding his exact intentions in East Asia.

Similarly, the Potsdam meeting held in July 1945 outside the blasted former capital of Nazi Germany dealt with war termination and postwar issues. Harry S. Truman, now U.S. president, confirmed Stalin's promises regarding entry into the Pacific War. By this juncture, though, many of the president's advisers were openly distrustful of the Soviets, and some even hoped that the new atomic bomb would make Russian participation in the war with Japan unnecessary. Both Russia and the United States were engaged in sophisticated espionage efforts in each other's countries. Even the Japanese observed the growing rift between the Americans and Soviets and hoped that they might be able to play the two off against each other. Just as Stalin's spies had told him of the atomic bomb before Truman "officially" informed him of its existence at Potsdam, the Americans knew, before the Soviets told them (because they were reading all of the Magic intercepts from Japan), that the Japanese ambassador had approached Soviet foreign minister Molotov in hopes of arranging a visit from former Prime Minister Konoe to discuss Soviet intercession with the Allies on Japan's part.

Clearly, though, as late as July 1945 both the United States, who now possessed the bomb, and the Soviets, who were fairly well informed as to the bomb's potential, were still intending to engage in a massive invasion of the home islands. The bomb was not expected to end the war on its own. Other options for bringing Japan to its knees had also been explored and rejected by this time as well. The military factions in Japan appeared to be dedicated to a policy of national suicide and no official offer of negotiation or surrender had been forthcoming. Costly as it appeared, invasion was still seen as the only way to ensure Japan's full submission.

American Military Plans for Victory

While Japanese military strategists prepared for one last decisive battle, American planners anticipated a series of brutal engagements at the very least. Magic intercepts revealed that early in 1945 the Japanese had begun draining the empire, especially China, of troops and returning them to the home islands. Allied prospects for eventual victory were not seriously diminished, but the expected cost for the victory continued to rise with each transfer of forces. The Allied campaign of blockade and bombardment was doing a good job of depriving the Japanese war machine of everything but willing recruits. If indeed the Japanese could be forced to surrender short of total annihilation, it would be in spite of a large, well-trained, and willing defense force.

War Plan Orange and other earlier scenarios of the Pacific War did not automatically assume an invasion of the Japanese home islands. The Orange plans anticipated a Japanese surrender following decisive American naval victories. Other plans tended to be nonspecific on the exact series of events that would lead to Japanese submission. Consequently, different military planners and the various service representatives held a variety of opinions on the best means for securing victory. American naval planners like Secretary of the Navy James Forrestal and Chief of Naval Operations Ernest King advocated a more gradual solution to the conflict by calling for an expanded blockade and a stepped-up bombing campaign. Nimitz suggested taking smaller surrounding islands as well as key locations on the China coast and eventually Kyushu, but not risking a direct assault on Honshu. Many sources, including some from inside Japan, were certain that given a relatively brief span of time, the Japanese simply would not be able to continue the war for lack of materiel. The casualty figures that resulted from the Iwo Jima and Okinawa campaigns supported the wisdom of such tactics. Once again, Magic intercepts provided valuable information to American planners. By reading nearly all messages originating in Japan, regardless of their intended audience, the Americans knew that the submarine and mining efforts had all but strangled Japanese industry, and what was left was daily being burned and bombed out of existence.

The overwhelming destructiveness of the firebombing campaign actually began to work against the supporters of a siege and bomb policy, as LeMay himself was forced to admit that few targets of any value would remain after December. The Twenty-first bomber command had been so successful and so systematic that most Japanese cities, even the smaller ones, were heavily damaged. Between March and August 1945 Lemay's bombers destroyed over 50 percent of Tokyo, 40 percent of Osaka, 50 percent of Kobe-Yokohama, 90 percent of Ammoi, and rained similar levels of destruction on nearly every urban center in the home islands. Only the imperial palace grounds and the handful of cities specifically removed from the target lists had been spared. If this level of destruction continued, all that LeMay would have to target in 1946 and following were rice paddies and small hamlets. If the total destruction of their urban centers along with a great host of their population did not bring the Japanese to the negotiating table, it is hardly likely that blasting the rice crop and scattered village populations would prove successful in doing so.

Even so, Japan showed few signs of military collapse. Indeed, most of the official correspondence proceeding from Japanese sources was of the *banzai* variety and called upon the Japanese people to prepare to sacrifice themselves as one. The Japanese citizenry appeared prepared to do this in the face of a stepped-up bombing campaign, and in the case of Allied ships' ability to cruise within shelling range of Japanese harbors and shore installations. American bombers even began dropping leaflets in late July warning Japanese civilians to abandon cities that were slated for destruction. The Allies and the Japanese engaged in a psychological war designed to break one another's will. The Japanese hoped for a hurried assault or miscalculation so they could inflict one serious defeat on the Allies, while the Allies hoped to convince the Japanese that they had no hope of repulsing an invasion.

However, when the Joint Chiefs of Staff (JCS) met with Truman in June it was not to decide whether or not an invasion was necessary, but rather what form it should take. Plans had been drawn up for an assault on the southernmost island of Kyushu preparatory to a direct advance on the Kanto plain region around Tokyo. Some planners had suggested "hopping" past Kyushu straight to Honshu, but this was not seen as prudent. Air force planners suggested bypassing both southern islands and capturing the relatively lightly defended Hokkaido, but again this was seen as overly risky and unwise. Possibly to offset lingering disagreements over the next phase of the war, the Joint Chiefs characterized Operation Olympic, the invasion of Kyushu, in terms of both invasion and siege. Regardless of whether or not Tokyo was eventually stormed and taken, bases on Kyushu would prove vitally important to a continued strangulation or a direct assault on Honshu. The JCS presented Olympic as the logical next step in the move toward the heart of Japan, as well as one that would position Americans to force Japanese realization of the hopelessness of their position and also allow U.S. troops to beat the Russians to Tokyo, should it come to that. In this, even the navy representatives concurred.

Ironically, American planners were beginning to fear exactly what the Japanese had hoped for in 1941—weakening American resolve. Leaders like King, Marshall, Leahy, Grew, and others feared that Americans would lose the will to prosecute the Pacific War, especially after the fall of Germany. With hundreds of thousands already dead and billions spent, American leaders feared that the American public would tire of the hardships, just as the Japanese had predicted, albeit after a much greater sacrifice than Tokyo had anticipated. World War II had already lasted longer than all American wars

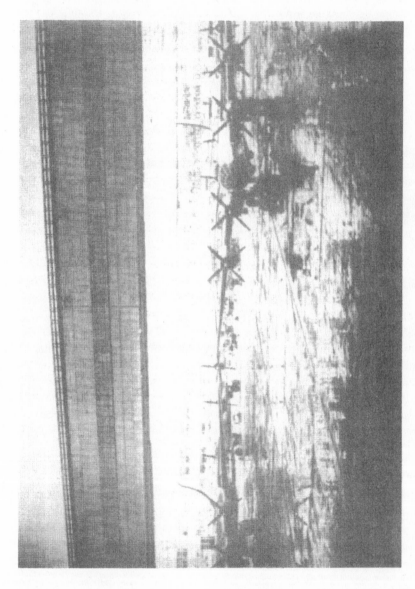

B-29s at the Boeing plant in Seattle, Washington, spring 1945. (*United States Army*)

except the Revolution, and had cost more American lives than any other war in the nation's history, save the Civil War. It now appeared that Japan's defeat was assured, though no one could say just when that would become official. Therefore, American government, military, and news agencies launched a campaign to reinforce the necessity of staying committed to the war against Japan. And while Americans did seem to be tiring of conflict, there was little doubt that victory over the Japanese would take time and a great deal of sacrifice. Polls revealed that most Americans, including General MacArthur, believed that war would continue in the Pacific until at least 1946, while many soldiers grimly quipped "Golden Gate in '48," indicating their belief that the war would last at least two to three more years.

The foregone nature of Japan's defeat coupled with the mounting and disagreeable cost of the war led to an increased belief on the part of Americans that any means that could bring about a speedier end of the war were acceptable. This is evident from the relatively modest protests to the firebombing campaign, as well as the growing popularity of battlefield tactics that included extensive use of flamethrowers and other especially brutal weapons. Popular sentiment ran that if these weapons and tactics could reduce the number of American casualties and shorten the war, then they were acceptable. The Japanese determination to continue the fight to the point of national suicide became a cause for Americans to view them as alien or inexplicable and therefore less comprehensible and rational than themselves, or even the other Axis forces. Besides, many Americans believed that the Japanese *deserved* this as revenge for the heinous attack on Pearl Harbor as well as the numerous incidences of atrocities against American servicemen during the war. Given this atmosphere, Truman's decision to employ the atomic bombs against the Japanese seems almost indisputable. In fact, Marshall believed that it might take as many as nine atomic bombs before the fanatical Japanese finally capitulated.

Marshall, as well as generals MacArthur and Arnold, advocated the use of chemical weapons on the Japanese also. They justified this highly controversial decision on the basis of previous Japanese actions. Once again, the "sneak" attack on Pearl Harbor and incidents like the Bataan Death March were cited as reasons why the Japanese deserved no better than gas warfare. Before his death, Roosevelt had vehemently opposed the use of chemical weapons and vowed to employ them only in retaliation for Japanese use of the same. Prior to the German surrender, the British had also discouraged the use of chemical weapons as they feared retaliation from Japan's Axis partners in Europe. American popular opinion was split on their use. Many people adopted the subhuman descriptions of the Japanese when justifying the use of chemical weapons and claimed that in a sense gas was more humane when putting down a dangerous or wounded animal than was fire or explosives. Others agreed with Roosevelt and believed that as a moral, as well as military leader of the world, the United States was obligated to refrain from such barbaric measures. Truman was not firmly committed one way or another on the issue, but refrained from initiating chemical warfare if for no other reason than it would have meant a major shift in tactics at a crucial stage in the war. The firebombing campaign and build-up to invasion were well in progress by July 1945 and a switch to chemical warfare would have meant a great deal of refitting of Allied troops and stockpiling and rearming of Allied bombers.

As the dates for the Olympic operations neared, disturbing information came from Magic as well as other sources. Many of the early projections for Japanese resistance on Kyushu had left the Americans with a comfortable numerical superiority in combat troops. Also, planners, especially MacArthur, had speculated that the Japanese would commit a substantial number of the troops on the island to defense of the northern beaches, thus leaving the best southern regions more vulnerable. However, intercepted radio traffic showed that not only had the Japanese managed to get more troops onto the island than had been anticipated, but that those troops were some of the best units remaining and were disposed evenly around the island and in position to offer maximum resistance to the landing forces. It even appeared that the Japanese would possess numbers roughly equal to the planned attacking force. The last time this had been the case, at Okinawa, the Americans had suffered a nearly 35 percent casualty rate. These numbers did not include the expected civilian defense forces either. If the attack proceeded as expected in November 1945, the Americans could expect to meet a nearly equal force of well-entrenched, professional troops as well as a large number of irregular, largely suicidal conscripts.

American Diplomatic Efforts for Peace

Acting Secretary of State Joseph Grew offered Truman one potential solution for ending the war more rapidly without a high cost in lives and fortunes: modification of the unconditional surrender policy. Grew, who had served for a decade as the ambassador to Japan, had a better insight on the workings of the Japanese leadership than most of the president's advisers. Though he tended to be overly confident in the power of the Japanese intelligentsia and assumed the existence of a larger anti-war faction than truly existed, he still had a greater knowledge of the state of affairs in Tokyo than nearly any other person in Washington. Grew suggested assuring the Japanese that the emperor's position would not be compromised by surrender. He informed Truman that the Japanese system did not allow Hirohito much participation in the decision making process, but held the emperor's office in great esteem nonetheless. If the United States were willing to allow that one exception to unconditional surrender, it might be enough to allow the peace faction to hold sway. This decision would not have been particularly popular with the American public, though, most of whom wanted to see Hirohito tried and hanged as a war criminal. Nor was it even the prevailing sentiment within the State Department, where the old "China hands" as well as Assistant Secretary of State Dean Acheson and former Secretary Cordell Hull were in favor of making an example of the emperor.

Much to Truman's relief, he never had to make that decision. As it happens, certain members of the Japanese government were thinking similarly and even made inquiries along these exact lines. Putting the question in almost the precise terms that Grew had proposed, during early July, Japanese ambassador to Russia Sato Naotake asked Togo if a guarantee of the emperor's retention would make surrender acceptable to the cabinet. The response he received stated that no form of modification to the unconditional surrender policy was currently acceptable. Once again, Magic delivered the news to American planners. In this instance, neither the Americans nor the Japanese had made any official statement or offer, but the war continued and an opportunity for negotiation and investigation of peace passed untried. Ironically, Secretary of State James Byrnes would later grasp at the same offer, first at the Potsdam meeting and later when dealing with the Japanese response to the atomic bombings, and it would eventually become the unofficial exception to unconditional surrender.

Certainly by July 1945 Roosevelt's politically expedient unconditional surrender policy had become a dangerous luxury for the Truman administration. Rumors of Japanese peace feelers and growing war weariness led some Americans to begin to question the intended aims of the ongoing Pacific War, while others suggested that a clarification of the exact meaning of unconditional surrender was long overdue. Truman received great support when he pledged his administration to continuing the hard line policy, while at the same time issuing assurances to any who would listen that unconditional surrender did not mean the subjugation or enslavement of the Japanese people. Several of Truman's advisers pointed out that the policy was almost certainly responsible for lengthening the conflict and that some Japanese might be willing to embrace self-destruction rather than submission because they feared the Allies would impose an occupation on the home islands similar to that enacted by the Japanese upon the conquered nations of East Asia. Most Americans agreed than no harm could come from a clear delineation of Allied terms for peace to replace the rather unclear unconditional surrender policy. Clearly defined war aims did not necessarily mean a "soft" peace or a demeaning of the sacrifice made by so many Allied soldiers already. The list of Truman's advisers who supported clarifying war aims and moving away from unconditional surrender, at least rhetorically, included Marshall, Stimson, Grew, and most of the rest of the cabinet save recently appointed Secretary of State James Byrnes, who feared Truman would be "crucified" by public opinion.

The center of much of this discussion became the role of Hirohito specifically and the imperial institution in general in the postwar world. Opinion was sharply divided among the American populace as to the part the emperor had played in initiating the conflict and his potential value in helping smooth the transition to a postwar Japanese society. The debate defied easy answer and presented a potentially dangerous political issue for the administration. Truman refrained from personally entering the debate fearing that he might be being duped by the Japanese and would suffer in the public eye by appearing weak or indecisive on the threshold of victory.

Further complicating the situation were several unauthorized attempts by Japanese officials in the Soviet Union and Switzerland to sound out American willingness to negotiate the specifics of unconditional surrender. Word of these contacts leaked out and provoked calls for full disclosure of Japanese efforts and clarification of Allied war aims. On July 10 Grew issued an official statement explaining that the United States had received no sanctioned overtures from the Japanese government and that the policies of the government remained the same as before, stating:

> We have received no peace offer from the Japanese Government, either through official or unofficial channels. Conversations relating to peace have been reported to the Department from various parts of the world, but in no case has an approach been made to this Government, directly or indirectly, by a person who could establish his authority to speak for the Japanese Government, and in no case has an offer to surrender been made. In no case has this Government been presented with a statement purporting to define the basis upon which the Japanese Government would be prepared to conclude peace. . . .
>
> The nature of the purported "peace feelers" must be clear to everyone. They are the usual moves in the conduct of psychological warfare by a defeated enemy. No thinking American, recalling Pearl Harbor, Wake, Manila, [and] Japanese ruthless aggression elsewhere, will give them credence.
>
> Japanese militarism must and will be crushed. . . . The policy of this Government has been, and will continue to be unconditional surrender. . . .

Grew went on to warn that the rumors and false leads might have been intended to weaken Allied resolve and that Americans could not afford to give credence to every rumor of peace that came along. The *Washington Post* countered that the reason the U.S. government was so reluctant to fully announce specific terms for peace was because it had not actually formed any. As if to support Grew, propagandist radio announcements in Japan cited the acting secretary's remarks as proof that American resolve was flagging.

The conference at Potsdam in late July was the final forum for official Allied reconsideration of the unconditional surrender policy. Truman and Byrnes represented the United States at this altered version of the Big Three (Churchill suffered defeat at the polls and was replaced mid-conference by new British prime minister Clement Atlee, leaving Stalin the only original member of the Big Three present for the close of the summit.) The Americans stuck to unconditional surrender, and the resultant policy statement, known as the Potsdam Proclamation, simply reiterated the former policy while making specific reference only to further death and destruction if surrender were not immediately forthcoming. No specific mention was made of the atomic bomb, though Truman had received confirmation of its successful test in the New Mexico desert early during the conference. In fact, Truman had authorized use of the weapon before the declaration was sent to the Japanese, a fact that later critics of the bomb's use focused on to demonstrate the administration's desire to employ the device in the face of evidence of Japanese leaders struggling to bring about peace.

The official reaction of the Suzuki cabinet to the Potsdam Proclamation justified continued prosecution of the war and made the use of the atomic bombs inevitable. A brief disagreement arose among military planners regarding the most appropriate site for the deployment of the first bomb. Kyoto, the ancient Japanese capital, had been removed from the target list early during the B-29 campaign and remained largely undamaged. It was also the largest city on the list. General Groves preferred to target it in order to demonstrate the bomb's devastating capabilities against a major urban area. Stimson disagreed, claiming that the social and cultural significance of the city justified its preservation, and argued until he finally secured Truman's sanction to remove Kyoto from the list of potential targets. The persuasive argument may have been that destruction of the ancient capital could actually serve to strengthen the Japanese resolve to resist surrender rather than drive them to embrace it. Therefore, the target for the world's first atomic bomb became Hiroshima, home to an army general headquarters and a substantial port facility.

The Soviet Union Enters the Pacific War

The atomic bomb deployed over Hiroshima not only destroyed that city and claimed over 100,000 lives, it also hastened Soviet participation in the Pacific

War. Soviet entrance into the war against Japan was no surprise. Indeed, President Roosevelt had worked very hard to make it come about. The Russians were under no obligation to enter the struggle against Japan simply because their allies in Europe were engaged with that foe. In fact, the Russians enjoyed a neutrality treaty with the Japanese that was not scheduled for termination until spring 1946. However, Stalin had become interested in the prospect of fighting Japan soon after the Nazi advances into the USSR had been blunted and the eventual fall of Hitler assured. Stalin saw the Pacific War as an opportunity to avenge Russia's humiliating 1905 loss to the Japanese. Victory would also afford Russia a share of the spoils and the chance to extend Soviet influence into the Pacific.

To this end, Stalin had responded favorably to Roosevelt's call for Soviet entry into the war as soon as Germany was defeated. Stalin had agreed at the Yalta Conference in February 1945 that the Soviet Union would enter the war in the Pacific within three months of the collapse of the Nazis. He also instructed his foreign secretary, V.M. Molotov, to inform the Japanese that the neutrality pact would not be renewed in 1946. Stalin reconfirmed the Soviet intention to enter the war against Japan during his meeting with Truman at Potsdam in July. By this time, however, though outwardly Truman welcomed the Soviet leader's assurances, many U.S. officials had begun to doubt the wisdom and necessity of involving the Soviets in the Pacific.

As early as January 1945 Roosevelt's military advisers had warned the president that in all likelihood Stalin would bring the Soviet Union into the Pacific War after German surrender, with or without America's invitation. Many members of the administration had begun to harbor serious reservations about Stalin's trustworthiness and hoped to distance the United States from further entanglements with the Soviet leader. Roosevelt justified his invitation to Stalin and its subsequent price, Sakhalin, influence in Mongolia and Manchuria, and northern Korea, by claiming that at least these concessions would put some limit on Stalin's grasp at war's end. By the time of Potsdam, many of Truman's advisers saw Roosevelt's bargain as a "devil's deal" at best. The atomic bomb promised to give the Americans the weapon they needed to force Japanese surrender without the enormous cost of a full-scale invasion of the home islands. Overestimating the bomb's power to force Japanese capitulation, American planners now found Soviet participation not only unnecessary, but also unwelcome. The Americans were appalled at Soviet behavior in determining the fate of divided Germany and believed any Russian participation boded ill for the future of Japan and the northern Pacific as well.

Stalin began building up troop strength in Siberia in April 1945. By August the Soviets had 1.5 million troops along the Manchurian border under the command of Gen. Aleksandr Vasilevsky and supported by 26,000 guns, 5,500 tanks, and 3,800 planes. Most of these forces were battle-hardened veterans transferred from the European theater and had participated in the recent defeat of Germany. On paper it appeared that they would be facing a formidable Japanese host, but much of the Japanese strength had been drained to confront the Allied advance through the Pacific and was now defending the home islands. Gen. Yamada Otoza had 900,000 troops, of whom 300,000 were Manchuko puppet soldiers and quite unreliable. Yamada's real weakness lay in equipment though. Not only were the Soviet guns, tanks, and aircraft superior to the Japanese, but Yamada faced a nearly 2 : 1 deficit in every category. In fact, the solid defensive perimeter that had been constructed in Manchuria in preparation for this very event was, by 1945, a hollow shell both under-gunned and nearly unmanned.

Though the Japanese knew the Soviet threat was imminent, they assumed that Stalin would await the actual April termination of the neutrality act before striking. It is ironic that Japan learned of Soviet entry into the Pacific War just at the Japanese ambassador was delivering another note asking for Soviet assistance in negotiating peace. On August 8 Ambassador Sato and Molotov exchanged notes, Sato's a request for Soviet good offices, Molotov's a Soviet declaration of war. The invasion of Manchuria began within hours of the exchange. Upon leaving Molotov's office, Sato remarked that now the duration of the war truly would be short.

The Soviet troops drove into the outclassed and outnumbered Japanese defenders from three directions. The poor quality and inability of the Japanese troops to deal with the Soviet heavy armor showed as the defensive line collapsed upon itself and the Japanese retreated toward strategic lines around Mukden. The Soviet advance was so rapid and well organized that several Japanese army groups were cut off and destroyed piecemeal. The Japanese continued to retreat into northern Korea and the Soviet forces pursued them until official surrender came nearly a week later.

The Soviet advance was as effective as could have been hoped by the Allies and as threatening as the Japanese had feared. The day following Soviet entry into the war, the United States deployed its second bomb, a nuclear device, over the Japanese city of Nagagsaki. The combined devastation of the Soviet attack and the second atomic bomb forced the Japanese to drastic measures and led the peace faction to press its point and call for imperial intercession on its behalf. Hirohito was willing to oblige, in part because he feared the effect of a Soviet invasion and occupation of Japan as much as the continued use of atomic weapons on his cities and his people. As the wheels of bureaucracy turned in Tokyo, the Allies made their final strokes of the war.

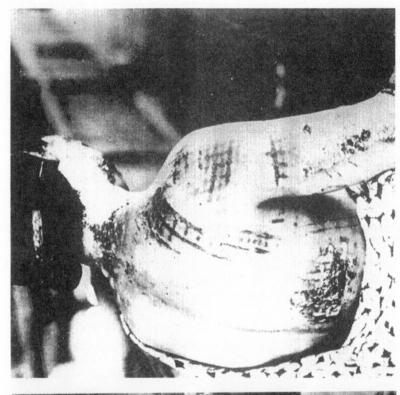

Three views of the dawn of the nuclear age at Nagasaki as witnessed from the air and at ground level. (*National Archives*)

Full-scale bombing missions continued after the bombing of Nagasaki. The United States did not want to give the impression that it had used its whole arsenal. On August 10 and 11 several large B-29 raids and assorted carrier-based attacks proceeded to further reduce Japanese cities. On August 11 the Japanese transmitted word of the acceptance of the surrender terms to the Allied capitals through their embassies in Sweden and Switzerland. Even this did not end the flights of American bombers over Japanese cities though. On August 13, after having received no further official contact regarding Japanese capitulation, B-29s dropped over 5 million leaflets on Japanese cities citing the Japanese offer of surrender and the Allied response. This prompted the last full measure of acknowledgement from the Japanese government that now allowed the emperor himself to inform the people of the war's end. The series of events that led up to that unprecedented event will be covered fully in the final chapter.

Suggestions for Further Reading

The best study of the American approach to the end of the war comes from Richard Frank's *Downfall: The End of the Imperial Japanese Empire* (New York: Penguin Books, 1999), on which the author has based much of this chapter. Also very valuable to this study was Leon V. Sigal, *Fighting to a Finish: The Politics of War Termination in the United States and Japan 1945* (Ithaca, NY: Cornell University Press, 1988). See also Stanley Weintraub, *The Last Great Victory* (Old Saybrook, CT: Konecky & Konecky, 1995). Much ink was spilled, and many hard feelings created, during the 1990s regarding the decision-making process and eventual use of the atomic bomb. The nexus of the debate circled around the Smithsonian Institution's controversial display of the *Enola Gay*, the B-29 that dropped the bomb. The scholarly debate has produced several highly charged and interesting studies, including Gar Alperovits, *The Decision to Use the Atomic Bomb* (New York: Vintage Books, 1996); Robert James Maddux, *Weapons for Victory: The Hiroshima Decision Fifty Years Later* (Columbia: University of Missouri Press, 1995); Barton Bernstein, *Judgment at the Smithsonian: The Bombing of Hiroshima and Nagasaki* (New York: Marlowe, 1995); and Ronald Takaki, *Hiroshima: Why America Dropped the Atomic Bomb*, vol. 1 (New York: Little, Brown, 1996).

12

Japan Surrenders

The Emperor and the Japanese Cabinet

The saga of Japanese surrender both begins and ends with the attitude and influence of the emperor, which must be explored in order to comprehend the surrender decision. Since the time of Meiji, the first constitutional monarch, the emperor of Japan has technically been only a ceremonial figure who reigned but did not rule. Constitutionally and by common practice, the monarch's chief functional role became diplomatic and ceremonial. He was head of state but not head of government. He received (or did not receive) diplomats more or less as he pleased. But in actual fact the powers of the monarch became popularly intertwined with the respect accorded him. Hence his position, as defined by Shintoism, the state religion, made him the spiritual leader of the nation.

The emperor commanded total respect. Children were taught that he was half human, half descended from the sun goddess. Prior to 1945 teachers taught their students that they would be struck blind if they looked him in the face. When he left the palace on ceremonial occasions, the upper portion of all buildings along his route had to be cleared lest someone look down on him. Further, the Emperor Hirohito in particular had a reputation for being fairly strong-minded concerning personal matters: witness that Hirohito had insisted on selecting his own wife, and chose a noble lady not on the list drawn up by the imperial household officials, much to their distress.

Of course, the military could also rationalize disobedience to the throne under the doctrine of *gekokujo*, which meant in effect that if they thought the emperor was being badly advised, military leaders could disobey the imperial will in order to serve the true needs of the empire. Therefore the emperor could easily find himself in what Americans now would call a catch-22 situation.

Hirohito had read a poem to his ministers and armed services chiefs several months before Pearl Harbor:

> If all men are brothers,
> Why are the winds and waves of the world so troubled,
> Why cannot all men live in peace?

The emperor clearly had substantial reservations about the war from the very beginning. Then, only three days after Pearl Harbor, while the military situation was still fluid, at least in the emperor's mind, Hirohito asked his ministers at a cabinet meeting about exploring the possibilities of a negotiated peace. No record of a discussion by the cabinet exists. But that Hirohito still entertained reservations about the wisdom of the conflict cannot be doubted.

During January 1942, Foreign Minister Togo told the Diet that he was ready to negotiate peace. His statement aroused a storm of protest from the more militant deputies. As each new victory became known, Premier Tojo received generic phone calls at his private residence, all of the congratulatory *banzai* variety. The fall of Singapore on February 15, 1942, convinced the emperor that Japan had a good chance of winning the war, for its forces had succeeded against all odds in the book, and for that matter, ahead of schedule in every instance. By the end of March 1942 Hirohito was convinced that Japan had won. In the spring of 1942 the throne announced that the conflict was over. The defeat at Midway in June was at first unknown to the emperor, for Tojo, who intensely disliked the navy, gave out the following statement concerning the Midway encounter: "The navy anticipated that hegemony in the Pacific would be decided in one great battle, and indeed it has been." Thus, many Japanese believed that Japan had won the fateful naval confrontation.

Just four days after the defeat at Midway on June 4, 1942, the former Japanese ambassador to Great Britain, Yoshida Shigeru (who later became premier during the occupation) called on Privy Seal Kido in his office within the palace. He proposed sending former premier Konoe to Switzerland, the most neutral nation of Europe, where he could have no specific mission but to keep in touch with everyone he could and try to determine if there were any rumors of peace proposals that would be to Japan's advantage. Nothing came of the suggestion, but it does show that there were important people in Japan who desired an end to the conflict.

After the defeat at Guadalcanal in early 1943, Prince Konoe began meeting with other senior and former premiers at the Dai Ichi building in Tokyo. They discussed the means of removing Tojo from office or, conversely, how to place someone in the cabinet who would oppose continuation of the war. They decided that the relatively moderate Adm. Yonai Mitsumasa should assume the post of minister of the navy. The plan did not succeed, but the meetings demonstrate that some among the civilian ruling elite hoped to terminate the war soon. And Hirohito could scarcely have been unaware of their doings. One must therefore assume that he approved, however tacitly.

In January 1943 the American and British leadership had met at Casablanca. During an informal luncheon conversation, Roosevelt remarked to Churchill that he was going to issue an "unconditional surrender" statement that would rally the Allied forces. Churchill agreed, suggesting that it would make the Axis leaders "squirm." Thus did Roosevelt issue his famous unconditional surrender formula, which dismayed all of the Axis powers. But probably least dismayed was Japan, where a Samurai code that embodied a "no surrender" philosophy already held sway. Then on December 1, 1943, at the first Cairo Conference, the unconditional surrender policy was confirmed, while Roosevelt inspired a declaration that assured that all territories taken by Japan since 1895 by "violence and greed" would be restored to their rightful owners—this in part to placate the Chinese. What the reaction was in Japan is not known, but the Japanese leadership could not have been pleased.

The emperor observed the New Year's Day festivities of January 1944 with greater than usual solemnity. The Imperial Army in general and Premier Tojo in particular had now become *the* power in the land. Tojo had managed to accrue such power, in part because he was also Minister of the Army, that everyone envied him. No previous premier had exercised such prerogatives. Then in February 1944 he also temporarily assumed the duties of chief of the army general staff. His wife joined him in unpopularity. In an era long before women's rights were given consideration in Japan, she shocked the nation by appearing in factories and urging women to work harder. Public reaction to her radio address was even greater. People began calling Tojo's home and inquiring, "Why hasn't Tojo committed suicide yet?" As his wife sadly observed, these were probably the same people who telephoned on Pearl Harbor morning to cry *"banzai"* into the receiver. Tojo had nearly fallen from power in June 1944, when two cabinet ministers resigned over his conduct of the war. A month later, when Saipan fell to the Americans, the end was in sight.

Tojo had held power for a record time, since October 1941. Kido, among others, expressed displeasure, and Tojo was faced with near-open revolt by several of his ministers. Everyone knew Kido spoke for the emperor. Clearly, Tojo's days in power were numbered. He was even ridiculed within the army hierarchy, where he was known as the "superior private," a rank directly above that of private first class. On July 18, 1944, after much bitter debate and rancor, Tojo resigned.

The ensuing cabinet crisis was the last occasion on which the emperor expressed hope that the war might still be won. Kido and members of the *jushin*, the council of former premiers, were well aware of the problem of interservice rivalry in the imperial forces: it was worse than in any of the Allied military establishments, and they determined that it was one of the primary causes of Japan's military decline. As a possible solution they discussed a co-premiership utilizing an army general and a navy admiral, although the army general would clearly have greater power. Admiral Yonai was their choice as the navy candidate if the position materialized. But the navy man in particular would be in some danger from the army's secret police, the dreaded *kempeitei*, which had been behind several actual assassinations as well as a host of unsuccessful ones.

The result was a compromise. The candidate chosen as premier was Koiso Kuniaki, a general. He was known to be studious and religious but suffered from poor health. He had been dubbed the "tiger of Korea" from his last post as governor general of Korea (like all Japanese military governors of Korea, Koiso had ruled with an iron hand). When Koiso arrived in Tokyo he was summoned directly to the palace. Word had evidently leaked to him, for he had contacted several politicians and military figures and inquired concerning their willingness to serve in a cabinet. Koiso agreed to form a government, and Yonai accepted the posts of navy minister and deputy premier.

The emperor received them simultaneously to invest them officially with seals and authority of office; he urged both of them toward greater cooperation between the Imperial Army and Navy. He also advised that they do nothing to disturb normal relations with the Soviet Union.

From the first, Koiso's strong-mindedness and independence were evident. However, the new premier did attempt to cooperate with the navy to a greater degree than had any of his immediate predecessors. Koiso also implemented a replacement for the old Liaison Conference in the guise of the "Big Six" body, comprised of himself, the foreign minister, the ministers of war and navy, and chiefs of the army and navy general staffs. The Big Six was unofficial, and its findings had to be ratified by the cabinet, but it did represent a genuine start at something like a greater measure of interservice cooperation.

Koiso had scarcely assumed office when the conduct of the Soviet ambassador in Tokyo grew questionable. In the Kremlin Stalin himself had made several public pronouncements as well as private remarks to neutral members of the diplomatic corps in Moscow that explicitly classified Japan as a fascist state, suddenly treating Japan as if it were little better than Nazi Germany. This represented a departure from the usual Soviet propaganda line and greatly upset the Japanese. Tokyo's neutrality pact with the Soviet Union was still in force, but Kido observed to the emperor that if Russia triumphed over Germany—and it was well on the way to doing so—they might decide, and/or the Allies might persuade them, to enter the war against Japan. Both Kido and Hirohito viewed such a prospect as the greatest calamity that could befall Japan. They both believed Japan could and would survive an American occupation, but the Soviets, once entrenched on the home islands, would destroy Japan's national polity and cultural essence, for they would never willingly withdraw their troops.

By New Year's Day 1945 the emperor was reasonably certain that 1945 would be the last year of the war. Early in the new year he decided to consult with his *jushin*. There were six former premiers still alive with whom he could talk, including Tojo and Konoe. For his part, Konoe had experienced a definite maturation of attitude and action as a result of the war. Unlike his leadership in the years before war with the United States, Konoe now demonstrated cool-headed realism and a sense of purpose and a potential for self-sacrifice. The emperor had them come separately to the palace that January, lest the *kempeitei* be alarmed.

The advice the emperor would value most was that of Konoe, who had been virtually his only wartime friend and political confidant, except for Kido. Konoe prepared his remarks in advance, for obviously Kido had told him that the monarch was seeking his opinion on the conduct of the war. Faithfully reconstructed by historian Robert Butow, Konoe's remarks are illuminating. Hirohito must have found them sobering indeed.

Konoe told Hirohito that unconditional surrender was, in effect, something Japan would simply have to accept. The United States and Great Britain, he evidently reasoned, would respect Japan's culture and ultimately its sovereignty. Konoe then mentioned one of his greatest fears, a possible communist revolution if the war were not terminated quickly. He urged Hirohito to seize the initiative and end the conflict soon. Konoe intimated that only the emperor's power could compel the military to accept surrender. The Imperial Army was the power in the land, and only Hirohito might persuade it of the wisdom of surrender. The emperor and Konoe might well desire peace, but unless the Japanese army concurred, nothing could be done effectively to implement a surrender policy. A few of the civilian ruling elite might desire peace, but until the army could be moved to accept the concept of surrender, the elite's opinion simply did not matter.

Before anything of further consequence happened in Japan itself, on Easter Sunday, April 1, 1945, the Allies invaded Okinawa. The repercussions were immediate. The general feeling throughout the civilian and, more importantly, the military elite was that the Koiso regime was bankrupt. Koiso tried to rally support, but even the emperor remained neutral. Kido then indicated imperial displeasure with the current regime. On April 5 Koiso returned the seals of office. Another cabinet crisis was at hand. On that same day word reached Tokyo that the Soviet Union would not renew its neutrality pact with the Japanese. This meant that the agreement would expire on April 13, 1946, and was disturbing news indeed. It greatly colored the politics of the ensuing cabinet crisis.

Some historians have argued that the Russian notification of nonrenewal of the neutrality pact meant little, since the Soviets assured the Japanese that they would abide by its terms until the actual expiration. But this promise belied common sense. Why had Stalin refused to renew it? Soviet promises had meant little in the past, and there was no reason to believe that the Stalin regime had suddenly turned over a new leaf.

The emperor was determined that this would be the last cabinet crisis of the war, and so was Kido. The difficulty now would be to find someone who would work to end the war while publicly declaring that he intended to prosecute the conflict to a successful conclusion. The specter of Russian participation in the conflict and also in the eventual Allied occupation of the nation was chilling indeed. But the Imperial Army remained unmoved. Hence the intention to surrender had to remain a secret, lest the *kempeitei* assassinate the next premier.

Kido quickly conducted a search for a suitable replacement for Koiso. He hit upon retired Adm. Suzuki Kantaro, who commanded almost universal respect throughout the ruling bureaucracy. Suzuki stated that he would be willing to play *haragei*, or "the stomach game," as he termed it. He would declare openly for continuation of the conflict, while his gut feeling, in the pit of his stomach, told him that the war was lost and peace was desirable. Suzuki fully realized that if he were not convincing in his role as military leader of the country anticipating victory, the *kempeitei* would probably threaten or kill him. He would have to pretend outwardly to support the war while quietly and discretely laboring for peace. It was a situation that would be both difficult and potentially fatal, should his intent leak to the army.

Suzuki made his job all the more difficult by insisting that former minister Togo Shigenori return to office to help him in any eventual bargaining with the Americans. Suzuki evidently believed, rightly or wrongly, that Togo was a skilled negotiator who would be trusted by the Americans. Togo was perceived as something of a dove by the military. Hence his appointment as foreign minister might betray the true intent of the Suzuki government. Togo had gone into a self-imposed retirement in late 1942 after a disagreement over the handling of the empire. He agreed to return to office only after he learned Suzuki's actual intent. Togo too would have to play the stomach game to avoid arousing suspicion.

The first crisis the Suzuki government had to face was the surrender of Germany to the Allied powers in early May 1945. The subsequent division of Germany by the Allies forewarned the Japanese of what they could expect in the event of a full-dress Allied invasion and conquest of the home islands (some warning of this division had been transmitted by Ambassador Oshima Hiroshi earlier, for the Germans themselves were privy to it before they surrendered). The division of Germany among the victorious powers appalled Hirohito. He correctly predicted that once Soviet troops were in occupation of German soil, German unity would be but a memory for many decades to come. Thus, the emperor informed Kido that Japan must avoid a similar fate at all costs. In a remarkably prophetic statement, the emperor also remarked to Kido that he feared Germany would never again be united in their lifetimes.

Peace Feelers

Meanwhile Japanese diplomats in several foreign capitals had jumped the gun by approaching American envoys to inquire concerning possible terms of surrender. In Switzerland, Japanese diplomats sought out Allen Dulles, an OSS operative, with questions about what terms the Allies would be willing to accept in return for a Japanese capitulation. The same "peace feelers" were reported by the American embassy in Stockholm, Sweden. In no case, however, were the overtures made officially. The U.S. State Department, under Acting Secretary of State Joseph Grew, was uncertain how to interpret these reports. Grew was, however, sympathetic to the Japanese, having served as ambassador in Tokyo from 1932 until Pearl Harbor.

The military in Japan were privy, at least at the highest level, to the next ploy the Japanese leaders used. They decided to turn to their greatest potential enemy, the Soviet Union, evidently as much to determine Russian intentions as to ask that they mediate with the Allies for peace. Former premier Hirota Koki approached the Soviet ambassador in Tokyo, Jacob Malik. Their first meeting took place on June 24. Malik proved unhelpful. Finally, on July 7, 1945, the emperor decided to dispatch an envoy directly to the Soviet Union. His choice for this unenviable task was Konoe. On July 12 Konoe appeared at the palace, accepting the emperor's mandate but stating in effect that he desired carte blanche to negotiate as he saw fit. Hirohito agreed, informing Konoe that the mission would be dangerous and that he would be risking his life. Konoe waved these considerations aside.

In the Soviet Union, Foreign Minister Vyacheslav Molotov and Premier Josef Stalin were busy preparing for the upcoming Allied conference to be held at Potsdam, a suburb of Berlin, during the last two weeks of July 1945.

Thus, the Kremlin postponed replying to the Japanese request that Stalin receive Konoe as a special envoy of the emperor.

When the Japanese learned of the Potsdam Conference and the Allied proclamation concerning possible Japanese surrender, they realized they would have to respond. Premier Suzuki in particular could not ignore it. Suzuki unknowingly played into the military's hands. He used the word *mokusatsu* to describe his feelings toward the Potsdam proclamation. He literally meant to state that he wished to "kill with silence" the ultimatum. Perhaps the English phrase "no comment" comes closest to Suzuki's intended message. Newspapers received instructions simply to reproduce the premier's literal text with no comment of their own. But several prominent Japanese papers did editorialize, opining that Suzuki believed the Potsdam document was laughable or "beneath contempt." Thus, the Allies became convinced that Suzuki was far from ready to consider surrender. Even the *New York Times* told its readers that this was Suzuki's intent or meaning. This was true as far as the Japanese military were concerned, but it did not convey the true feelings of the civilian ruling elite.

The Decision to Surrender

Consequently Japan was condemned to atomic attack. As mentioned in the previous chapter, Truman decided that fission weapons should be used against the Japanese and it was widely anticipated that the bomb would compel surrender and thus save both American and Japanese lives. The first bomb was detonated above Hiroshima on August 6, 1945, at 8:15 A.M. It took a full day for word of the catastrophe and its possible cause to become known in Tokyo. Only on the morning of August 9 did Minister of the Army Anami Korechika definitely learn that a single bomb had destroyed the city. Just before had come news of a proclamation by President Truman, monitored by Japanese radio, stating that it was indeed an atomic device, which had cost the United States $2 billion to develop. No one in Tokyo was sure it was really an atomic explosion, so the head of Japan's own atomic bomb project, Dr. Nishina Yoshio (later a Nobel prize winner), was dispatched to the city. He surveyed Hiroshima from the air and then inspected the damage on the ground. Nishina promptly concluded that only a uranium bomb could have caused such damage.

In the early morning hours of August 9 (August 8 in Europe) Stalin kept his pledge, and Soviet troops invaded Manchuria. Later that same morning news came of the Nagasaki bomb. But contemporary members of the cabinet and Kido affirmed that the essential impression was made by Soviet intervention. The British official history of the war, *The War Against Japan*, states that Russian participation in the Pacific conflict brought home to the Japanese government that "the last hope of negotiated peace had gone and there was no alternative but to accept the Allied terms sooner or later." Suzuki himself told General Anami:

> If we don't act now, the Russians will penetrate not only Manchuria and Korea, but northern Japan as well. If that happens, our country is finished. We must act now, while our chief adversary is still the United States.

Hirohito was impressed with the military potential of the bomb, as well as with the peacetime uses of atomic energy. This would perhaps provide part of the motivation to name it in the documents pertaining to surrender. But the emperor later confided to Kido that his basic reason for surrender was the threat of Soviet occupation. The United States, he believed, would eventually withdraw from the country, but the Soviets would never leave. This may seem to betray extraordinary foresight on the part of the Japanese, and in a sense it does; but all Japanese governments since the Meiji Restoration have thought in terms of years, decades, and even centuries when making decisions, and Hirohito was merely following this tradition. The military dismissed the new American weapon as something like a magnesium "flashlight" device. Even when among themselves the military chiefs refused to acknowledged its true nature, claiming that if civilians were properly clothed in white garments they would not be harmed. In the end, they issued several official pronouncements on the bomb, dismissing it as "routine." They might not have seriously meant this, but at the very least the dismissal indicates the samurai code and the mind-set that it engendered.

Sometime early on the morning of August 9, before the world's first true nuclear device exploded over Nagasaki, the emperor and Kido decided that this was the day to implement a surrender policy. The most influential body in the land was the semi-official Big Six, whose members included Premier Suzuki, Foreign Minister Togo, Minister of the Army Anami, Minister of the Navy Yonai, Chief of the Army General Staff Umezu Yoshigiro, and Chief of the Naval General Staff Toyoda Soemu. As in cabinet meetings, Kido and one or two others sat in as unofficial, nonvoting members. And meetings were held in the presence of the emperor, who listened but, following tradition, refrained from speaking.

Normally Hirohito was the servant of the Big Six. Now he decided that the time had come to break precedent and demand that Japan surrender. Kido sent a young secretary of the prime minister to acquire the signatures of all the members so that an extraordinary meeting could be called at an unspecified later date. Anami warned the lad that this had better not be one of Kido's tricks to implement a surrender policy, or he would kill the first man to mention surrender. The excuse was given that this was the only way to ensure, in the event of an emergency that might prevent some or all of the members from being reachable, that a meeting of this influential body could be called within the hour.

Upon receipt of the documents, Kido immediately called a meeting and instructed the members of the body to come to the imperial palace. They gathered in the underground *obunko* complex, a small area used to house some of the emperor's books, a little before midnight on August 9, the meeting having been delayed by several false air raid alerts. The weather was hot and oppressive, and the meeting was held in this underground complex partly for comfort's sake. At ten minutes before midnight the emperor arrived and the meeting was called to order. The final chapter of the war was about to be enacted.

Anami, Umezu, and Toyoda took the line that the atomic bomb could be successfully defended against, if the proper anti-aircraft measures were taken. No other mention was made of the device. The military agreed that the situation was desperate but maintained that they could still win. Their logic is difficult to grasp. After two hours of discussion, which indicated that the group was evenly divided on the question of surrender, Suzuki deemed it time to play his trump card. The premier had foreseen this development. By prearrangement, knowing that Anami, Umezu, and Toyoda, all ardent hawks, would deadlock the proceedings if it came to an actual vote, the emperor had agreed to speak. He had prepared a brief unwritten statement for the occasion. At this juncture, Suzuki called on the throne to express an opinion, since the body was deadlocked. Due to a hearing impediment, Suzuki failed to hear the emperor's initial response and asked a second time. The emperor motioned for Suzuki to sit down and all remained silent as Hirohito rose to address them as never before.

He then began his address. In a high-pitched, emotional voice he told the group: "I have given serious thought to the situation at home and abroad and determined that my people must suffer no longer." The emperor went on to compare the situation to that experienced by Japan during the Triple Intervention of 1895, when France, Germany, and Russia prevented Japan from gaining Korea, which it had won from China. He told those assembled that once again Japan would be forced to bear the unbearable, and that his ministers and his people had better prepare "to drink their own tears." The fact that his subjects were willing to die for him had not escaped his perception, but he could not require such a sacrifice. The very survival of Japan as a nation was at stake. Immediate surrender was the only means to assure that Japan would live on as a unified nation after the conflict.

When the emperor finished speaking, the decision had been made. Many of those assembled left in tears. The official decision to surrender had to be approved by a meeting of the entire cabinet. It met that same morning and quickly approved the surrender policy. Virtually the entire government and military elite silently agreed, as if by an instinct, that in only one sense could Japan's surrender be less than unconditional: the emperor must retain his throne. A proviso was therefore added to the surrender decision to this effect. Had the Allies rejected this condition outright, all agreed that Japan would continue the struggle to the bitter end.

That same morning, just after the cabinet meeting, Anami was evidently so moved by the Soviet entrance into the conflict that he issued a statement contending that the unity of Japan was so important that a "Holy War" should be waged against the Soviet Union. He would later claim that this message was sent out by accident. This may have been the case, but it made Kido and Togo quite angry nonetheless.

The next task for Togo and Kido was to inform the Allies of Japan's willingness to surrender. Unfortunately, the normal civilian radio stations were being monitored and censored by the army, and no one could be sure that a militant officer might not invoke the doctrine of *gekokujo* to block the broadcast. That evening the message was sent out via the Domei news agency in Morse code, which somehow was not subject to censorship. It was in that manner that the Allies learned of the Japanese decision.

Popular opinion in the Allied nations favored trying the emperor as a war criminal, probably because of a lack of understanding of his true role in Japanese politics. Truman himself appears to have had no strong convictions on the matter. He offered no objection when U.S. secretary of state James Byrnes (appointed April 1945) told the American nation that "the ultimate form of government of Japan" would be determined "by the freely expressed will of the Japanese people," as had been envisioned at the Potsdam Conference. This message was then dispatched via the Swiss government to Japan. The Japanese had already learned of this policy in the early morning hours of August 12 via an English-language radio broadcast.

In Japan, Foreign Minister Togo and several legal experts in his ministry somehow determined that the phrase "the government of Japan" did not include reference to the emperor. Hirohito himself stated that he accepted the proclamation. He did not fear that his people would vote against retaining him as monarch if the Allies put the question to the test in a plebiscite during the forthcoming occupation. The Allied military continued its campaign of bombing and strafing Japanese cities after the announcements were made. The rumor was even spread—no one knew its origin—that Tokyo itself would receive an atomic bomb attack on August 15.

Generals Umezu and Anami refused to accept Togo's opinion that the American reply did not include the emperor. Anami in particular began to back out of his silent acquiescence to the surrender decision. He argued that it would be better to wait until the Allies attempted an invasion. Once an initial landing had been thrown back into the sea, he reasoned that Japan would have greater bargaining power. In fact, Admiral Onishi, founder of the kamikaze corps, opined that if 20 million lives were sacrificed in a special suicide mission, Japan could yet win the war. He did not, however, reveal what sort of special kamikaze attacks he had in mind. On the morning of August 13 the Americans precipitated matters by dropping leaflets on Japan, stating that the Japanese government had agreed to surrender and giving the essential terms of Byrnes's reply.

At a little before noon on August 14, 1945, the emperor convened the Big Six and the cabinet as one body. Hirohito stated simply but very firmly that all present had already agreed to a surrender decision; it displeased him that a second meeting was necessary to enforce the decision. As soon as the meeting terminated, Togo rushed to the Foreign Ministry and dispatched plain text, uncoded messages to his ambassadors in Bern and Stockholm, stating that the Japanese government accepted the Allied terms of surrender. As Togo doubtless had anticipated, they were read by prying eyes before delivery at their destinations. Wire services the world over soon carried flash stories to the effect that Japan had capitulated. The world's costliest war was over.

Here the story should end, but it does not. Some of the younger Japanese army officers viewed Russian entrance into the conflict as more of a challenge than a threat. This was especially true of some of the lower-grade staff officers in Tokyo. The emperor realized that this might be the case. He took necessary precautions. His brothers had spent several days assuring the military that the emperor desired surrender, and certain war heroes—Fuchida included—had devoted their energies to similar ends. Still the effect proved unavailing in one sense: troops on far-off islands could not be reached, and staff officers in Tokyo still busied themselves in preparing for disobedience.

Thus, on August 14 the emperor decided to broadcast a surrender rescript to the nation. Since every conflict was ended by an explanation by the throne, this one could be no exception. But the emperor would read it himself. Then, later in the day, Hirohito decided he did not trust his emotions. He asked Kido to arrange for him to record his message. This the lord privy seal proceeded to do with dispatch. Technicians from station NHK were sent for, came to the palace, and set up recording equipment. They did so in the Imperial Household Ministry, within the 500 acres that comprise the palace grounds. This was the natural place for the recording, since the military might attempt to stop the talk.

These precautions were not in vain. Indeed one staff officer in Tokyo had spent the last several days in plotting the undoing of the emperor's surrender policy. General Anami's son-in-law, Maj. Hatanaka Kemji, was privy to the emperor's commands via Anami. He determined to stop the surrender himself. Hatanaka was without officer transportation, and spent a lot of time on his bicycle garnering support among other officers for a palace revolt. Anami sympathized with his son-in-law's efforts but refused to support him. On the other hand he also did nothing to stop him, which as a superior officer he could have done with one word of command.

At 11:15 P.M. on August 14 Hirohito arrived at the Imperial Household Ministry to make the recording. He had never before spoken on the radio. Only once, in 1928, had the imperial voice been broadcast, and that was an accident. Hirohito came with the rescript in hand. It took less than twenty minutes to read. Placed in a room with a microphone, he became nervous. He spoke in a high-pitched voice, virtually shouting, evidently under the impression that the louder he spoke, the greater the number of his subjects who would be able to hear him.

Thus, the first recording was not a good performance. A second was necessary. The emperor was told he could use his usual speaking voice, which he did. But now he was hoarse, and he skipped several syllables. Kido managed to signal the technicians that a third attempt was out of the question. The second recording was labeled "original" and the first "copy." The ten-inch disks were taken back to the residential portion of the palace grounds for safekeeping. They were to be played to the nation the next day, August 15, 1945, at noon.

Major Hatanaka knew that a surrender recording was being made, but he did not know the details. At 11:00 P.M. on the evening of August 14 he called on Lt. Gen. Mori Takeshi, commander of the Imperial Guards Division. Mori evidently sensed that his interlocutor was up to no good, for he immediately launched into a monologue on his philosophy of life. Hatanaka listened with rising impatience. At 1:30 A.M. he drew his pistol and shot General Mori dead. Hatanaka then appropriated the general's seal and forged an order placing himself in temporary charge of the entire Imperial Guards Division.

Hatanaka proceeded to the palace, where he blundered into a portion of the imperial residence itself. He demanded to know the location of the surrender recordings but was unable to find them. Kido, however, became so nervous that instead of sleeping, he spent the night destroying documents that he feared Hatanaka might find and somehow use. At dawn Hatanaka's little drama ended, in part because an unsympathetic general arrived and ordered Hatanaka's men to disperse. Hatanaka seconded the order, leaving the imperial residence. After making an attempt at NHK to stop the playing of the recording, Hatanaka took his own life.

At 7:21 A.M. on August 15 NHK announced to the nation that the emperor would address his subjects at noon. The rescript was written in official court Japanese, which was a mixture of Japanese and Chinese characters. It was generally unintelligible to the masses, especially if read without an accompanying printed text. The people would be forced to determine the emperor's meaning from the tone of his voice and such portions of the rescript as they could comprehend. Add to this the distortion inherent in cutting a ten-inch Bakelite recording at 78 rpm and it seems doubtful indeed that his actual words were fully understood.

When the emperor's broadcast began, many expected to hear that the Allies had begun the invasion of the home islands and that they were to resist to the last. Only such an important message would require the emperor himself to address the nation. When Hirohito's recording began, the people were surprised by the high-pitched quality of the emperor's voice, but his tone betrayed the content of the message. Instead of aiding in the repulsion of an invasion, they were to suffer an even less enviable fate—surrender. Many wept. Now Japan would be forced to endure a conqueror's rule for the first time in its history.

The imperial rescript is worth reproducing in full, for it not only implements the surrender policy but provides a recipe for the future, one which in effect the Japanese are still implementing to this day:

> To Our good and loyal subjects: After pondering deeply the general trends of the world and the actual conditions existing in Our empire today, we have decided to effect a settlement of the present situation by resorting to an extraordinary measure.
>
> We have ordered Our government to communicate to the government of the United States, Great Britain, China, and the Soviet Union that Our empire accepts the provisions of their joint [Potsdam] proclamation.
>
> To strive for the common prosperity of Our subjects, is the solemn obligation which has been handed down by Our imperial ancestors and which we keep close to Our heart. Indeed, we declared war on America and Britain out of Our sincere desire to ensure Japan's self-preservation and the stabilization of East Asia, it being far from Our thought either to infringe upon the sovereignty of other nations or to embark upon territorial aggrandizement. But now the war has lasted for nearly four years.
>
> Despite the best that has been done by everyone—the gallant fighting of the military and naval forces, the diligence of Our state servants and the devoted service of Our hundred million subjects—the war situation has developed not necessarily to Japan's advantage, while the general trends of the world have all turned against her. Moreover, the enemy had begun to

employ a new and most cruel bomb, the power of which to so damage is indeed incalculable, taking the toll of many innocent lives. Should we continue to fight, it would not only result in the ultimate collapse and obliteration of the Japanese nation, but also would lead to the extinction of civilization. How are we to save Our subjects? By accepting the joint [Potsdam] proclamation of the powers.

We cannot but express deep regret to Our East Asian allies who have cooperated with us. The thought of those officers and men as well as civilians who died in the battles or air raids pains us day and night. We have suffered unspeakably, and we hope you will accept Out imperial apology for all of this. We can only hope that future generations will enjoy peace. Having thus safeguarded and maintained the Japanese nation, we feel at one with Our people. Do not engage in outbursts of emotion which might have international significance, or in any internecine contention and strife, which might cause us to lose the confidence of the world. Let the entire nation continue as one family from generation to generation, ever firm in its faith that Japan will always exist, and mindful of the many trials and tribulations ahead.

Unite your total strength to construct the future. Cultivate the ways of rectitude; foster nobility of spirit; and work with resolution so as to enhance Japan's glory and *keep pace with the progress of the world*.

[Emphasis added]

Perhaps the myths began as soon as the rescript was published in the evening paper, and people were able to study it fully. Kido's testimony as well as that of several cabinet members makes it clear that the Japanese surrender came in response to the Russian entry into the war and the fear of a Soviet occupation of the home island. But Hirohito had not mentioned this in the rescript for fear that any such reference might encourage the vengeful Allies to allow the USSR to participate in the postwar control of Japan. Also the new American weapon provided a convenient, face-saving excuse for capitulation.

The importance of the atomic weapons' role in terminating the conflict vanishes when one considers the lengths to which the Japanese had gone in preparing for the Allied invasion of the home islands, as well as the zeal they had displayed during the final months of actual fighting. The fanatical resistance that had characterized Japanese determination on Iwo Jima and Okinawa demonstrated that the Japanese still had a lot of fight left in them. The organization of a kamikaze corps designed to destroy the American navy at a tremendous cost in lives shows the length to which the Japanese had already gone to prevent defeat. A national guard of 27 million had been organized and armed with primitive weapons to drive the Allied invasion of the home islands back into the sea.

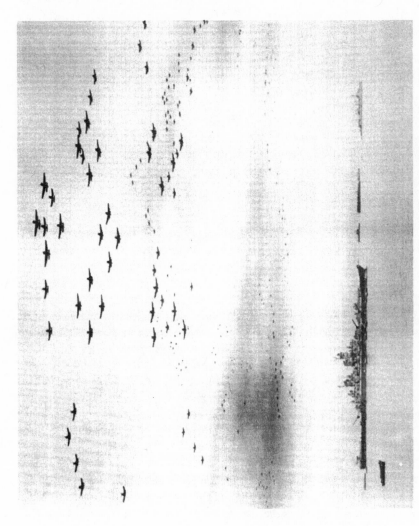

A small sample of the United States aerial might is displayed above American warships in Tokyo Bay.

Since March 1945 the home islands had been subjected to the most mur-derous bombing campaign mankind had yet witnessed and hundreds of thou-sands of civilian lives had been lost monthly. Japan had failed to significantly disrupt any of the aerial bombardments undertaken by the Allies. Its willing-ness to absorb horrendous losses had already been established. The intro-duction of a more efficient weapon, even the atomic bomb, was not significant enough to bring about Japanese capitulation. Only the military intervention of the Soviet Union had moved the Japanese military to consider the un-thinkable—surrender. And witness that even then, Hirohito had to twice com-mand his generals to lay down the sword before the decision became actual Japanese policy.

Further, a United States Army intelligence study conducted after the ter-mination of the conflict reinforces and verifies these conclusions. As sum-marized in the *New York Times* (August 3, 1989), the 1946 report concluded that the bombing of Hiroshima and Nagasaki provided a "pretext" for sur-render, "seized upon by all [Japanese] leaders as the reason for ending the war," but that Japan's motivation to surrender came in the form of the Soviet participation in the conflict, which the report described thus: "the disastrous event which the Japanese leaders regarded as [an] utter catastrophe and which they had energetically sought to prevent at any cost—Russia declared war and began moving her forces into Manchuria." How widely known this re-port was at the time remains unclear, but a section of the Pentagon bureau-cracy evidently realized that Russia, which had compelled Japan to modernize in the 1860s, had similarly compelled it to surrender in 1945. Only the threat of communism and Soviet domination, the fear that Japan would suffer a Soviet occupation while losing both her unity and national identity in the process, was enough to overcome the samurai mindset.

Never Look Back

On August 27, 1945, General MacArthur arrived at a kamikaze air base, Atsugi Field, located near Tokyo. His entourage was small, in part because he wanted to demonstrate his trust in the Japanese people. He established his office in the Dai Ichi building in downtown Tokyo and his actual living quar-ters in the American embassy. His office faced the imperial palace and also the square in which a radio propaganda broadcaster had once assured her listeners that MacArthur would be hung.

The official surrender ceremony took place aboard the battleship *Mis-souri* on September 2, 1945, in Tokyo Bay. Hirohito had to personally ask the Japanese delegates not to commit suicide, lest their taking of their own lives seem to Americans to invalidate their signatures on the surrender docu-

The conclusion of Japan's formal Instrument of Surrender, signed September 2, 1945, on board the battleship *Missouri*. *(United States Army)* ment. As the delegates came aboard, they were horrified to see rising suns painted on gun turrets, evidently denoting aircraft downed by *Missouri*'s anti-aircraft guns, although it is also possible that they had been painted on simply for effect. MacArthur conducted the ceremony. He and Adm. Chester Nimitz signed for the United States. Representatives of the other major Allied, now United Nations, powers, also signed. There was considerable resentment among America's Allies, however, because MacArthur had ruled that prisoners of war not liberated in the course of hostilities had to await the formal signing on that day before being freed from POW camps. There are many Australians in particular who to this day do not forgive MacArthur for that decision.

The cost to the various belligerents was awesome. The Japanese suffered 1.5 million battle deaths, and well over 3 million civilian deaths from the air raids, including the bombings of Hiroshima and Nagasaki. Total American casualties, killed and wounded in the Pacific, was later placed at 296,148. British, Australian, and other empire/Commonwealth forces suffered 185,000 battle deaths. At least 4 million Chinese had also been killed. The suffering of those who lost their homes and families is incalculable and cannot be shown on any chart or graph.

In Japan itself all now wondered what the Americans would be like. The Japanese truly adopted a "never look back" philosophy; rather than rationalizing their defeat, newspapers filled their columns with advice on how to get along with the Anglo-Saxons. Some women, perhaps victims of wartime propaganda, nonetheless husbanded poison capsules especially issued by the government. Or perhaps they anticipated the sort of treatment Japan would have given a conquered nation under the samurai code.

General MacArthur was later to be criticized for not trying the emperor as a war criminal. But he did not do so for very practical reasons: he came to realize that he would probably face civil insurrection at the least if Hirohito were put before a tribunal. Indeed, he told the American leadership as much when they complained of his decision. Perhaps knowledge of the Japanese government "folkways" motivated him as well. The military had not informed the emperor in 1931 when they invaded Manchuria, and a small army clique had tried to invoke the doctrine of *gekokujo* to overturn the surrender decision before it was broadcast to the Japanese nation. Hirohito, for all of his theoretical power, was no more than a bystander to the conflict; he was trained to reign, not to rule. He could not prevent war in China, which was begun without his knowledge, or war against America, which he regarded as the greatest tragedy of his life.

For many years the Japanese referred to the period of the subsequent American occupation of the home islands as "the period in which we had

An impromptu victor celebration on the streets of New York after the official announcement of Japanese surrender.

visitors." Only recently have the Japanese come to grapple with the true history of the war and their subsequent defeat. Even with the physical and economic ruin caused by the fighting, the Japanese in a sense long refused to acknowledge the war's bitter legacy.

This can be better understood when one examines the aftermath of the conflict and the continued suffering the Japanese endured at the hands of their American conquerors. In one respect, General MacArthur did a poor job of attempting to ready Japan for self-rule during his tenure as Occupation commander. Giving little thought to the immediate welfare of those under his jurisdiction, he set about attempting to reform the government in what he thought was the correct manner.

The most obvious example of his neglect, from a Japanese standpoint, was the diet that was mandated for the general populace. The meager few ounces of rice and one or two potatoes per week on which they were expected to live were simply insufficient to sustain life. The Japanese were forced to turn to the thriving black market, which expanded tremendously in occupied Japan, to secure their daily bread. For some, it may well have consisted largely of Spam and Hershey bars if there was an American base or PX nearby. Still the Japanese were grateful to MacArthur. At the very least, he was better than having Soviet troops on Japanese soil.

Although the Greater East Asian Co-Prosperity Sphere could never be realized through overt, aggressive means that stretched the Japanese military beyond its limits, it is arguable that what the Japanese could not achieve through war they have more than managed through peaceful means. And while the Americans did indeed crush all of their foes in 1945, standing unrivaled in economic and military strength, they have seen their relative position in the world diminish. Few seem to realize that the Japanese "economic miracle" was predicated on peace; in a war, the Japanese economy would suffer very severe reverses, particularly if Japan's supply of imported oil were interrupted. As in 1941, almost all of Japan's raw resources today are imported, and anything like an effective naval blockade would quickly decimate the Japanese economic infrastructure.

But let no one doubt the zeal of the Japanese leadership and its people to think of policy planning in terms of years and decades rather than weeks or months. The Japanese people and their leaders have indeed followed the advice given in Hirohito's surrender rescript: *"Keep pace with the progress of the world."*

Suggestions for Further Reading

The standard work on Japan's surrender is still Robert Butow's *Japan's Decision to Surrender* (Stanford, CA: Stanford University Press, 1954), from which the authors have derived a considerable amount of factual information. Some primary source material of considerable importance is contained in the Pacific War Research Society's *Japan's Longest Day* (New York: Ballantine, 1972); the quote by Premier Suzuki to General Anami, "If we don't act now . . ." is found in this volume. Thomas Coffey's *Imperial Tragedy: Japan in World War Two—The First Days and the Last* (New York: The World Publishing Company, 1970) also contains some interesting material on the subject. See also *The Day Man Lost* (New York: Kodansha, 1981) by the Pacific War Research Society, and Leon V. Sigal, *Fighting to a Finish: The Politics of War Termination in the United States and Japan, 1945* (Ithaca,

NY: Cornell University Press, 1988), which approaches the surrender from the standpoint of a political scientist who analyzes the process involved. Eugene Soviak, ed., *The Wartime Diary of Kiyosawa Kiyoshi* (Princeton, NJ: Princeton University Press, 1999), tells the story of the Japanese empire's decline and collapse from the point of view of an increasingly dissenting observer. Important eyewitness material may be gleaned from Michihiko Hachiya, *Hiroshima Diary* (Chapel Hill: University of North Carolina Press, 1955). The actual mechanics of the formal surrender are recorded in Toshikazu Kase, *Journey to the Missouri* (New Haven, CT: Yale University Press, 1950). Those portions of the text recounting the surrender in John Toland, *The Rising Sun: The Decline and Fall of the Japanese Empire, 1936–1945* (New York: Bantam Books, 1970), are reliable and have supplied interesting detail to this narrative. The official British history concerning Japanese surrender is Woodburn S. Kirby et al., *The War Against Japan* (London: Her Majesty's Stationary Office, 1969). A revealing account of Japan during the occupation can be found in John Dower, *Embracing Defeat: Japan in the Wake of World War II* (New York: W.W. Norton, 1999).

Index

About the Authors

Mark D. Roehrs received his Ph.D. in history from the University of Tennessee, Knoxville, in 1998. His specialty fields include United States diplomatic and military history. He is currently an assistant professor at Lincoln Land Community College in Springfield, Illinois.

Willliam A. Renzi received his Ph.D. from the University of Maryland, College Park, in 1969, where he studied under Pacific War specialist Gordon Prange. His other works include *In the Shadow of the Sword: Italy's Neutrality and Entrance into the Great War, 1914–1915*. He was an associate professor at the University of Wisconsin, Milwaukee, until his death in 1991.